Whole-Faculty
Study Groups

Whole-Faculty Study Groups

A Powerful Way to Change Schools and Enhance Learning

Carlene U.
Murphy

Dale W.
Lick

Forewords by
Dennis Sparks
Ron Brandt

CORWIN PRESS, INC.
A Sage Publications Company
Thousand Oaks, California

For information:

Corwin Press, Inc.
A Sage Publications Company
2455 Teller Road
Thousand Oaks, California 91320
E-mail: order@corwinpress.com

SAGE Publications Ltd.
6 Bonhill Street
London EC2A 4PU
United Kingdom

SAGE Publications India Pvt. Ltd.
M-32 Market
Greater Kailash I
New Delhi 110 048 India

Printed in the United States of America

Library of Congress Cataloging-in-Publication Data

Murphy, Carlene U.
    Whole-faculty study groups: A powerful way to change schools and enhance learning / by Carlene U. Murphy, Dale W. Lick.
        p. cm.
    Includes bibliographical references and index.
    ISBN 0-8039-6726-8 (cloth: acid-free paper)
    ISBN 0-8039-6727-6 (pbk.: acid-free paper)
    1. Teacher work groups—United States. 2. Teachers—in-service training—United States. 3. School improvement programs—United States. 4. Academic achievement—United States. I. Lick, Dale W. II. Title.
    LB1731 .M866 1997
    370'.071'55—ddc21   98-9025

This book is printed on acid-free paper.

98 99 00 01 02 03 10 9 8 7 6 5 4 3 2 1

Production Editor: Astrid Virding
Editorial Assistant: Karen Wiley
Editorial Assistant: Kristen L. Gibson
Cover Designer: Susan Mathews
Designer/Typesetter: Rebecca Evans
Indexer: Jean Casalegno

Contents

Tables and Figures

Snapshots

The Snapshots are true stories from whole-faculty study group schools that illustrate key points in the chapters of this book.

Foreword

Imagine a school that has committed itself to high levels of learning for all its students. The school has declared that it will educate all its students to meet national standards in the core academic areas. And the school recognizes that the knowledge and skills of its teachers will be its most important resource in meeting this lofty goal. Put another way, high levels of learning and performance on the part of all teachers will be the key to high levels of all learning and performance for all students.

The challenges faced by such a school are immense. As Carlene Murphy and Dale Lick point out in their preface to *Whole-Faculty Study Groups: A Powerful Way to Change Schools and Enhance Learning,* "Like other organizations, schools are not naturally open or amenable to major change." What processes will perturb the status quo, create sustained commitment to innovative practices, and provide a means for learning that will enable teachers to plan the change effort and alter their day-to-day instructional practices?

Although no single professional learning process can measure up to that challenge, whole-faculty study groups are an essential element in the mix of strategies that can lead schools to high levels of learning for all students and staff members. Such groups involve the entire faculty in sustained, rigorous study of the innovations they will implement and in working through the problems that inevitably accompany such innovation.

The use of whole-faculty study groups is, the authors point out, "a holistic practical process for facilitating major schoolwide change and for enhancing student learning in the schools." These groups make it possible for teachers "to explicate, invent, and evaluate practices that have the potential to meet the needs of their students and the community their schools serve," Murphy and Lick write. "As teachers work together in these study group approaches, they alter their practices to provide new and innovative opportunities for their students to learn in challenging and productive new ways."

Consider the power of whole-faculty study groups in improving student learning. The faculty begins by committing itself to extended study by an overwhelming vote in favor of the study group process. The faculty gathers and analyzes data to determine the focus of its efforts. The teachers form groups that will meet weekly for about an hour to discuss research, consider alternatives for actions, and acquire instructional skills. Because everyone is involved in the study, the faculty develops a common vocabulary and strategies to address the student learning goals it has identified. Because of the meetings, barriers that isolate teachers are removed, and norms of collaboration, experimentation, and risk taking are nurtured. Whole-faculty study groups teach their participants through example that professional learning must be an ongoing, focused process if it is to affect student learning.

In such a school, the principal is a skillful leader who is a "keeper of the dream" and a holder of high expectations for students and staff. This person values continuous improvement and models this behavior by participating in a study group. Surrounding the school is an infrastructure of district support in the form of resources and visible district leadership and pressure in the form of high expectations and accountability for high levels of learning for all students.

If school reform efforts are to succeed, individuals who occupy various roles in the educational enterprise must be knowledgeable about the benefits and processes of whole-school study groups. Leading the list would be teachers, principals, and district leaders, such as superintendents, directors of staff development, and curriculum specialists. Education professors and consultants who work for educational agencies would also benefit from a deeper understanding of this process.

Carlene Murphy and Dale Lick bring a unique combination of experiences to this book. Murphy has distinguished herself as a national staff development leader and a consultant to numerous schools. She is familiar with both the practical day-to-day realities of school change and the theory and research that support those efforts, a special combination that makes this book a rare blend of theory and practice. Lick brings a background in organization development and leadership that rounds out the knowledge and skills required to transform schools and school systems. Together, they have written a book filled with practical advice for those most closely involved with educational reform.

It is difficult to imagine a school seriously committed to high levels of learning for all students and staff members that does not use some form of whole-faculty study. *Whole-Faculty Study Groups* provides the theory, strategies, and examples schools need to begin such a journey.

DENNIS SPARKS
Executive Director,
National Staff Development Council

Foreword

This book is about a simple but powerful idea: people working in small groups to improve their professional performance. It's not a new idea; social psychologists have recognized the power of small groups for decades. But most organizations, especially schools, have not made effective use of that power.

We have committees, of course. Every educational institution at every level has them—with varying results. Teachers know that what appears to be a sensible device for getting things done can be fruitless and frustrating instead. And even when committees function well, their perspective is outward, not inward. Their focus is the task, not the growth of participants themselves.

The small-group process explained in this book is different. Members of whole-faculty study groups are concerned with what they themselves do and what they might do differently. If they find an idea appealing, they must decide how it applies to them and what they should do about it.

That can be threatening, but it can also be exhilarating. What could be more relevant to any professional than his or her own performance? And what responsible person wouldn't like to hear new ideas and learn new methods, if they can be freely discussed and evaluated?

The problem for many teachers is that they are already overwhelmed by the demands of their jobs, so they are unlikely to want to attend more meetings, no matter how apt. An eager few may voluntarily form study groups on their own. Most will need encouragement.

The authors understand this and offer sound advice on how to set up study groups that teachers will enjoy and support. They are supremely well-qualified to do so. Dale Lick, who has been president of three respected universities, is a scholar of organizational change, a researcher, and consultant. Here, he teams with Carlene Murphy, who originated and managed an extensive program of faculty study groups when she was director of staff development for the Richmond County, Georgia, Public Schools.

In recent years, Murphy has consulted with schools in numerous other districts, including Cobb County, Georgia, where principals report dramatic changes. Teachers, they say, are less likely to avoid important issues with small talk and more often discuss educational matters. One principal says teachers consider study groups the most important aspect of their school. "They'd do without me before they'd give up study groups," she jokes.

Teachers elsewhere may not be quite that enthusiastic, but many will find study groups satisfying, because they are a refreshing antidote to the professional isolation that characterizes most schools. Observers bemoan the fact that teachers spend their days engaged with students and seldom interact with other adults. The study group format changes that, putting teachers in regular communication with a handful of colleagues. Researchers say this "professional community" is at the heart of successful school reform. Karen Seashore Louis and her coauthors Kruse and Marks (1996) write, "By collaborating on common objectives, sharing developmental activities and concerns, and reflecting together on the technical aspects of their teaching, teachers come to own in common the consequences of their joint work for students' intellectual progress" (p. 180).

A skeptic might ask why, if study groups are beneficial, so few schools have them. Part of the answer may be that recognizing the value of something is only the first step. To make it work, you need to know how. That is the contribution of this book. The authors provide detailed, practical advice that will help educators avoid missteps that could lead to misunderstandings and rejection. How large should the groups be? How often should they meet? Who decides what they will talk about? How can administrators keep informed and be responsive? What if most teachers are willing but a few are not? The authors answer these and other questions based on successful experience in schools large and small, urban and rural, elementary and secondary.

Educators seeking school improvement—especially principals and superintendents but also teachers, central office staff members, and others—will welcome this book, because it outlines a process by which promising reforms can become realities. Whole-school study groups have value in themselves, contributing to faculty solidarity and a climate of professionalism. Beyond that, they are a vehicle for implementing the many other changes that must be made if schools are to meet the challenges of a new century.

RON BRANDT
Former Assistant Executive Director of the Association
of Supervision and Curriculum Development and editor
of the journal **Educational Leadership**, *now retired*

Preface

Need and Purpose

School reform and the improvement of schools are not as simple as the last decade of general and educational rhetoric would imply. Well-intentioned societal leaders and school personnel have talked about the necessity to change and improve, and schools and their personnel have attempted a wide variety of what appeared to be logical and progressive solutions. Unfortunately, most of these have failed or, at best, been only partially successful. This failure or limited success happened because change, even positively perceived change, is difficult to bring about in long-standing, well-established organizations. Like other organizations, schools are not naturally open or amenable to major change.

To successfully reform, improve, and transition schools to meet tomorrow's needs will require approaches and processes that are different than most attempted during the last decade. We must not only decide what changes or reforms are required, but we must also put in place a significant transition process to help negotiate the societal, organizational, cultural, and people barriers in and affecting schools.

One of the most successful and exciting new approaches to reform and change in education today is that involving professional whole-faculty study groups. The key element in these efforts, and unique to this book, is the "whole-faculty" involvement. Not just study groups, but whole-faculty study groups, where all of the faculty are committed to the effort, actively involved in it, and responsible for an important part of the total effort. Where whole-faculty study groups have been properly implemented, they have been unusually successful. The whole-faculty study group approach is a holistic, practical process for facilitating major schoolwide change and for enhancing student learning in the schools. This book presents a detailed discussion of whole-faculty study groups, their application, and the underlying change principles necessary for such study groups to be successful in the school environment.

Based on our work in managing major change and our experiences in over 100 schools and 1,000 whole-faculty study groups in those schools, this book provides both (a) the practical knowledge required to implement and successfully use the whole-faculty study group approach in schools and (b) the theoretical foundation to understand the key change elements involved and how these can be applied, using whole-faculty study groups, to facilitate schoolwide change and enhance student learning. Furthermore, the book contains a generous collection of relevant and illustrative examples, "snapshots" of real-world situations, and a detailed, step-by-step practical methodology for the development of successful professional whole-faculty study groups in schools.

In particular, this book grew out of a wide array of real-world whole-faculty study group efforts and experiences, encompasses the existing relevant literature on study groups, and significantly extends this knowledge base through (a) new up-to-date information and refinements of processes, procedures, and approaches, (b) new experiences and applications from user schools across the country, and (c) the unique integration and use of practical and theoretical concepts regarding change and change management approaches.

Who Should Read and Use This Book?

This book should be read and used by anyone who is interested in facilitating important change in the schools and increasing student learning. A primary audience for the book should be the personnel in schools (kindergarten through 12th grade)—all teachers, administrators, and staff.

For schools that choose to introduce the whole-faculty study group approach, all school personnel will be involved in their schoolwide effort. Consequently, in such schools, each faculty, administration, and staff member should have a copy, or many copies should be shared generously for school personnel, allowing full and convenient access across the school.

In addition, the book holds special potential for individual teachers and administrators and groups of teachers and administrators who are considering new options for seriously improving their schools.

Other important audiences for this book include

- Central office personnel in school systems, especially for consideration and possible implementation of study groups in their school systems
- College of Education faculty in colleges and universities, for understanding this new and successful process for schoolwide change and enhanced student learning as well as for possible use as a textbook or reference book in their classes relating to teacher training and school enhancement
- Community college faculty and administrators, for consideration of study groups and their application in their institutions for collegewide change and improving student learning
- School, community college, college, and university libraries
- Individuals and groups in national and international workshops on study groups and their application in education, from small seminars to large groups
- Individuals and groups in corporate, community, and governmental organizations involved with schools, education, and training

Knowledge Base of the Authors

Both of us have spent successful careers in education as teachers and administrators. Carlene U. Murphy has an extensive background as a teacher and staff development director. During her 17 years as the administrator of a large school district's comprehensive staff development programs, the whole-faculty study group process was implemented in 10 of the district's schools.

In 1993, she began working at the national level with faculties who wanted to initiate the whole-faculty study group process in their schools. She is a past president of the National Staff Development Council; regarded as the national leader in the whole-faculty study group movement; a recipient of several related state and national awards; creator of the Whole-Faculty Study Group Collaborative, a national organization for those interested in areas relating to whole-faculty study groups; and the most prominent national researcher, practitioner, and author on whole-faculty study groups (e.g., see typical publication examples in the bibliography). During her role as a private consultant who has narrowed her focus to schools implementing the whole-faculty study group process, her work has taken her to schools in urban, suburban, and rural areas; elementary, middle, high, and vocational schools; and schools with as few as 10 teachers and as many as 250 teachers. Her association with ATLAS Communities, one of the seven design teams funded by the New American Schools Cooperation, has put her in the center of the nation's major national reform initiatives.

Dale W. Lick has been a faculty member and educational administrator for over 35 years, at nine colleges and universities, including three college and university presidencies. Included in 33 national and international biographical listings, he is the author of a book, over 50 professional articles and proceedings, and 285 original newspaper articles. Over the years, his work and responsibilities have been directly and indirectly related to teacher preparation, school operation, and school improvement. More recently, he has been a researcher on the statewide school enhancement initiative, "Florida Schoolyear 2000," served as a school consultant, and offered national and international educational workshops. In addition, he presently teaches and does research on educational and transformational leadership, managing organizational change, and learning organizations, especially as related to education and the schools. He is also formally trained and certified in Change Management (in the three certification areas: Change Knowledge, Trainer, and Consultant) and may be the only person in the country so certified to be working in the school improvement areas and with whole-faculty study groups.

Organization and Contents

The book is organized so that its chapters logically build on each other with each laying a foundation for those that follow. The contents include the key elements in the whole-faculty study group and change processes and their implementation and a large number of real-world examples and illustrative cases. The book is written so that it can serve as a textbook, a detailed reference book, or a stand-alone guide for the effective initiation, comprehensive implementation, and successful completion of the whole-faculty study group approach in schools.

Chapter 1 discusses the school reform environment and the potential of the whole-faculty study group approach serving as a major change process to improve schools and student learning and enhance schools as learning organizations. This chapter also summarizes fundamental faculty-student-school-teaching-research-support relationships and approaches.

The concept and nature of study groups, their strengths and weaknesses, and their ability to serve as vehicles for change and the creation of collaborative work cultures are described in Chapter 2.

Chapter 3 helps the reader differentiate between "means" and "ends" and keeps attention focused on the desired "ends," namely, enhanced student learning and school improvement. The whole-faculty study group approach is the "means" that modifies the culture and innovative processes, changes the ways teachers learn about new instructional models and strategies and transfer new skills to the classroom, and creates more of a learning organization environment.

The principal function of the whole-faculty study group approach, as described in Chapter 4, is to effectively manage change and transition schools and their processes, including curricular and instructional innovations, coherence of instructional practices and programs, identification of schoolwide needs, research on teaching and learning, and assessment of the impact of innovations on students and the workplace.

Chapter 5 addresses the context for schools (i.e., the organization, the system, and the culture) in which study groups must function. Especially key among the school-context-related topics discussed are the change concepts of building commitment, developing effective sponsorship, dealing with human change and resistance, using the roles of change, understanding assimilation capacity, and modifying school-related cultures, as well as applying the important, overarching Universal Change Principle.

The process for the whole-faculty study group approach, unfolded in Chapter 6, allows educators to acquire and develop the knowledge and skills necessary to increase student performance and improve schools. Toward these ends, 14 study group process guidelines are discussed, 14 procedures are established for the creation of communication networks and strategies, and 24 study group "work time models" are provided.

The heart of the study group process, the content, detailed in Chapter 7, is what teachers study, what teachers investigate, and what teachers do to become more skillful in the classroom with students. This chapter discusses staff development content; academic knowledge, instructional strategies, instructional skills, management, and belief systems; a decision-making cycle, involving data collection and analysis, student needs, prioritization of needs, organization around student needs, plan of action, implementation, and evaluation; and 14 suggested recommendations for dealing with groups that seem to be stuck.

Effective study groups are effective teams. Teamwork is what differentiates an effective study group from a typical committee or other work group. Chapter 8 describes how to use the study group process to build effective teams and teamwork in schools. Discussed and illustrated in this chapter are the key elements of synergistic team building, including synergistic relationships; prerequisites of synergy—common goals, interdependence, empowerment, and participation—and the synergy creation, process-interaction, appreciative understanding, integration, and implementation; and a synergy checklist for diagnosing and correcting teamwork problems.

The resources also include additional important and helpful nuts-and-bolts information for the effective application of the whole-faculty study group approach, including examples of study group action plans, a set of study group logs, and exhibits from whole-faculty study group schools.

It is hoped that the material in this book will inspire you and help you understand and use whole-faculty study groups in your work to develop more effective schools for the new century and create learning environments that significantly enhance student learning.

Acknowledgments

Joseph Allison Murphy III
Marilyn K. Lick

Rachel Brown
Ernest Clements
Daryl R. Conner
Bruce R. Joyce
Beverly Showers
William R. Snyder
John P. Strelec

Richmond County Public Schools, Augusta, GA

Richmond County's Models of Teaching Cadre (1987-1992)

Richmond County's Models of Teaching Schools

1987-1993:

Barton Chapel Elementary School—Audrey Wood, Principal
Wheeless Road Elementary School—John Black, Principal
East Augusta Middle School—Lee Beard, Principal

1988-1993:

Morgan Road Middle School—Vivian Pennamon, Principal
Murphey Middle School—Winnette Bradley, Principal
Tubman Middle School—Tracey Williams, Principal
Laney High School—William Holmes, Principal

1989-1993:

Copeland Elementary School—Eddie Robinson, Principal
Hains Elementary School—Nathaniel Dunn, Principal
Hornsby Elementary School—Thelma Williams, Principal

ATLAS Communities

Linda Gerstle, Director
Ronald Walker, Associate Director
and ATLAS schools in: Memphis, TN
CHAIN Cluster and Strawberry Mansion Cluster in Philadelphia, PA
Everett, Northshore, and Shoreline School Districts in Washington state

Americus City Schools, Americus, GA

Patricia Turner, Visionary
Sarah Cobb Elementary School

Cobb County Public Schools, Marietta, GA

Tricia Mingledorff, Executive Director
Addison Elementary School
Bryant Elementary School
Murdock Elementary School
Sky View Elementary School

Baltimore County Public School, Baltimore, MD

Arbutus Elementary School

Boyle County Public Schools, Danville, KY

Pam Rogers, Assistant Superintendent
Perryville Elementary School
Woodlawn Elementary School
Boyle County Middle School

Decatur City Schools, Decatur, GA

Gloria Lee, Director
Clairmont Elementary School
College Heights Elementary School
Fifth Avenue Elementary School
Gleenwood Elementary School
Oakhurst Elementary School
Westchester Elementary School
Winnona Park Elementary School
Renfroe Middle School
Decatur High School

Imperial County Public Schools, Holtville, CA

Holtville High School
Holtville Middle School

Lyons Unified School District 405, Lyons, KS

Montgomery County Public Schools, Mt. Sterling, KY

Liz Petitt, Assistant Superintendent
Mt. Sterling Elementary School

Round Rock Independent School District, Round Rock, TX

Edna Harris, Director
Brushy Creek Elementary School
Deepwood Elementary School
Forest North Elementary School
Round Rock High School

San Diego Unified School District, San Diego, CA

Carol Leighty and Mariam True
Birney Elementary School
Fulton Elementary School
Johnson Elementary School
Jones Elementary School
Toler Elementary School
Mission Bay High School
Garfield High School

San Diego County Board of Education, San Diego, CA

Karen LaBlanc and Shirley Mills
Sweetwater High School
Ramona High School
Washington Middle School

Washington County Public Schools, Sandersville, GA

> Grace Davis, Assistant Superintendent
> Sandersville Elementary School
> Elder Middle School

Woodford County Public Schools, Versailles, KY

> Sue Bowen, Assistant Superintendent
> Sheila Hollin, Director
> Huntertown Elementary School
> Northside Elementary School
> Simmons Elementary School
> Southside Elementary School
> Woodford County Middle School
> Woodford County High School

Weld County School District 6, Greeley, CO

> Jackson Elementary School with special recognition to Barry Shelofsky,
> Principal, for charting his own journey

and all of the faculties at the whole-faculty study group schools listed above

For Sarah Zemulaw Louise (Moore) Usry,
my mother, whose joy in me made me all I am and
who taught me by example how to be a mother,
a grandmother, and a great-grandmother.

—Sarah Carlene (Usry) Murphy

About the Authors

Carlene U. Murphy lives in Augusta, Georgia, where she worked in the public schools in her hometown for 22 years as a classroom teacher and the administrator of the district's staff development programs. She also was a classroom teacher in Memphis, Tennessee, for 13 years. From 1978 to 1993, she was director of staff development for the Richmond County Public Schools in Augusta, Georgia, and the work was recognized at the state and national levels. In 1991, Richmond County received the American Association of School Administrators' and the National Staff Development Council's Award for Outstanding Achievement in Professional Development. Also, in 1991, she received the National Staff Development Council's Contributions to Staff Development Award. Since her retirement in 1993 from the Richmond County school district, she has narrowed her work to schools that want to implement the whole-faculty study group process. This work has taken her to more than 100 schools in which she has had contact with over 1,000 study groups. These have been high schools, middle schools, elementary schools, and vocational schools; schools with a range from 250 teachers to schools with 10 teachers; schools in urban, suburban, and rural areas; and schools in all regions of the country. She is a staff member of ATLAS Communities, one of seven design teams funded by the New American Schools Corporation; based in Boston, it is a collaboration of four of the nation's leading reform efforts: Harvard University's Project Zero, Brown University's Coalition of Essential Schools, Yale University's School Development Program, and the Education Development Center. Because all ATLAS schools are also whole-faculty study group schools, her work with ATLAS is to train and support faculties in the study group process. She has written extensively about her work in *Educational Leadership, The Journal of Staff Development,* and *The Developer.* She has led numerous professional development institutes for the Association of Supervision and Curriculum Development, for the National Staff Development Council, and for several state organizations. She and her husband, Joe, who is a former principal, district administrator, and college dean, have two children and three grandchildren who also live in Augusta.

Dale W. Lick is a past president of Georgia Southern University, University of Maine, and Florida State University and presently, is University Professor and Associate Director of the Learning Systems Institute at Florida State University. He teaches in the Department of Educational Leadership and works on projects involving education, transformational leadership, managing organizational change, and developing learning organizations. He is an active school and higher education consultant and researcher on transformational changes in education, and he offers educational workshops nationally and internationally. Included in 33 national and international biographical listings, he is the author of over 50 education-related books, articles, and proceedings, and 285 original newspaper columns. He received his bachelor's and master's degrees from Michigan State University, and a PhD degree from the University of California, Riverside. Also, he is probably the only educator in the United States with his educational experience to hold all three levels of formal training and certification for Managing Organizational Change—Change Knowledge, Instructor-Trainer, and Consultation Skills—from the international change research and development organization, ODR, Inc. He and his wife, Marilyn, live in Tallahassee, Florida, and have three grown children and two grandsons.

Introduction **1**

The past several years have helped us see more clearly than ever before that school reform and the improvement of schools are not as simple as the last decade of general and educational rhetoric would imply. Over and over, well-intentioned societal leaders and school personnel have talked about the necessity to change and improve, and schools and their personnel have attempted a wide variety of what appeared to be logical and progressive efforts. Unfortunately, most of these efforts have failed or, at best, been only partially successful.

Why? Why have seemingly well-thought-out initiatives of change and improvement failed so frequently? The simple answer is that change, even positively perceived change, is difficult to bring about in a long-standing, well-established organization. Our schools are clearly among such organizations, and their cultures, the ones that have given us so much success and stability in the past, are deeply ensconced and rigid. Like all other such organizations, they are not naturally open or amenable to major change. Can we bring about meaningful reform and major change in our schools? The answer is "absolutely yes," and many such changes will be essential in the future! However, to do so will require approaches and processes that are different from most of those attempted during the past decade. We must not only decide what change or reform is required, but we must also put in place a significant transition process to help us negotiate the societal, organizational, cultural, and people barriers in and affecting the schools.

Major change in our schools, as is true in other types of organizations, requires active and effective sponsorship—support, encouragement, pressure, and accountability—from the leadership (e.g., boards, superintendents, principals, and directors). With strong sponsorship at each level in the school, teachers and other school personnel feel a greater sense of empowerment and, as a consequence, are more comfortable with the change and more willing to attempt seriously new major projects and processes.

If genuine reform is to come from within our schools, then teachers and school personnel must be importantly and intimately involved. In particular, teachers must be perceived, treated, and held accountable as educational professionals. To treat them as such requires that teachers enjoy the latitude to invent local solutions and to discover and develop practices that embody central values and principles rather than to implement, adopt, or demonstrate practices thought to be universally effective (Little, 1993). One of the most exciting new approaches to reform and change in education is that involving professional study groups. A properly implemented professional study group process encompasses the change characteristics discussed earlier as well as several others, including collaboration and synergy; individual, team, and organizational resilience; elements of learning organizations; and culture modification.

The professional study group process allows teachers the freedom and flexibility to explicate, invent, and evaluate practices that have the potential to meet the needs of their students and the community their schools serve. As teachers work together in these study group approaches, they alter their practices to provide new and innovative opportunities for their students to learn in challenging and productive new ways.

Effective study groups are a complex mixture of many activities happening simultaneously. The study group approach is a holistic, practical process for facilitating major schoolwide change and for enhancing learning outcomes in the schools. In particular, the study group approach to professional development in schools and for educators includes the following:

- Planning and learning together, testing ideas, and sharing and reflecting together
- Providing support for each other
- Grappling with what broad principles of teaching and learning look like in practice
- Engaging in the pursuit of genuine questions, problems, and curiosities over a period of time in ways that leave marks on perspectives, policies, and practices
- Constructing subject-matter knowledge versus merely consuming it
- Immersing in sustained work with ideas, materials, and colleagues
- Experiencing the frustrations of dealing with "what is" while envisioning "what could be"
- Functioning not only as consumers of research but also as critics and producers of research
- Contributing to knowledge and practice
- Struggling with the fundamental questions of what teachers and students must learn and know

The materials that follow provide a generous collection of relevant and illustrative examples and snapshots of real-world situations and a detailed, step-by-step practical methodology for the development of professional study groups in schools for facilitating schoolwide change and enhancing learning processes and outcomes.

Strengths and Weaknesses

Snapshot 1   A Vehicle for Change

Sarah Cobb Elementary School draws its 692 third-grade, fourth-grade, and fifth-grade students from a small, rural community. Forty-nine percent of the children are on the Aid to Families with Dependent Children list; 75% of the students are eligible for free or reduced-cost lunch. Only one third of the students live in traditional, two-parent homes.

Two years before schoolwide study groups were implemented, the school had undergone a major change. The school that had housed grades five and six for 15 years became a third-grade through fifth-grade school. Two thirds of the faculty were new to the school, and the faculty was led by a new leadership team consisting of a principal and two assistant principals. Year 1 was a time for blending the two faculties and assessing student needs. In Year 2, the faculty focused on examining student achievement and the effects of the school's curriculum and its delivery. One recommendation resulting from an examination of the school's needs was that the teachers receive more support in the implementation of the many initiatives that were aimed at student success. In the fall of the third year, after the school's new grade structure was initiated, whole-faculty study groups became the design to provide teachers a structured support system.

The results of the whole-faculty study group design after 1 year were these:

- Teachers examined strategies and materials that had been the content of staff development programs, practiced and used the strategies and materials with each other and in their classrooms, and reported classroom results to each other.
- Teachers petitioned the State Board of Education to approve a waiver to allow early release of students 1 day per week for teacher study. The waiver was approved and implemented in January of the first year.
- Discipline referrals declined.
- The number of books read independently by students increased, as did media center circulation.

The results at the end of the second year were as follows:

- Teachers designed and implemented a back-to-the-basics plan called "Immersion in Basic Skills."
- All teachers committed to and began participation in a 2-year, site-based training program that included immersion in the theory and practice of

three key teaching strategies: concept attainment, inductive thinking, and mnemonics. Study groups were the vehicles for practicing and demonstrating these strategies and discussing their effects on students.

- Iowa Test of Basic Skills (ITBS) results indicated growth for every grade and in every area tested.
- Discipline referrals continued to decline.
- The number of books read independently by students increased dramatically.
- Surveys indicated a high level of teacher satisfaction.

The results for the third year of the whole-faculty study group design were these:

- All of the earlier results continued.
- Chapter 1 and Title I students posted significant National Curve Equivalent gains in all areas, with substantial growth recorded in reading and mathematics problem solving.

Study Groups Defined

Organizing teachers into small groups, study groups, to promote collegial interchange and action is not a new idea. Such study groups have existed for individuals who, for instance, take courses together; read, discuss, and reflect on the contents of a publication; explore new research findings; and introduce a new instructional technique.

The study group concept is an important approach to professional development. Professional study groups of teachers seem like a simple notion, and yet, they have the potential of facilitating major change and significant school improvement.

A formal definition of a study group in education might be the following:

A *study group* of teachers is a small number of individuals joining together to increase their capacities through new learning for the benefit of students.

The study group process grows in complexity as we examine what the group does and how the group functions so that members will actually implement new practices, change behaviors, and demonstrate new skills, knowledge, and activities in the job setting.

We encourage professional study groups in schools as a vehicle to integrate individual and organizational development with a challenging and supportive set of personal relationships. The desired end result of these collegial relationships is increased success for all students. The end result of any professional development approach is to more effectively serve students.

Ideally, professional study groups bring individual needs and organizational needs together. The purpose of a school, an organization, is to create the conditions and circumstances where young people can learn to their fullest potentials and capacities.

Creating conditions for continuous improvement of students is a goal that provides a common purpose to all of the individuals who participate in professional study groups. We classify professional study groups into two categories:

1. Whole-faculty study groups
2. Independent or stand-alone study groups

Whole-Faculty Study Groups

As we mentioned earlier, organizing teachers into small groups to promote collegial interchange and action is not a new idea. However, organizing the entire school faculty into study teams, whole-faculty study groups, to bring about schoolwide improvement is unusual.

Whole-faculty study groups is a term used when all faculty members at a given school are members of professional study groups. Such study groups have an organizational focus. The faculty, through a consensus process, has decided that each certificated staff member will be a member of a study group that meets regularly to support whole-school improvement. In these schools, study groups are part of a schoolwide design and are a regular and legitimate part of the school organization.

In forming study groups, the faculty has gone through a process of analyzing student and school data to determine what study groups could do to improve student learning. Once the area of need or problem to be lessened or solved has been identified, the key to the study group process is to determine what teachers will study, investigate, and become skillful at doing to address the need or problem area. Often, this means examining what will enable teachers to effectively use new and refined instructional practices and materials in the classroom. As each classroom improves, the whole school improves.

The goal of whole-faculty study groups is to focus the entire school faculty on implementing and integrating effective teaching and learning practices into school programs that will result in an increase in student learning and a decrease in negative behaviors of students, as reflected in related, relevant data sources.

Whole-faculty study groups bring individual needs and institutional needs together in an organizational setting. As a result, whole-faculty study groups can become important vehicles to assist schools in meeting their primary objective of creating the conditions and circumstances where students learn to their fullest potentials and capacities, as illustrated in Snapshot 1. Without substantive content, however, the study group process will not have the desired effects—increased student achievement. The power in the whole-faculty study group process rests in the promise that teachers will become more knowledgeable and skillful at doing what will result in higher levels of student learning. Study groups that function simply to satisfy interests of group members often lack adequate content focus to boost the goal of the school. The primary goal of schools is to meet student needs. Therefore, it is the collective energy and synergy from the whole faculty that propels the whole school forward. To our knowledge, the documented effects of study groups on students and the learning environment are limited to situations involving whole-faculty study groups focusing on instruction. Schools that have successfully initiated the whole-faculty study group design have many differences, such as those reflected in student age and level, location (e.g., rural vs. urban), the socioeconomic circumstances, and size. Even with the many demographic differences in schools, we have not seen these differences make for significant differences in how the adults in the schools work together in study groups.

For study groups, there are at least two factors that are constant in all of the schools. First, all of the individuals in the study groups are adults learning together and developing their instructional skills together. Second, faculties initially worry about the same logistical concerns, such as time for groups to meet, how groups will be organized, and what groups will do. These logistical considerations are what make each school different in how study groups function. It is not the size of the school, the grade levels in the school, or the types of students the school serves. The differences are reflected in how each faculty decides to initiate and implement the process. And the fact that each faculty does initiate and implement the process is the success factor. That is why the whole-faculty study group process—having all faculty members involved in study groups that are focused on the needs of the school's students—is successful in a wide variety of settings. In Chapter 6, we offer logistical suggestions, not a recipe, for initiating and implementing the study group process.

The whole-faculty study group process is *not* advised unless

- The whole faculty has an understanding of the process
- The whole faculty acknowledges that if at least 75% of their number endorses the process, that percentage obligates everyone
- The whole faculty participates in analyzing student data and identifying student needs that can be addressed through faculty study groups

A discussion concerning decisions about what groups will do and how groups will be organized is described in Chapter 7.

Whole-Faculty Study Groups: Strengths

The most obvious strength of whole-faculty study groups is the support the groups give each other within the same organizational structure. The structure ensures an acceptable and supported study group routine, meaning that the meetings of study groups become a routine for the school and for the individual members. With this strong, schoolwide sponsorship, study groups take on an additional sense of importance, and members are less likely to miss meetings of their study groups, especially if time is given for study groups to meet during the workday.

Frequency and regularity of meetings are key elements for successful study groups. Successful study groups are groups that achieve the intended results. Because, in the organizational context, study group members are part of the same organization, they have common goals and serve children from the same community. Communication between meetings of study group members is easier, and resources can be shared. Because implementation of innovations is a key function of study groups, proximity is important. Teachers who work in the same building and have had common training can more easily work on implementation concerns together.

When professional study groups are part of a schoolwide design, the principal's pressure and support, his or her sponsorship, are positive forces for action and success. Pressure is typically perceived as a negative force or pain. However, change often occurs because some pressure or pain has built up to the point that it leads to action (Fullan & Steigelbauer, 1991).

How the school is organized so that the adults in the school can engage in serious and purposeful learning requires adjustments in scheduling activities, a form of pressure or pain, and allocating resources, a form of support. Fullan and Steigelbauer (1991) asserts that it is increasingly clear that both pressure and support are necessary for change efforts that alter the fundamental ways in which organizations work. The whole-faculty study group process is such a change effort, altering existing structures and roles. In this process, interactions among administrators and teachers serve to integrate both pressure and support in a seamless way through expectations of attendance and of completing tasks, sharing and developing lesson plans, and practicing lessons.

In every school where study groups have become a routine feature of the workplace and where changes in teacher and student behaviors are evident, the principal is the key factor (i.e., providing effective sponsorship). The principal, the primary and sustaining sponsor of school change, is the source of the pressure and support that makes it possible for teachers to have the willingness and skill to establish and maintain collaborative work cultures. Study groups operating outside of a school-wide design seldom have the level of organizational sponsorship, such as pressure and support, that connects teacher learning and student learning.

A strength that is often overlooked in the study group approach is that all members are expected to be leaders and that the success of the study group is measured in terms of the collective energy, participation, and synergy of the whole group. Another strength is that being a member of a professional study group becomes a norm of the workplace and its organizational culture; this helps the organization become a more effective *learning organization*—an organization continually enhancing its capacity to learn, create, and effectively act.

The question is not, "Will you be a member of a study group?" Instead, the question is, "Which study group will you join?" This understood and accepted attitude strengthens the norms of collegiality and collaboration (synergy) and continuous improvement. As whole-faculty study groups meet, the changes that are initially most evident are the cultural norms that underscore a collegial and collaborative work culture in the school.

Whole-Faculty Study Groups: Weaknesses

There is a perceived weakness in framing study groups within the context of the organization. The perception is that individuals have no choice and that the individual's interest or need is not considered or is secondary to the needs of the organization as a whole. However, this perception will be lessened if the decision-making cycle described in Chapter 7 is followed. A rationale for what individuals will do in study groups is established when all of the faculty participate in analyzing data, identifying and prioritizing student needs, and specifying what teachers will do to address those needs. Another perceived weakness is that, because the groups meet during the workday, the membership of the groups is often determined by the schedule. This means that individuals may be with other individuals that, initially, they do not know very well and feel they have little in common with. However, once a study group gets started and becomes immersed in the content, individuals usually see their differences as a plus. Individuals soon discover that within the small groups, they are, in fact, in the driver's seat, making all decisions about how the group will function and what the group will do.

Leadership for the Whole-Faculty Study Group Effort

As in any major change, strong leadership is a requirement (see the section on Effective Sponsorship in Chapter 5). It is usually the principal that first gets information about the functions and structure of the whole-faculty study group process. The principal has the choice of whether or not to inform the school's faculty. If the principal chooses to take that step, the faculty as a whole has a choice, understanding before voting that if at least a given percentage, usually at least 75%, wants to initiate the process, that decision will obligate everyone. Typically, if the response is positive, the principal would invite a team of teachers, called the *focus team* (Murphy, 1995), to learn exactly how to go about initiating and implementing whole-faculty study groups. There are several ways that this might be accomplished.

One approach is for the principal and focus team to ask a consultant to work with them. The consultant works with the focus team to help them

- Understand the purpose and functions of whole-faculty study groups
- Review the procedural guidelines that are discussed in Chapter 5
- Experience the decision-making cycle described in Chapter 6
- Develop a step-by-step plan for how the focus team will work with the whole faculty to implement the whole-faculty study group process

After the focus team leads the faculty through the decision-making cycle and the study groups get started, the consultant continues to support the focus team by meeting with them at intervals during the first and second years of implementation. The focus team serves as the cheerleaders for the study group effort and uses the information from their training to assist the study groups and keep them focused on student learning. The focus team usually has about five members and, in most schools, there would not be a focus team member on every study group. Because focus team members choose what student need they would like to address, as do all teachers in the school, two focus team members could be on the same study group. The leadership of a study group is assumed by each member of the study group on a rotating schedule.

Another approach to training a team from the school is for the principal to predict how many study groups the school could have. If the principal predicts that there will be 10 study groups, the principal will ask 10 teachers to be study group leaders during the initiation stage. Those selected leaders would be trained in the process and content of study groups. Under this system, one individual would remain as the leader for an extended period of time.

Still another approach to initiating whole-faculty study groups would be to have one or more persons attend workshops at the regional or national level. Those attending would return to the school and organize the effort.

Initiation and implementation of the whole-faculty study group structure could also be done after reading about how to implement the whole-faculty study group process, such as after reading this book. Whether implementation occurs as a result of reading this book or attending a workshop, it will take a major team effort to actually lead the whole faculty through the decision-making process and keep the process moving in the desired direction. A team composed of the principal and four or five teachers will need to carefully plan for every step of the decision-making cycle found in Chapter 6.

Additional leadership issues are discussed in the section on Process Guidelines for Study Groups in Chapter 6 (see Item #15). In that section, the roles of the instructional council, a leadership group, are discussed. It is recommended that representatives from each study group meet about once every 4 to 6 weeks to discuss what each study group is doing, address concerns, set expectations, review current data,

Table 2.1 Roles and Responsibilities in the Whole-Faculty Study Group Process

The Principal

- Is the sponsor, the advocate, the agent
- Is an active participant in training and planning sessions
- Receives the Action Plans and responds to the plans, as appropriate
- Receives the Study Group Logs and responds to the logs, as appropriate
- Establishes the conditions that facilitate the process, e.g., time for groups to meet, internal communications networks
- Uses the study groups as the primary units to implement the school's improvement plan
- Communicates what study groups do to district leaders, parents, and the general community

The Focus Team

- Is the principal and a representative group of teachers
- Represents the faculty in training sessions that are designed to facilitate the successful initiation and implementation of study groups.
- Leads the whole faculty through the decision-making cycle
- Shares with the faculty information that supports the successful functioning of the study groups
- Is the advocate group for the whole-faculty study group process, the change agents
- Initiates different forms of communications to keep everyone informed about what all groups are doing.

The Study Group Leader

- Rotates weekly, every 2 weeks, or monthly so that leadership is a shared responsibility among all study groups members
- Sees that the study group log is given to the appropriate person(s)
- Confirms logistics with study group members (e.g., date, time, location, resources needed)
- Starts and ends the meeting on time
- Keeps the study group focused on the content of the study

Individual Study Group Members

- Respect norms established by the study group
- Take turns serving as leader (all teachers are leaders)
- Take turns representing the study group at meetings for representatives from all study groups
- Take responsibility for their own learning and for seeking resources for the study group

and share resources. In most schools, this group is called the *instructional council* (see Snapshot 13 in Chapter 6). However, any established group may serve those functions (e.g., site-based council). Successful institutionalization of whole-faculty study groups is a complex task. Teachers must feel the advocacy and sponsorship, discussed in Chapter 5, from school and district leaders. They will require technical assistance from school, district, and external sources. No matter how successful the study groups are for a year, 2 years, or even longer, when teachers feel that the process is no longer valued and participation is no longer expected, the study group process will falter. See Table 2.1 for a look at the roles and responsibilities involved in the whole-faculty study group process.

Independent or Stand-Alone
Study Groups

An independent or stand-alone study group is one that does not depend on organizational support. It is a group of individuals that have a common interest and will consider themselves a study group until, as individuals, they satisfy their need for the group. There are unlimited possibilities for professional study groups to function other than in an organizational setting. Study groups may form within or outside of the context of a school or district. Study groups emerge as a result of individuals' interests or needs and are less structured. Independent or stand-alone study groups serve a very important role in the growth of individuals and should not be minimized.

Independent Study
Groups: Strengths

The major strength of an independent study group is that individuals are the initiators and that no larger unit controls or directs the group. A group of teachers who decide that they have a common need and agree to get together to address that need may have more early successes than groups that are part of the whole-faculty study group design. Also, in study groups that are not part of a schoolwide design, individuals can choose who they want to include in the group. The options for study may be more varied because choices are generally not aligned with specific student needs. Meeting times are more flexible because the group is not tied to a school schedule. Teachers are often from different schools and can also meet in the evenings or on weekends. Locations of meetings are more varied. Individuals frequently use their own resources and have wide latitude as to what they study and do.

Independent Study
Groups: Weaknesses

A major weakness is that an independent study group is less likely to apply its study and results to the school or district setting. Other weaknesses of independent study groups include the following: They often do not keep to set routines, absenteeism is higher, intended results are less clear, motivation may be centered around "what the group can do for me," and a terminal point is more evident. Once the individuals satisfy personal needs, they usually stop attending study group meetings. Leadership often rests with the individual who brought the group together, and members tend to look to that person for making the arrangements and getting needed materials. When the study group is initiated by an individual, separate from an organization, there is usually little commitment to a larger body or greater purpose. In the long run, however, one cannot separate himself or herself from the workplace. The independent study group may function outside of the school or district but the effects of what is learned will most probably affect the organization in some way. We strongly encourage independent study groups to agree on a study group action plan and follow most of the guidelines in Chapter 6.

Table 2.2 Comparison of Whole-Faculty Study Groups, Independent Study Groups, and Committees

	Whole-Faculty Study Groups	*Independent or Stand-Alone Study Groups*	*Committees*
Focus	Organizational	Individual (not part of a whole)	Administrative
Need	What's good for the whole school?	What's good for me?	Predetermined purpose
Purpose	Classroom instructional improvement centered on need of students	Individual's improvement centered on his or her interest or need	Centered on assigned task
Audience	All inclusive; whole faculty	Selective; based on choice of individual	Selective; based upon others' appointment or assignment
Process or product	Ongoing	End point	End point
Size of group	4-6	3 or more	3 or more
Role of participant	Active	Active-passive	Passive-active
Expectations	Implementation of new instructional skills; changes in classroom behavior	Individual growth; increased personal knowledge	Recommendations made for others to implement
Leadership	Scheduled by group members; rotates among all members with shared responsibility for success	Based on dialogue with group; tends to flow among all members with shared responsibility for success	Leader appointed or elected leader who has primary responsibility for success

A Study Group Is Not a Committee

Study groups are vehicles for self-improvement for the benefit of the individual and the whole organization. It is not an appointed group with an assigned job or task. Committees have appointed or elected leaders who usually assume the major responsibility for the success of the committee. Study groups generally focus on professional development issues and not administrative issues. Committees are often larger than study groups, and an end point is assumed. Generally, committees come up with recommendations for someone else to implement. Study groups implement and try out the perceived solutions to a problem, collect information about the degrees of change, and share their information with the whole faculty.

A comparison highlighting the key characteristics of whole-faculty study groups, independent study groups, and committees is given in Table 2.2.

Differences in Types of Meetings

Similar to the differences shown in Table 2.2 is the question of how study groups differ from the usual grade level meetings in elementary schools, team meetings in middle schools, and department meetings in high schools. The following lists distinguish the differences.

Grade level and departmental meetings generally

- Focus on managerial or logistical directives from the school, district, or state
- Have an agenda that is determined by directives from the school, district, or state

- Are leader driven by a grade chairman or department chairman
- Have a "talk to" format, meaning that the leader presents information and the participants primarily respond to topics generated by the leader

Study group meetings generally

- Are aimed at the professional development of the members
- Focus on"what I need to do and learn to change how I teach and what I teach."
- Have an action plan that is the group's agenda
- Are driven by member needs
- Rotate leaders, with the leader not being responsible for the content of the meeting or what the group will do
- Recognize all members as being equal in status and responsibility

Study Groups as Vehicles for Change

We find that most major learning and behavioral change projects attempted in the schools fail or are only partially successful. Why is this true? As we briefly discussed in Chapter 1, the simple answer is that major change efforts, especially those relating to the well-entrenched learning and behavioral processes, are extremely difficult to accomplish in a culture, the professional school culture, that is rigidly tied to past education-related assumptions, beliefs, and behaviors, as we describe in Chapter 5. Even under the best of circumstances, bringing about major change in the schools is hard and quite simply will require far more "change management" appreciation, understanding, and application than that used in the past.

On the other hand, the beauty of whole-faculty study groups is that the methods and processes implemented in a well-designed and properly coordinated effort provide an effective change management approach. The process itself is a management system for bringing about major school change and learning improvement.

Research Supports Collaborative Work Cultures

The value of the whole-faculty study group concept is well documented. Susan Rosenholtz's (1989) research, included in her book, *Teachers' Workplace: The Social Organization of Schools,* reported on an investigation of social organizational features in 78 elementary schools in eight school districts in Tennessee. Rosenholtz's investigation included school and classroom observation; interviews with teachers, principals, superintendents, board members, and parents; data collection from 1,213 teacher questionnaires; and the analysis of student achievement. Rosenholtz concluded that schools could be categorized as "moving" (i.e., learning-enriched environments) or "stuck" (i.e., learning-impoverished environments). The comparison to follow summarizes the characteristics of the two categories:

Moving	*Stuck*
Learning enriched for students and teachers	Learning impoverished for students and teachers
Higher levels of student achievement	Lower levels of student achievement
Teachers worked together	Teachers worked alone, rarely asking for help
Teachers shared beliefs about on-the-job learning	Isolation, self reliance, and turf issues predominated
High consensus on the definition of teaching	Low consensus on the definition of teaching
Shared instructional goals occupied a place of high significance	Inertia seemed to overcome teachers' adventurous impulses
Teachers had a marked spirit of continuous improvement in which no teacher ever stops learning how to teach	Teachers less likely to trust, value, and legitimize sharing expertise, seeking advice, and giving help
80% of the teachers responded that their learning is cumulative and that learning to teach is a lifelong pursuit	17% expressed a sustained view of learning for themselves

The studies by the federally funded Center for Research on the Context of Secondary School Teaching at Stanford revealed that teachers' participation in a "professional community" had a powerful effect on how successfully they were able to adapt their instructional strategies to meet students' needs (Bradley, 1993). In one study, described by Bradley, McLaughlin and Talbert, in-depth research was conducted in 16 high schools in seven school districts in California and Michigan. One case cited (that of Rothman, 1993) was of two high schools in the same California district. Both served roughly the same student population and lived under the same rules and regulations. The study found, however, that one school had high student failure and drop-out rates, whereas the other had among the highest test scores in the state and sent 80% of its students to college. The difference was reflected in the professional characteristics of the schools. A summary of the factors associated with student achievement from the work of McLaughlin and Talbert (as cited in Bradley, 1993) follows:

High Student Achievement	*Low Student Achievement*
High levels of collegiality	Low levels of collegiality
	High norms of privacy (no sharing of resources or materials)
High levels of innovation	
High levels of opportunity for adult learning	No support or opportunity for adult learning
Subject matter seen as dynamic	Subject matter seen as static (canons were not to be challenged)
Commitment to success for all students, publicly declared	Large number of students fail
High standards for all students	Low standards for students
High degree of commitment to the school as a whole	Low commitment to the school workplace
More positive views of students	More negative views of students

Saphier and King (1985) identified 12 norms of school culture that should be strong in order to create a healthy school culture. The norms were (a) collegiality; (b) experimentation; (c) high expectations; (d) trust and confidence; (e) tangible support; (f) reaching out to the knowledge base; (g) appreciation and recognition; (h) caring, celebration, and humor; (i) involvement in decision making; (j) protection of what's important; (k) traditions; and (l) honest, open communications. If these norms are strong, then improvements in instruction will be significant, continuous, and widespread, say Saphier and King. But if these norms are weak, then improvements will be infrequent, random, and slow. Of the 12 norms, Saphier points to 3—collegiality, experimentation, and reaching out to a knowledge base—that have the highest correlation with changing the school environment and improving student achievement. Saphier (as cited in Richardson, 1996), president of Research for Better Teaching, stated that current data continue to support the 1985 Saphier and King study.

Linda Darling-Hammond (as cited in Lewis, 1997) of Teachers College, Columbia University, has worked extensively with schools around professional development. She and her colleagues have recommended in a September 1996 report to the National Commission on Teaching and America's Future that new policies are needed to accomplish the following:

- The redesigning of school structures to support teacher learning and collaboration around serious attention to practice

- The rethinking of schedules and staffing patterns to create blocks of time for teachers to plan and work together

- Making it possible for teachers to think in terms of shared problems, not "my classroom" or "my subject"

- Organizing the school into small, collaborative groups

Joyce and Calhoun (1996) synthesize and illustrate, through five case studies, new understandings about the conditions of teaching and learning that are necessary for creating substantial improvements in student achievement. The five in-depth case studies represent a very diverse set of educational challenges and settings. Joyce and Calhoun, through the case studies, show that real changes in what students learn can occur, often more rapidly than expected, if we can think and act smarter about school renewal and professional development. What the five case studies make clear is the release of synergy when well-articulated models of teaching are linked to a norm of pervasive staff development within an educational community committed to and structured around inquiry.

Murphy's research, discussed in the Snapshots in this book, also validates the impact that high norms of collegiality have on student learning. The research cited earlier leaves little doubt that effective schoolwide change and enhanced student learning require a structure or a process for greater collaboration among teachers. Furthermore, it is unlikely that the desired cultural norms described earlier will happen without a deliberate strategy. Knowing general educational research and acknowledging the validity of the research will not by itself change anything. Faculties must be given a change and process framework that is flexible enough to give them the latitude necessary to transform the research into practice. The whole-faculty study group process is such a framework. It provides a structure that creates forward-moving, learning-enriched schools.

In the remaining chapters of this book, we discuss in detail the development and application of study groups and show how they use the key elements of change and change management for the improvement of schools and enhancement of student outcomes.

3 The Results

Enhancing Student Learning

Snapshot 2 Ends and Means

At the beginning of the 1987-1988 school year, East Middle School and two other schools in the same district were the first schools to implement the whole-faculty study group design. East Middle School is located in an urban area where a staff of 40 teachers served approximately 550 sixth, seventh, and eighth graders. Ninety percent of the students qualified for free or reduced-cost lunch. The faculty agreed to engage in a whole-school improvement effort with the desired results, the ends, being an increase in student achievement and a decrease in negative student behavior. The means to those ends was a massive staff development initiative involving whole-faculty training in several models of teaching and organizing the entire faculty in study groups to support themselves in the implementation of the new teaching repertoires.

Ends and Means

One of the confusing problems we face in education is differentiating between "means" and "ends." The whole-faculty study group process is a means to an end: increased student learning.

In education, when someone asks about the success of our educational efforts, we often tell them about our teachers, our facilities, our libraries, our technology, and our curricula. However, what they were really asking about were the outcomes of our efforts, such as percentages of students graduating, the levels of student accomplishment, and graduate preparation for college or work. The former (i.e., teachers, facilities, libraries, technology, and curricula) are means, the way to deliver ends, whereas the latter (i.e., graduation rates, academic accomplishments, and graduate preparation) are ends, the results, consequences, accomplishments, and payoffs of our efforts.

Means and ends are not the same! Means are the ways to deliver ends, including resources (e.g., time, money, students, teachers and administrators, the Parent-Teacher Association (PTA), the community, technology, and facilities) and methods (e.g., teaching, collaborating, self study, learning, thinking, planning, and developing).

Some typical means and ends are as follows:

	Means	Ends
Classrooms and laboratories	X	
Libraries	X	
Financial support	X	
Inservice education	X	
Graduation		X
Board of education	X	
Teachers	X	
Study groups	X	
Graduate employment		X
Collaborative learning	X	
Strategic planning	X	
Shared governance	X	
Course grade		X
Technology	X	
Outcome-based education	X	
Graduate competence		X
Policies	X	
Accountability	X	

In education, as in other professional areas, the ends are the "what" to be accomplished, whereas the means are the "how" to accomplish the desired results.

Unfortunately, in education, we have a tendency to spend most of our resources on the means without first clearly determining the desired ends. If you don't have a target (a desired end), it's hard to find means that will help you hit it. If you want to enhance success, first, clearly determine your desired results (ends) and then, select your means based on the ends you wish to achieve.

Starting with means before identifying desired ends is backward and usually ineffective. One of the chief reasons for lack of real success in educational reform over the past decade has been the spending of most of our time and money on means without having well-defined goals that the means were to have successfully addressed. Test your own school's record; in your school's educational mission, decide what the means and ends are and observe how much attention has been given to the means.

Means are to help accomplish ends but are not ends! The definitions are as follows:

- End: A result, outcome, output, or product
- Means: The tools, methods, techniques, resources, or processes used to achieve an end

Kaufman, Herman, and Watters (1996) remind us that one of the six critical success factors in education is this: "Differentiate between ends and means" (p. 18)—focus on the *what* (the desired ends) before selecting the *how* (the means).

The Desired Results: Enhancing Student Learning

The overarching goal of each school is student learning. Consequently, the fundamental end we seek with the introduction of any new means, such as study groups, is enhanced student learning.

As a result, whole-faculty study groups focus on whole-school improvement efforts that engage the staff in a study of how to help students learn more effectively. That is, the goal of study groups is to center the entire school faculty on implementing, integrating, and managing effective teaching and learning practices that will result in an increase in student learning and a decrease in negative behaviors of students.

Whole-faculty study groups bring individual needs and institutional needs together in an organizational setting. The purpose of schools is to create the conditions where young people can learn to their fullest capacity and potential. Therefore, the goal of all study groups at a school is to collectively meet that organizational goal.

We offer a caution at this juncture. When strong advocates of professional study groups want to organize them simply for the sake of having study groups, a disservice is done to the effort, the school, and the coerced faculty. Advocates need to understand and project to others that study groups are a means to an end and not an end in and of themselves. The desired end of professional study groups is positive change in student learning and the learning environment. When increased student success is the vision and guiding principle, individuals and study groups are motivated, work harder, and take responsibility for the successful implementation of the required processes and procedures.

> *The question that guides all decisions:*
> What is happening differently in the classroom as a result of
> what you are doing and learning in study groups?

Snapshot 3   Enhancing Student Learning

In the East Middle School illustration of Snapshot 2, the desired ends were an increase in student achievement and a decrease in negative student behavior. The means to those ends was a staff development effort involving whole-faculty study groups that included the following:

- Administrators and teachers attended a 2-week training program during the first summer of the initiative, focusing on several models of teaching.
- Administrators and teachers learned the theory, observed demonstrations, and practiced four key models of teaching: concept attainment, inductive thinking, mnemonics, and cooperative learning.
- Administrators expected the teachers to use the models or strategies frequently and appropriately throughout the school year.
- Teachers met weekly for about an hour in study groups of five or six members to jointly plan and practice lessons using the models.
- Teachers made video tapes of their teaching on a regular basis.
- Administrators and teachers attended similar training programs for the next two summers and continued to meet in study groups during the school years.

- Virtually all teachers learned to use the teaching models and strategies to a mechanical level of competence, and some reached higher levels of skill by the conclusion of the first year.

The models and strategies of teaching were new to almost all of the teachers and students, requiring substantial amounts of new learning. Administrators scheduled time for study groups to meet, teachers practiced the strategies in the classrooms, and teachers taught the students how to use the teaching strategies as learning strategies. Some study groups were comfortable planning and sharing; others were anxious. New teachers hired during the 3 years had to be integrated into the process. The degree of change that occurred was dramatic:

- Only 34% of the students reached promotion standards the year before the whole-school improvement effort began. That number rose to 72% after the first year of implementation and 94% after the second year.
- At the conclusion of the first year of implementation, the number of promotions by exception dropped from 33% to 13%, and the number of students retained dropped from 33% to 15%.
- The eighth graders taking the state's Eighth Grade Basic Skills Writing Test scored the lowest (11th) in the district the year study groups were initiated; the students who were sixth graders that year went on to score 3rd in the district when they were eighth graders.
- Out-of-school suspensions were reduced from 343 the year prior to the training and study group implementation to 124 during the year of implementation.
- The ITBS battery in social studies was administrated to the sixth graders at the conclusion of the first year of the initiative and again 2 years later, when these same students were eighth graders. Their rate of growth was 6 months more than their past rate would have predicted.

During the first year of implementation of the staff development program described in this Snapshot, all other factors at the school stayed the same as they were during the year prior to the initiative. There were no changes in the administration, facilities, or curriculum; no increase in instructional funds; and no additional personnel. The only interventions were the study group design and the training in the models and strategies of teaching.

When teachers in the East Middle School, illustrated in Snapshots 2 and 3, were organized into study groups to help them learn new teaching models and strategies, their students' achievements and behavior improved remarkably (Joyce & Calhoun, 1996). The school developed an improvement program based on principles derived from research, including the following:

- Modification of the culture of the school and the processes of innovation
- The ways that teachers learn new instructional models and strategies
- The ways teachers transfer new skills to the classroom
- The creation of more of a learning-organization environment in the school

Their design restructured the workplace (the means) by organizing teachers into collegial study groups, providing regular training on teaching, and inducing faculties to set goals for school improvements (the ends) and strive to achieve them.

4 The Function

Accomplishing Many Purposes

Snapshot 4   Change Transition

As a result of implementing the whole-faculty study group design, 12 schools in five school districts in central Kentucky have found that transformation plans are now more "real" to the teachers who transition the plans into classroom practice. A focus team from each of the 12 schools attended whole-faculty study group training in the summer. Each team spent 3 days developing a plan for initiating and implementing study groups. The teams worked with their faculties in August during preplanning days in designing how the study groups would be structured. It was assumed that the study groups in the schools would be organized around causes of instructional problems that had been specified in the schools' transformation plans developed the prior spring. When the teachers looked at their plans from the perspective of what teachers would study, investigate, and do to enable students to achieve at higher levels, they saw a general lack of clarity and specificity in the plans. Seeing the discrepancy in what was stated and what teachers would actually do in collaborative groups to address the causes of instructional and curricular problems created frustration and anxiety. As teachers began to write action plans for what they would do in the study groups, they saw more clearly what to include in the schools' transformation plans that would transform the schools. At the conclusion of the schools' first year of having all teachers in study groups addressing the causes of curricular and instructional problems, the schools used the study groups to tie student development to teacher development. Making this shift made the transformation plans living documents. As the schools began the second year of using the study group design, the groups worked more authentically from the schools' transformation plans.

Another outcome of the whole-faculty study group design in the 12 schools was the realization that professional development is inclusive of various models that interact with each other to make a more dynamic whole. At the beginning of the first year, schools saw study groups separate from the professional development days. They saw study groups and professional development days as separate from whole-faculty or individual training needs. And they were likely to see all of the before mentioned as separate from attending conferences and doing independent activities. By the conclusion of Year 1, when the schools' professional development committees met, the committees were more able to design professional development plans that had the various development strategies or models feeding (i.e., interdependent with) each other. The faculties were clear in saying that it was the study groups that enabled them to plan more integrated and holistic approaches to professional development.

Change Transition

When initiated, implemented, and managed properly, professional study groups are impressive and effective. Whole-faculty study groups allow for the creation of individual, team, and schoolwide processes that increase student achievement and school accomplishment. And all of this can be done without substantial additional costs.

Why are whole-faculty study groups so effective? Why are whole-faculty study groups such good vehicles of change?

Genuine school reform, especially increased student achievement and school improvement, is difficult to accomplish and represents major change. It must deal with the natural resistance to change of people and organizations and the rigidities of an educational and social culture that has been in place for centuries.

For example, for a long time, our schools have been geared to preparing students to work in the Industrial Age. Now, we are being confronted with a very different era, the Information Age, with new kinds of educational, technological, and workforce needs and demands. Simultaneously, we have reached the productivity and quality capacity of many of our existing educational processes (Branson, 1987).

As a consequence, significant improvements in our schools are going to come very hard. Frankly, most processes now being tried to bring about change and reform are just not capable of bringing about such massive change.

On the other hand, properly initiated, implemented, and managed professional, whole-faculty study groups are effective processes of change. As we shall illustrate in the remainder of this book, they encompass the key elements of change management for the transformation of processes and organizations. These include the following elements:

- Effective change sponsorship
- The building of individual, team, and school resilience (i.e., the ability to demonstrate both strength and flexibility in the face of disorder and change) so that people and schools can be more change adaptable
- Collaboration and synergy—common goals, interdependence, empowerment, and participative involvement
- Modification of the educational and school culture

These factors, not fully contained in most change efforts, are critical to bringing about major change in any complex organization, such as a school, and will be discussed in detail and applied in subsequent chapters.

Whole-faculty study groups, though complex and requiring a substantial, broad-based commitment, are among the most effective and applicable processes available to bring about school reform and help enhance student achievement and school improvement.

Functions and Purposes

Professional study groups serve many functions and purposes, including the major ones whose descriptions follow, and some of these simultaneously.

1. *Supporting the implementation of curricular and instructional innovations*. The implementation of new learning is affected by the fact that our individual abilities to understand and use new curricular and instructional ideas frequently encountered in courses and workshops vary considerably, as do our personal assumption, values and beliefs, and experiences. By providing teachers of varying attitudes, knowledge, and skills with the opportunity for their support of each other, new learning will more likely be used in the workplace. Study groups create such opportunities, increasing the implementation of new practices learned in courses and workshops and the effectiveness of new curricula and educational materials.

For instance, teachers are trained to use new instructional strategies that are backed by a strong research base and apply to a wide variety of curriculum areas. Such strategies or models may include cooperative learning, inductive thinking and concept attainment, and mnemonics. These strategies are often categorized as higher order thinking skills. The expectation is that all of the teachers in a school are to reach high levels of appropriate use of these strategies in their classrooms. This is not likely to happen if the workplace is not designed to prepare teachers to support each other in the immediate and sustained use of the new practices. The leaders of such a training effort might ask study groups to

- Share lessons and materials already used so others could use the plans or materials and thus cut down on preparation time

- Observe each other trying the new strategies to learn from each other and study student responses to the strategies

- Plan future applications of the strategies within their curriculum areas in an attempt to integrate new strategies with existing repertoires and instructional objectives

If teachers do not have a schoolwide structured support system, teachers will often delay using the new practices. When they do use them and a lesson goes poorly, it will be an even longer time before they try again. If there is any fear or skepticism about the new procedure, delay gives anxiety time to develop, and practice will not ensue. Thus, a major training effort fails to achieve its intended results.

However, if the school has a schoolwide design that encourages sharing successes and failures, there will be a high degree of comfort in practicing lessons together and doing joint work in preparing lessons. As a teacher's comfort level rises, so does the level of use with students and the assurance that new strategies and new materials will have a positive impact on the students in the school.

2. *Integrating and giving coherence to a school's instructional practices and programs*. A charge given to study groups that has schoolwide benefits is for teachers to attempt to integrate new objectives, strategies, materials, and programs with those currently in existence.

Schools and teachers are continually bombarded with innovations. At any point in time, teachers are confronted with questions concerning (Guskey, 1990) these issues:

- Ongoing, year-after-year technical assistance

- How the various innovations are similar and different

- How similarities can be used to positively influence different aspects of classroom application of the innovations

A professional study group is a vehicle for answering these questions and making sense out of past, current, and future instructional initiatives. It is also a vehicle through which instructional innovations are made more coherent by teachers who are expected to implement them. By exploring the theoretical and research bases of the various instructional models that routinely confront teachers, study groups can identify the critical attributes to see how the programs or practices are alike and how they are different, which would duplicate current efforts, and which would compromise or lessen the impact of current initiatives. This analysis would minimize or avoid the traditional layering of initiatives, bringing coherence to all-to-often disjointed efforts.

For example, whole language, cooperative learning, and critical thinking skills are typically perceived as three separate strategies or programs, because they are usually introduced to teachers in three separate and distinct packages or by three different trainers. Frequently, it is left up to the teacher to try to figure out the relationships and the common attributes of the three strategies. A group of teachers who regularly meet over a period of time, a study group, to synthesize the new information and innovations and together develop lessons that incorporate all three strategies will have an improved chance of attaining the strategies' intended results.

3. *Targeting an identified schoolwide need.* The term *whole-faculty study group* means that at all times, the focus is on every student, by every teacher, every administrator, every grade level, every curriculum area, and every student service. *Whole* should be interpreted as schoolwide.

Making the whole school better for all of the students it serves is a constant function of all of the study groups in a school. It is the collective energy and synergy that is generated from all of the groups that propel the school forward. A student does not excel as a middle school student because a student had a great fourth-grade teacher. The reason is more likely to be because the student had outstanding learning opportunities as a kindergartner and first through fifth grader. The middle schooler continues to excel because all of the teachers have an extensive repertoire and are masters of the content they teach. The cumulative effect of good teaching over years of schooling produces a high school graduate that can be expected to continue as a learner. When all of the teachers in a school are in study groups that target good teaching practices, a range of schoolwide needs will be met. To focus on a schoolwide need, data from all of the grades and a look at the effectiveness of all of the curricula must be examined. The fourth grade is not singled out because it is the grade where the state tests are administered. If the standardized tests administered in the fourth grade indicate that reading comprehension is a problem, then that is a problem for all grades in the school.

After the whole faculty analyzes information about the whole school and its students, the school may identify several areas that need attention and have study groups form around those areas of need. Or one area is given priority, and all of the groups take an aspect of that problem. If the repertoire of teachers is too limited, then expanding those repertoires would be the target of all study groups. If the school has just adopted a new mathematics textbook, then all teachers may want to target the new mathematics curriculum.

4. *Studying research on teaching and learning.* An important aspect of the study group process is the reflection on research that describes effective teaching and effective schools, allowing the faculty to make wiser, research-based decisions. In professional study groups, teachers increase their contact, understanding, and application of

new innovations from educational research in the United States and abroad, providing for better use of funds and an improved educational environment. Teaching is often perceived as being so personal to a particular teacher and classroom that the teacher does not feel that what happens with another class has any significance for him or her. This reality was made evident in a district committed to increasing student achievement through the training of staffs in several models of teaching. At the beginning of the effort, teachers were given examples of successful efforts of schools in California that used this approach to school improvement. The teachers responded, "That's California, not here." The next year after successful implementation of the program in one middle school in the district, the success was shared with another middle school in the same district. The teachers responded, "That's East Middle School, not here." The school did decide, however, to join the school improvement program. The next year, after successful implementation in most of the classrooms in the new middle school, the success one teacher had in her classroom with her students was shared with another teacher in the same school. The teacher responded, "That's Mrs. Brown's classroom, not mine." It seems no matter how close to home examples of success are, the feeling that "my classroom and my students are different from anyone else's" is so pervasive that it is hard for many teachers to learn from what others have done or are doing. The personalization of teaching is one of the barriers broken when teachers meet routinely in study groups and share teaching practices. As teachers become more open and objective about teaching and learning practices, they feel and become less isolated. Contact with a broad base of relevant research encourages teachers to take more seriously what other districts are discovering about general improvement strategies and to be more actively involved in the collection and analysis of data that come from their own schools and classrooms.

For example, one study group decided that its members could best meet the diverse needs of their students by collecting information and data on several approaches to school improvement. The group read and discussed the work of Bruce Joyce, Lawrence Lazotte, James Comer, Henry Levin, and Theodore Sizer. Taking a school year for readings, visitations, attending conferences, and viewing videos gave the group members an opportunity to analyze and determine how to apply the new knowledge to improve their school. Study groups that take this approach, taking a year to gather information, should do so with the understanding that schoolwide change will be delayed. It will be delayed until action is taken on what was learned through the data gathering. It is action, changed behaviors, in every classroom that creates schoolwide change, not the reading about change programs and the gathering of information.

5. *Monitoring the impact of innovations on students and on changes in the workplace.* Prior to initiating an innovation, members of a study group might review information and other data that could lead them to the identification of specific student needs. During the information collection stage, data could be organized and interpreted about student learning and about the learning environment.

When student need is defined, the group agrees on an instructional intervention aimed at increasing the students' proficiency in the area of need. For example, if students are not using technology for a variety of purposes, the teachers plan lessons and deliberate opportunities for students to use technology in language arts, mathematics, science, music, and other content areas. Given such focused attention, teachers chart the students' use of technology when the students are given choices as to how assignments may be completed. Teachers also chart student use of available software in a wide range of subject areas. Then, students are asked to respond to questionnaires that reveal their comfort and proficiency levels in using technology. At points along the way, teachers can track changes in student behavior. Taking action on a student need and monitoring the effects of that action is often referred to as *action research*. The collection and analysis of information over a period of time will tell the teachers in the study group whether or not the intervention is having its intended result.

6. *Acting as a vehicle to accomplish many purposes.* We often use "vehicle" in relation to study groups. Study groups carry, push, and support many schoolwide needs. Study groups transport abstract information to concrete classroom practice. Study groups move information and training from district offices to every classroom in a school. Study groups provide vehicles to do what is already expected that teachers will do, with the study groups giving support and companionship in the doing of those expectations. Study groups are vehicles that enable members to

- Become learners
- Engage in the process of reflection, authentic teaching, and assessment
- Provide support to each other, encourage risk taking, and celebrate success
- Observe and share information about one another's work
- Question, prod, and critique each other in ways that expand the "comfort zone" of current practice
- Generate concrete and precise talk about teaching practices
- Create the forum for joint work (Little, 1990)

In summary, as a professional development model, whole-faculty study groups present an integrated learning experience for adults. It is an approach to learning characterized by the following learning principles:

- Whole-faculty study groups are teacher centered. The teachers in a group determine what they need to know and what they need to do more skillfully to meet the needs of their students.
- Whole-faculty study groups give teachers the opportunity to experiment. In groups, teachers try new materials, new techniques, new strategies, and new technologies.
- Whole-faculty study groups inspire reflection. As teachers talk about their practices, they reflect on what works and does not work and why a critical element for change in practice is to occur and be sustained.
- Whole-faculty study groups provide authentic learning experiences. The teachers are not following an instructor's syllabus or set of objectives presented to them. The experiences are designed by the group and tied to the teachers' classrooms and students. Because the group is addressing their students' needs, the work of the group is real and meaningful.
- Whole-faculty study groups focus on the whole. The needs of the whole school, the whole class, the whole art of teaching are brought into focus. Isolation, once the norm, is broken. Not only has isolation from each other been a common work condition, but instructional programs and strategies have often been viewed separately.

- Whole-faculty study groups support democratic behavior. All of the faculty members have an opportunity to decide if having the teachers work together in small groups will benefit their students. All of the faculty members have a voice in what the student needs are that the groups will address and the method that will be used to determine the membership of the study groups. And once the study groups are formed, each member of the group has a voice in determining exactly how the group will work and what the group will do.

- Whole-faculty study groups allow teachers to construct their own learning and their own meanings in what they read, hear, and see. The process validates a teacher's individuality and empowers a teacher to go beyond the boundaries that are usually set by others.

- Whole-faculty study groups give teachers the motivation to establish challenging and rigorous standards for themselves.

Embedded in these foregoing points are principles of integrated learning that are important for all learners regardless of age. As teachers are respected for how they learn best, it is hoped that the end result will be that the teachers will do the same for their students.

The Context

Building Commitment

The *context* addresses the organization, system, or culture in which the study groups exist. It is the organizational or cultural factors that facilitate or impede progress toward the organization's intended results. The context includes how the organization "feels" to the personnel, as well as the norms that govern their lives. It is often the informal structure of how things get done. The context will largely determine how psychologically safe individuals feel, how willing they are to take risks, what behaviors are rewarded and punished, and whether it is standard to work in isolation or with peers. The context of an organization is typically the first line of concern for sponsors or change agents.

On the other hand, *process* refers to the "how" of staff development. It describes the means for the acquisition of new knowledge and skills. And *content* refers to the actual skills and knowledge educators want to possess or acquire through staff development or some other means. Diagrammatically, context, process, and content are illustrated in Table 5.1, and these concepts are discussed in this and the next two chapters.

Snapshot 5   Building Commitment

Sweetwater High School is a large urban school with 110 certificated instructional staff members. The school serves a low-socioeconomic-status community. It is a year-round school using block schedules to meet the diverse needs of its students. In May 1993, by an 89% approval vote, the staff elected to participate in the whole-faculty study group process. In December 1993, 15 heterogeneous study groups of four to six educators were formed; they met for 1 hour each week within the professional duty day to study, reflect, and develop strategies that would strengthen their curriculum and instruction. As of this writing, 4 years later, a total of 18 groups continue to meet weekly for the first hour of a school day.

The 1-hour study group period once a week provided the environment to build a strong, collaborative work culture that enhanced the school's capacity to change. The groups considered genuine questions (e.g., What will the practice of constructivists' models look like in my classroom? How will portfolio assessment benefit my students and assist in evaluating my instructional program?). This left a mark on Sweetwater teachers' perspectives and created a climate for change in policy and practice.

Table 5.1 Diagram of Context, Process, and Content

Context:

Organizational or cultural factors that facilitate or impede progress toward intended results, such as a shared vision and norms of continuous improvement and collegiality

Process:

How individuals, groups, and the whole will function, behave, perform; procedures to be followed; the means for the acquisition on new knowledge and skills

Content:

What individuals, groups, and the whole will study, learn, or become skillful in doing to achieve the intended results; skills, attitudes, and knowledge to be acquired

The diversity of the study groups is substantial; for example, one study group, addressing the self-esteem of high school students, is made up of teachers from physical education, fine arts, mathematics, and social sciences, and a counselor.

The focus team, the overseer of the whole-faculty study group process, is very active at Sweetwater. The team is composed of seven teachers and two administrators who attended the initial training and follow-up training. The team puts out a monthly newsletter, called *FOCUS,* which shares what the study groups are doing. At the beginning of the year, the team establishes a calendar of study group events for the coming year. Once a month, the team disperses and meets with assigned study groups to serve as liaisons. The goal of the liaison is to promote communication among study groups and problem solve areas of concern. The team also serves on the school's instructional council, which meets once a quarter and is made up of the leaders of each of the study groups. Because leadership rotates among study group members, the one attending the council meeting is the one who is the leader the week the council meets. In this way, the composition of the council is very fluid and always changing. The focus team also plans schoolwide activities, such as the celebration of the 4-year anniversary of study groups at Sweetwater.

To assess the effectiveness of each year's study groups, a survey is distributed to all staff members during the last staff development day of the school calendar. The survey includes questions to be answered by study groups as teams as well as in-depth individual assessments. Feedback from both strands of the survey is used to further strengthen the tie between teacher learning and student learning. The focus team summarizes the information and shares the results with the faculty. Future decisions about how study groups will function and what they will do are based on this survey information and student data.

All of the energy emanating from the study groups produced dramatic improvements in student achievement. In 1992-1993, Sweetwater ranked 8th out of 9 schools in the high school district in grade point average (GPA) and second in failure rate. Through sustained study group engagement, these rankings were changed. In 1994-1995, Sweetwater's cumulative GPA was second highest in the district and course failure rates dropped 40% overall and 62% for students identified as limited English proficient. In April 1996, Sweetwater High School was notified by the Superintendent of Public Instruction in California that they has been selected as the 1996 Distinguished High School.

Building Commitment

In Snapshot 5, the initial context of Sweetwater High School was one that approved, by an 89% vote of the staff, the school participating in the whole-faculty study group process. This was a major commitment by the school's faculty and administration to the potential enhancement of their students and school and to the study group process. As positive results of study group efforts unfolded over the next few years, the Sweetwater High School context grew in its responsiveness and commitment to the study group process

In general, the more competent we become, the more committed we become. As teachers and administrators see that they are more competent in delivering instruction and the students show more competency on tests, the more supportive and committed they are to the study group process. What makes faculties want to continue the study group model year after year is its contribution to both the faculty's increased effectiveness and the positive measurable impact on their students.

As teachers and schools, through study groups, attempt to enhance learning for their students, they introduce alternatives and innovations in the structure, programs, processes, and practices of the school. These alternatives and innovations usually represent major changes in its systems and often become threats to the prevailing context of the school. Consequently, for study groups to be effective and for schools to improve their results, they must deal with the basic elements, concerns, and potential difficulties of major change within their school or district context.

One of the most important factors in dealing with major change is the building of commitment for the desired change projects of the study groups and their ramifications. That is, commitment building is creating in the study group context (i.e., in the environment of the study group) a foundation for personal, political, and institutional acceptance, encouragement, and support for the study group process. The more effectively the commitment is built, the more effectively will be the work and results of the study group. On the other hand, it must be recognized that it is almost impossible to bring about meaningful change in a context or environment that is nonsupportive!

In the balance of this chapter, we discuss a number of concepts and approaches that enhance commitment for study group efforts and help reshape the context to create an environment that is supportive of study groups and the changes resulting from them. As an important part of this commitment-building process, we discuss and illustrate, in Snapshot 6 and the following section, the four key roles of change: change sponsor, change agent, change target, and change advocate.

Snapshot 6   Roles of Change

A Kentucky cooperative invited its member school districts to attend a day's meeting in February to hear a consultant discuss how the whole-faculty study group approach to professional development could be a vehicle for schools to implement transformation plans. As part of the Kentucky Education Reform Act, all schools develop transformation plans targeted at increasing student achievement. The districts were invited to send a district leader, principals, and teachers to the orientation meeting. After the meeting, those in attendance from the district discussed the pros and cons of proposing the study group concept to other district leaders and to their faculties. The district representatives that decided to encourage the study group structure in their districts did so with the recommendation that the structure be put in place at the beginning of the next school year. Six districts decided to move forward. One district leader met with her superintendent and, later, the entire group that attended the orientation meeting met with the board of education.

After hearing from teachers and principals in all six schools in the district, the board voted in May to release students in all district schools 2 hours early one Wednesday per month for study groups to meet. On another Wednesday in the month, study groups were to meet in place of a faculty meeting. This schedule was to be effective in September when the new school year began. During that summer, the cooperative sponsored a 3-day training workshop for a team from each of the 12 schools in the six districts that would initiate study groups that fall. The six districts pooled resources to cover the expenses of the summer training and for the follow-up support for the consultant that would be in place during the school year. The cooperative continued to be the fiscal agent for the initiative and coordinated the initiative from a regional level. Each district had a strong advocate at the district level to ensure that resources were allocated to the schools to support the initiative.

Each school's principal and teachers that attended the summer training were advocates of the study group process and made sure that time was allocated during the preplanning days for the whole faculty to decide how the groups would function and what the groups would do. Teachers shared with students what they were doing in study groups. Parents were informed and kept abreast of progress through school and community newsletters. Everyone had a role to play in mobilizing support for the professional development study group innovation. Throughout the year, these roles interacted and crossed, keeping the momentum going. The district that released its students 2 hours early one Wednesday each month of the school year had no complaints from parents about how the time was being used.

Roles of Change

As schools attempt to build commitment for study group efforts that affect their people, processes, and outcomes, an understanding of the four roles of change—change sponsor, change agent, change target, and change advocate—is critical.

A *change sponsor* or *sponsor* is an individual or group who has the power to sanction or legitimize the change or efforts of the study group. In schools, depending on the specific change effort, a sponsor might be the school board, the superintendent, the principal, a department chair, or a combination of these individuals, because they, typically, are the ones who can sanction or legitimize study group efforts and change. Also, in a whole-faculty study group situation, where essentially the whole faculty has endorsed the study group initiative, the faculty itself becomes an important and potentially effective sponsor of the study group change process and the results coming from study group efforts.

Sponsors weigh the potential of study groups and their change implications and assess the opportunities and problems of the implementation of their possible recommendations. It is the sponsor's responsibility to decide what initiatives and changes will be authorized, communicate their decisions and priorities to the school and its personnel, and provide the appropriate encouragement, pressure, and support for the study group's efforts. Strong sponsors are key to the building of commitment for study group efforts and can create an environment in the school that enables their work to be effectively implemented and productive.

In Snapshot 6, notice the broad sponsorship that developed in support of the study group approach. It began with the Kentucky Education Reform Act providing an umbrella authority and expectation for reform in the Kentucky schools. This was followed by a Kentucky cooperative sponsoring a meeting to acquaint leaders, principals, and teachers in its member school districts with the whole-faculty study group concept. In those districts that chose to participate in study groups, superintendents, principals, and the board of education sponsored the implementation of the study group process and legitimized it, both through formal action and specific commitments, in those districts. This made the study group process both important to the schools and legitimate for principals, teachers, and others to invest time and serious commitment in. Also, notice how, by educating the parents and bringing them along with the effort, the parents, too, became, directly or indirectly, supporters of the study group approach, rather than resisters and opponents of it.

A *change agent* or *agent* is an individual or group who is responsible for implementing the desired change. Teachers and study groups often play the role of change agent in a school alteration or innovation, as do various administrators and supervisors. An agent's success depends on preparation as a change agent; relations with others in the school; and the abilities to diagnose problems, deal with the issues, plan solutions, and implement plans effectively. Properly prepared study groups can assist in commitment-building efforts for desired school change and have the potential to be especially effective change agents for the enhancement of student learning and the improvement of our schools.

A *change target* or *target* is an individual or group who must actually change. Targets are the people who must change if the alternation or innovation is to be successful. In school improvement projects, targets typically are students, teachers, or administrators who must change for students to be more successful.

For example, if the change calls for computer-assisted instruction, then students would be targets and have to change by learning how to use computers in an instructional mode. Probably, a number of teachers and administrators also would be targets and have to change somewhat to help students change.

As study groups are created and implemented, the individual members and the group find that for their efforts to be successful, they, too, must actually change (e.g., teachers might change in how they approach and study issues, in their relations with others, in their basic assumptions, beliefs, and behaviors about students and the learning process, and in their implementation of new practices and processes).

In addition, it is important that teachers see the relationship between their behaviors and the students' behaviors. Change in teachers' behaviors is the immediate target of study groups. As teachers work together in becoming more skillful in their

Whole-Faculty Study Groups'
Impact on
Student Performance

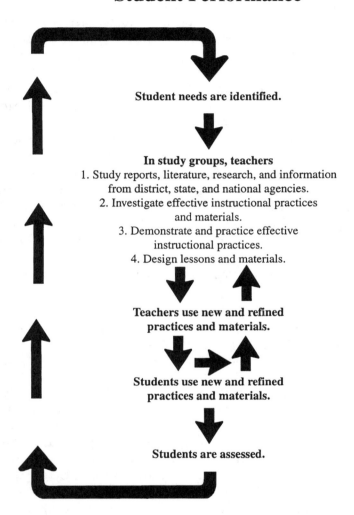

Figure 5.1. Whole-Faculty Study Groups' Impact on Student Performance
Copyright © 1997 by Carlene Murphy.

practices and in the materials they use, the focus shifts to students as targets and their becoming more skillful. It is doubtful that students will become more skillful if teachers continue to use practices that are not causing students to change. Student change is measured by increased learning and by differences in how they behave.

For example, teachers become skillful at using mnemonics in teaching information that students should memorize. As teachers use this strategy, students will use the strategy as they confront new information that they want to know "by heart." For the teacher, mnemonics is a teaching strategy; then, it becomes a learning strategy for the student.

Figure 5.1 depicts how changes in teacher behaviors precede changes in student behaviors. Student needs are identified and study groups are formed to address the student needs. In study groups, teachers study together, investigate new practices and materials, demonstrate to each other how they teach a concept, practice with each other a new skill, design lessons, construct materials, and share what works for them and what does not work. As a result of what the teachers do in the study group, the teachers use new or refined instructional practices and materials. After using the practices and materials in their classrooms, in the study group the teachers share and revise their work. Overtime, the study group's cycle of using and sharing creates the synergy for the teachers to change how and what they teach. As students experience more powerful teaching practices, the new teaching behaviors result in changes in how and what students learn. Student behavior feeds back into and determines how and what teachers do next. These inner cycles within Figure 5.1 is where the momentum is generated for improved student performance. A range of student assessments will continue to identify student needs that are to be continually addressed by teachers in their study groups.

As we relate to targets, those who are to change, it is important to remember that they are very much like us; they will be more responsive to our efforts if we put things in their frames of reference and help them fully understand the desired change, why it is important, what is expected of them, and the impact of the change on them and the school. Fullan and Steigelbauer (1991) state that people must be able to attach personal meaning to the experiences regardless of how meaningful the experiences may be to others. This is true for students as well as for teachers. Fullan and Steigelbauer go on to say that the mechanisms to address the ongoing problem, for the individuals expected to change, are critical to success, because it is at the individual level that change does or does not occur. The change agent, then, must be alert to how the meaning of change is communicated to the targets of the change.

A *change advocate* or *advocate* is an individual or group who desires a change but doesn't have the authority or power to sanction it. Frequently, faculty study groups, principal, or nonschool persons or groups, such as parents, play the role of advocate when they want something new to happen, but they do not have the power to approve it.

Advocates are typically those who recommend actions to an individual or group with the authority to approve or further recommend. For instance, a community person may advocate for a special resolution to the school board, or a department may ask the principal for a special budget consideration, or a principal might recommend a certain policy to the superintendent for school board consideration.

In different circumstances, an individual or group may play different change roles. We have described how study groups could play all four roles of change sponsor, agent, target, and advocate. In addition, various change projects might require an individual or group to serve in more than one change role. A typical example might be where a principal is an agent to the superintendent but a sponsor to the school teachers. The important thing to remember is to determine the role you are playing in the given situation and perform it well.

A summary of the roles of change and the situational roles in Snapshot 6 are given in Table 5.2.

Effective Sponsorship

All four change roles are necessary for the success of study groups and major change. However, the roles of those in leadership positions are especially critical. For major

Table 5.2 Roles of Change and the Roles in Snapshot 6

	Role of Change and Definition	*Roles in Snapshot 6*
Change sponsor:	Individual or group with power to legitimize the desired change	Board of education Superintendents Principals
Change agent:	Individual or group responsible for implementing the desired change	Principals Teachers
Change target:	Individual or group who must actually change	Teachers Students
Change advocate:	Individual or group who desires a change but doesn't have power to sanction it	Principals Teachers Parents

alterations or innovations to be successfully implemented in our schools, sponsors must demonstrate strong, decisive, and visible commitment to those efforts. Very simply, significant change will not occur without sufficient commitment and action by the sponsors, such as those by the board of education, superintendents, and principals in the schools illustrated in Snapshot 6 and Table 5.2.

Strong sponsorship is absolutely critical for major change! Sponsors must show strong commitment to ensure that agents and targets are effective in their roles. Often, the difference between success and failure in school efforts comes down to the quality of the sponsorship! Furthermore, anyone can be an advocate. We must be careful not to confuse "advocacy of change" with "sponsorship of change."

In his excellent book on change, Conner (1993) outlines the characteristics of a good sponsor. What follows is an adaptation of these sponsorship characteristics to the school setting.

- Power—Power in the school to legitimize the change with targets
- Pain—A level of discomfort with some area of the school that makes change there attractive
- Vision—A clear understanding of what change must occur
- Resources—An understanding of the school resources (e.g., time, money, and people) necessary for successful implementation and the capacity (i.e., willingness and ability) to commit them
- Long View—An in-depth understanding of the effect the change will have on the school
- Sensitivity—The capacity to appreciate and empathize with the personal issues raised by the change
- Scope—The capacity to understand fully the impact of the change
- Public Role—The capacity to demonstrate the public support necessary to convey strong school commitment to the change
- Private Role—The capacity to meet privately with key individuals or groups to convey strong personal support for the change

- Consequence management—The capacity to reward promptly those who facilitate the change or to express displeasure with those who inhibit it
- Monitor—The capacity to ensure that monitoring procedures are established that will track both the progress and problems of the transition
- Sacrifice—The commitment to pursue the transition, knowing that a price will most often accompany the change
- Persistence—The capacity to demonstrate consistent support for the change and reject any short-term action that is inconsistent with the long-term change goals

The forenamed criteria give a comprehensive set of characteristics by which to measure the sponsorship for whole-faculty study groups in a school or district. If most of these are met, there is a high probability for good sponsorship and support. However, if several of these are not satisfied, then there may be serious sponsorship problems; in such situations, leaders should work to improve sponsorship for the effort or replace the sponsors with stronger ones.

Whole-faculty study groups and their schoolwide efforts represent major change in the school. As a result, they will require the same strong and effective sponsorship as that outlined. If a major study group initiative does not have a reasonably high level of sponsorship commitment or if such cannot be developed in an appropriate time frame, then the initiative has a high risk of failure.

What should be done if sponsorship is weak? When sponsors are not fully committed to the study group process, don't fully understand it, or are unable or unwilling to provide adequate support, there are only three options: advocates must educate sponsors, find alternate sponsorship, or prepare to fail. Strong sponsorship is absolutely vital to the success of effective whole-faculty study groups and the change initiatives they hope to accomplish!

Human Change and Resistance

Human beings have a strong need for control. This is especially true when it comes to change. When we have a sense of control over change and its circumstances, we typically feel comfortable. So the change we initiate, understand, and have a sense of control over is a change that we feel good about and are comfortable with.

There are actually two types of control we all seek: direct control, where we have the direct ability to request or actually dictate outcomes that usually occur, and indirect control, where we have the ability to at least anticipate the outcomes of a change. People usually have the highest level of comfort when they have a sense of direct control.

Indirect control results in less, but some, comfort with change. For example, if I am not in direct control of some change but understand the change and know the implications of it, I then can anticipate what will occur. This again, is indirect control, and I will feel less threatened by the change than if I had no sense of possible outcomes.

What all this means is that if leaders of an innovation want people to feel comfortable with a particular change, the leaders must do whatever is appropriate and necessary to give them a sense of control, either direct or indirect, for the change effort. If this can be done, leaders enhance the chances that people will be supportive of and helpful with the change.

On the other hand, if people aren't given some sense of control over the change by feeling able to directly dictate or influence its outcomes or at least anticipate its outcomes, they may feel threatened. As a result, they will do what comes naturally when people don't understand or appreciate what is going on; they will resist the change, either openly and overtly or covertly. Human resistance to change is not an aberration or a reflection that something is wrong with someone. Instead, it is a natural reaction to change when one does not understand the change and its implications and so does not have a sense of direct or indirect control of the change. Consequently, if you do not want people to do what is natural relative to change (i.e., resist it), then, very simply, you must make them feel comfortable with the change by doing things that help them understand the change and its implications and that give them a sense of either direct or indirect control. The major change principle that describes how to do this is discussed in the next section.

Universal Change Principle

In this section, we describe a critical principle for dealing with and helping others deal with change. It gives an overarching approach for managing change and is applicable virtually everywhere. Because of its broad applicability, we call it the *universal change principle.*

For our discussion of change and the universal change principle, think of *learning* as gaining information, knowledge, or understanding for effective action relative to the change or the implications of the change under consideration.

Universal Change Principle: Learning Must Precede Change

That is, if people are to help bring about change, then they must be provided with the appropriate learning, in advance, so that they understand and appreciate the change and its implications. Providing the appropriate learning allows people to gain a reasonable sense of control with respect to the change.

Appropriate learning does not mean that the change agents have an answer for every circumstance in the initiation and implementation stages of the innovation. In any complex change effort, such as whole-faculty study groups, there will be holes and blanks that cannot be filled in by any but the implementers. Appropriate learning would include knowing theoretical and practical underpinnings that support the proposition that the new process, practice, program, attitude, belief, or material would bring about the desired change in a specific school or with a particular group of students. Teachers should know what disagreements or conflicts may exist among researchers about the new practice. When the initiators or change agents confirm with teachers that there are few clear answers that fit every situation, teachers are more likely to see themselves as the experts in their situation, given the latitude to find the answers for their students. Teachers with this attitude and that are part of a strong support system will be less likely to get frustrated and rebellious when the proposed change hits snags. The learning that precedes the change, then, includes a clarification of the meaning of the change and whatever information is required for the proposed implementers to agree to begin.

For example, a simple illustration of the universal change principle might be a driver who wants to make a turn ahead. He provides learning for those behind him by lighting his turn signal a few hundred feet before the turn. As a result, all drivers learn of the first driver's desired change and then have time to make their appropriate adjustments. In this case, learning preceded change for the success and safety of all.

Another example might be a principal who wants the mathematics faculty to use a new approach for teaching basic mathematics. If that principal just announces one day that starting next semester, the mathematics faculty will teach by the new method, probably most of the faculty will be unfamiliar with the new approach, not understand its value and implementation, not feel comfortable with this new change, and, as a consequence, resist rather than be helpful with what the principal desires to happen.

However, suppose the principal instead uses the universal change principle to guide the implementation of what he or she desires to have happen. Following this approach, the principal would first ask the question, "What learning must take place before this change can be successfully implemented?" In response, the principal would most likely involve the mathematics faculty in a series of discussions concerning what he or she is thinking about; why this is important to improving student learning, to the faculty and to the school; what the implications are for the students, faculty, and school; and how and when the new approach should be implemented. Doing all of this doesn't guarantee that everyone will be in favor of the change and that all resistance will be averted. It does, though, ensure greater understanding of what's desired; why it's important; and what the implications are for the students, faculty, and school and helps the faculty gain a sense of control for the project, making them feel much more comfortable with it and its implementation. As a result, the faculty are far more likely to help with it rather than resist the implementation of the desired change.

The proper application of the universal change principle does not guarantee that all resistance to change will be averted and that all desired changes can be accomplished. However, an appropriate application of the universal change principle does significantly enhance the likelihood of these desired things happening. The proper application of the universal change principle does take additional time and effort but generally pays off handsomely in terms of real accomplishment in the end.

The universal change principle and its applications are excellent examples of the concept of "slowing down to speed up"; that is, taking a little longer initially to do the right things and then being able to speed up the process substantially later on as a result of the earlier foundation that was laid.

Notice that the universal change principle also says, "No surprises!" If you want to bring about a desired change, don't surprise people with it. Their likelihood of reacting favorably to the change and assisting with it will be increased greatly if you take the time to provide people with a basis of understanding from which they can make the desired transition.

If L represents learning and C represents change, a nice way to symbolize the universal change principle is $L > C$.

Notice that this says that if there is to be a lot of change, then there must be a lot of learning that takes place first. In fact, if the change is really major, then several iterations of learning may be required at several different times, depending on the change, the circumstances, and the people involved. For large school changes, this is what typically must happen—there must be several applications of the universal change principle at different times and with different groups of people. In fact, it is helpful, in advance of the announcement of a desired change effort, to develop a plan, based on the universal change principle, to provide the appropriate and necessary learning iterations to precede the desired change. Snapshot 7 describes a specific case illustrating the implementation of a plan for the whole-faculty study model based on the universal change principle.

Snapshot 7   Learning Precedes Change

The principals in the San Diego Unified School District and districts in San Diego County received notification in March that a consultant for the whole-faculty study group model would provide an orientation on the concept the first week in April. Principals were invited to attend and to bring one or more teachers. Along with the memorandum, the principals were sent an article to read about whole-faculty study groups. At the orientation, the consultant shared the history of how the process became an effective school improvement strategy, defined terms, gave examples, and clarified purpose.

Representatives from the district offices explained to those that attended the orientation what they were to do if they were interested in initiating and implementing whole-faculty study groups. First, those attending from a school were to meet with their whole faculty and share the information they received at the orientation. The district representatives offered to assist with the planning of the meeting with the faculty, such as preparing overheads and handouts. Once the faculty received the information, the faculty was to vote as to whether or not they wanted to put the structure in place at their school. The understanding would be that if at least 70% voted in favor of the process, the vote would bind everyone. Over a period of time, 12 school faculties made the decision to proceed.

A team, called the focus team, from each of the 12 schools attended a week's training during the summer. On Day 1, the team reviewed a collection of research reports on the change process, building collaborative work cultures, and general school improvement strategies that showed promise. This review primarily pulled from the work of Bruce Joyce, Michael Fullan, Susan Rosenholtz, and Judith Warren Little. On Day 2, the teams did an analysis of school and student data that they brought to the seminar. After their review of the data, they identified, categorized, and prioritized the instructional problems. On Day 3, the teams examined ideas for what the content might be if the faculties chose to address the problems the teams had identified. Then, the teams looked at different approaches to organizing groups around the identified areas of study. Day 4 was a work day for the teams, a day to work independently on their implementation plans. On Day 5, the teams shared with each other and gave each other feedback and ideas. The teams understood on Day 1 that they would not go back to their schools and tell the faculties what they had concluded that groups would do and how the groups would be organized. Rather, the teams would lead their faculties through a mini version of what the teams had done. The faculties may or may not come to the same conclusions that the teams did.

When the new school year began in August, time was allocated on the preplanning schedule for the focus teams to work with the faculties. The whole faculties at the schools did a data analysis to confirm needs, identify areas of study, and determine how groups would be organized. When study groups began in October, teachers felt informed and that they had been part of making the critical decisions. A plan had been developed and implemented so that learning had preceded the change, and the whole-faculty study group process had been introduced and initiated in a positive manner and receptive environment.

Cultural Change

Schools have evolved over a long period of time, and our general approaches to schooling have been in place for centuries. As a consequence, schools have well-established cultures, a part of the context for the study group environment, that give them and their programs stability and govern how issues are addressed and what can happen in schools. On the other hand, school cultures are fairly rigid and make schools far less open to change than might be desirable when trying to introduce new concepts and practices for the enhancement of student learning and school improvement.

Among the best mechanisms for bringing about meaningful cultural change are professional whole-faculty study groups. When properly supported and applied, study groups have the potential to modify aspects of a school culture to allow for enough change so that educational processes and schools can be improved. Why is this so important? Because school cultures, like many others, are so very difficult to productively and qualitatively change. Although not all cultural change is valuable, positive school change will come about only when the school's culture is changed appropriately.

School culture is not always visible to outsiders and even to many from within, but it is always there and is always very powerful. *School culture* is the social and normative glue that holds together the educational and educationally related aspects of a school and creates the central features, structures, and approaches that characterize it (Birmbaum, 1988).

The culture is what sets one school distinctly apart from another; it is a school self-concept analogous to an individual's personality. The culture of a school, for example, establishes a unique set of ground rules, both stated and unstated, for how people in the school think and behave and for what they assume to be true.

The concept of school culture has generated many definitions and approaches to the subject. Because our interests in culture focus on the relationship of culture to change (e.g., student learning enhancement and school improvement), we shall use a definition that has proven helpful from a change perspective.

The following definition (Conner, 1993) has been used extensively and successfully in organizational research and change efforts: **School culture** reflects the interrelationship of shared assumptions, beliefs, and behaviors that are acquired overtime by members of a school.

The key building blocks of this definition are the assumptions, the beliefs, and the behaviors. If a school changes one or more of these cultural building blocks, it changes the school culture. What we are trying to do with study groups is to carefully alter some of these building blocks in schools so as to allow for the desired changes that will lead to the enhancement of student learning and school improvement.

Snapshot 8 Cultural Change

A teacher at Sky View Elementary School eagerly shared her reactions to being in a study group. The second-grade teacher said that she felt more like a professional than she had at any point during her 10 years of teaching. She was more confident, felt better about herself, felt she had contributed to the learning of her colleagues, felt proud to be a colearner with colleagues that shared new practices, and felt confirmed that her craft was based on a field of knowledge.

The teacher went on to give two examples of her improved self-esteem: She has put her diplomas and other professional certificates on the walls of her classroom for parents and students to see. She asked, "Physicians, lawyers, and other professionals do this, why not teachers? Why shouldn't parents and students see that teachers do have impressive credentials that verify that they have high levels of training?"

Another outcome of her positive feelings about herself came in the form of being more confident with parents. She said that she is now more assertive with parents in stating her evaluation of a student's work or behavior and what action she felt needed to be taken. Again, using medical doctors as a reference point, she said,

> Physicians tell us what their diagnosis is and what we need to do to get better. And we don't usually argue or second guess the doctor's opinion. Now, I speak with more professional confidence when I talk with a parent.

This teacher had changed some of her personal and professional assumptions, beliefs, and behaviors.

As other teachers at Sky View mirrored this teacher's feelings and actions, the change in the culture was felt and observable on entering the building.

Assumptions, Beliefs, and Behaviors

The building blocks of the culture of a school are the assumptions, beliefs, and behaviors of the school and its personnel. To change the culture of the school for its enhancement, we must change one or more of the assumptions, beliefs, or behaviors.

Assumptions in a school are the unconscious and, therefore, unquestioned perceptions concerning what is important and how people and things operate in and relating to the school. That is, the unconscious rationale for people continuing to use certain beliefs and behaviors. For example, teachers in schools often have the unconscious assumption that the lecture approach is a good form of teaching, whereas research tells us that this approach is one of the least effective methods for student learning.

Beliefs are the values and expectations that people hold to be true about themselves, others, their work, and the school. They provide a basis for what people in the school hold to be right or wrong, good or bad, and relevant or irrelevant about their school and its operation.

Belief statements in schools, for instance, relate to such things as the vital role played by the personal interaction of the teachers and students, value of the grading system, importance of lesson plans, and the need for staff development.

Behaviors are the ways people conduct themselves on a day-to-day basis. They are perceptible actions that are based on values and expectations and are ideally aimed at carrying out the school's mission. Whereas assumptions and beliefs often reflect intentions that are difficult to discern, behaviors are observable and can be noted objectively.

Behaviors of teachers, for example, might include such things as how they teach, prepare lesson plans, advise students, and use technology, whereas behaviors for administrators might include how they assess teaching, involve faculty in decision making, encourage innovation, and relate to other administrators.

In Snapshot 8, the teachers had unconscious assumptions about their self-esteem and professionalism. Their whole-faculty study group efforts helped them see themselves more like physicians and other professionals, changing their unconscious assumptions about their self-esteem and professional outlook dramatically. The change in these assumptions also brought about changes in the teachers' beliefs and behaviors. Teachers now believed that they had professional training that they could be proud of; that they were as professional as physicians, lawyers, and other professionals; and that they could and should function more like professionals in their activities and responsibilities. As a result, the behavior of these teachers changed substantially, including displaying diplomas and certificates, taking more responsibility for colearning with colleagues, having greater confidence in themselves, and functioning more professionally and assertively with parents. These were important changes in the assumptions, beliefs, and behaviors of the teachers and the school and so represented a positive, major shift in the culture of Sky View Elementary School.

School cultures can be realigned through a process called *cultural shift.* Such a cultural transformation requires realigning, in some measure, assumptions, beliefs, and behaviors to make them more consistent with the new directions of the school. No cultural shift can materialize without some modification of the assumptions, beliefs, or behaviors. One important strength of the study group process is that it has the capability to bring about a cultural shift and, through the shift, desirable changes in how a school functions.

Table 5.3 Study Groups Generate Cultural Changes and Student Changes

Study groups   →   Cultural change   →   Student changes

We will outline study group processes in later chapters and show how these processes lead to important cultural shifts in schools.

Assimilation Capacity

One of the major problems in schools (and most other organizations as well) is that they have too many change efforts going on at any one time. This is a serious problem for the personnel of the school, the various groups that are functioning in the school, and the school itself.

People and schools have only so much capacity or resources to deal with change, their *assimilation capacity.* The assimilation capacity is different for different individuals; some individuals have little capacity to deal with change, whereas others may have substantial capacity. The same is true for both groups and organizations, with some having limited assimilation capacity and others having much more.

When there is so much change that an individual's assimilation capacity is surpassed, then that individual's efforts are degraded, and the individual performs below his or her normal levels of productivity and quality. In such a case, we say the individual is dysfunctional; that is, his or her actions or feelings divert resources away from meeting productivity and quality standards. Dysfunctional individuals can continue to perform, but they perform at a lower level of productivity and quality. In a similar way, groups and schools can be dysfunctional; this happens when their assimilation capacities are surpassed, and they perform at lower than optimal productivity and quality levels.

Dysfunctional behavior in individuals ranges, for example, from low levels (poor communications, reduced risk taking, lower morale, and conflicts with fellow workers) to medium levels (lying, chronic tardiness, apathy, and interpersonal withdrawal) to high levels (covert undermining of the leadership, chronic depression, physical breakdown, and substance abuse). Simply put, if individuals, groups, or schools are asked to handle too much change in their total arena of action, including work, home, family and friends, community, and beyond, they will become dysfunctional and cannot perform optimally. The students, school, family, and others all lose. When this is true for all or most of the personnel in a school, then the loss is major and serious. Often, this represents reality today in our schools and other organizations in society.

Typically, schools are filled with an excess number of low-priority to middle-priority projects that have some value or would be nice to have but will have little real effect on the productivity and quality of the school. In fact, these low-priority to middle-priority projects actually stand in the way of accomplishing the ongoing and other potentially high-priority efforts.

An activity that will uncover or unload the sizable volume of initiatives that schools face is a very important part of the data collection process when faculties are conducting a self-study. This self-study may be for the purpose of determining whether study groups are an option the faculty wants to pursue or for the purpose of deciding what study groups will do. An example of such an activity follows.

Ask the faculty to form groups of six or seven individuals and to identify a recorder to write on the piece of chart paper that has been placed on each table. Tell the groups, when given the "go," to brainstorm all of the initiatives that the faculty has confronted during the last 5 years. They are not to debate or discuss the items as the initiatives are called out. The recorder will simply list the initiatives on the chart paper. After no longer than 10 minutes, stop them. Ask the recorder to count the number of initiatives. It is not unusual for the group to have listed as many as 30. At this point, you can almost hear a sigh of relief. Relief that the overload has been confirmed and affirmed. Use the following stages of change and the given number notation: initiation stage—1, implementation stage—2, institutionalization stage—3, and discarded or should be discarded stage—4. Have each group put the number for the stage beside each initiative that best describes its status (e.g., a 1 for an initiative that is in an initiation stage and a 4 for an initiative that has been or should be discarded). Note that stages are not consistent with lengths of time, because some innovations may still be in the initiation stage even though committees have been discussing them for years. Once the numbers are assigned, ask each group to count the numbers in each category. When teachers see a large number in the initiation stage, there is usually a big "Ah ha! That is why I feel so stressed." With a large number in the implementation stage, we know why we are doing only a few with any sense of satisfaction. The fewest number is usually categorized as being institutionalized. The realization is that we don't usually get to that point.

Another approach is to have each group categorize the list according to the levels of use (Hall & Hord, 1987), which are *preparation* (getting ready to do), *mechanical* (poorly coordinated), *routine* (establishing pattern of use), and *integrative* (coordinating use with others). Again, they see how many they are still getting ready to do and the number that they are struggling with to do skillfully.

A major outcome of these activities is that the teachers realize how far apart they are on any one initiative. They assume that everyone is where they are. They learn that some new teachers do not even know what an initiative on the list is. They begin to see duplications and conflicts among the initiatives. This activity nearly always brings a faculty to the point that they clearly see what study groups will do to diminish the sense of isolation and to provide support to their efforts to implement an initiative to the level that the effects on students are evident.

The discussions that come out of these activities show that most faculties have exceeded their capacities to assimilate all of the change and that many faculties as a whole are dysfunctional. Such discoveries bring clarity to what needs to be done and give a sense of hope to teachers. Now that we understand these assimilation and dysfunction concerns better, what can we do about them? A five-step process for dealing with such concerns follows:

1. Leaders must become aware of the concepts of limited assimilation capacities and associated dysfunctions and their serious potential impact on the people and the effectiveness of the school and its operation.

2. Before new projects involving major change are initiated, a thorough analysis of all existing projects should be undertaken and a list of them prepared.

3. The projects on the list should be prioritized, ranging from low to high priority (the imperatives).

4. All but the highest-priority projects (the imperatives) should be considered for termination or reduction in scope.

5. A plan should be developed and implemented in the school to eliminate or reduce in scope as many of the lesser-priority projects as is practical, timely, and cost effective.

Terminating or reducing in scope lower-priority initiatives could free up both financial resources and assimilation resources.

Whole-faculty study groups represent major change in and for a school. Their implementation should not be taken lightly. In fact, if a school is considering initiating study groups, it probably would be best to delay their implementation until such time as something comparable to the five-step process described has been completed or nearly completed. This would give a good picture as to whether the school had adequate assimilation capacity to take on another major change project as large as a whole-faculty study group effort.

District Influence and Sponsorship

Schools exist within the context of school districts. The school district is in fact the structural organization that typically shapes schools and schooling. It is the central board of education and the district administrators that are ultimately responsible for what happens in schools. The district can be one of the most important sponsors of innovation in the schools or a serious inhibitor of progress. The district level both constrains and facilitates. It provides a kind of "supported enforcement." The culture of the district is the underlying structure of meaning, and it permeates the schools. It facilitates or constrains school administrators' and teachers' perceptions, interpretations, and behaviors. The schools want the approval of district leaders and to be consistent and in compliance with district expectations. The district has influence that affects almost every major decision that school personnel make. Districts can reward or sanction. Often, that influence is invisible, not generally openly discussed. However, it is there. The district office is a critical sponsor of change; it creates the conditions for the process of change, establishes specific district goals, ensures accountability, and sets the time lines. It is the district that initiates most of the instructional innovations that confront schools. The district usually sets priorities for budgets. How much money schools will have for staff development, heavily influenced by district priorities, will determine what schools can do. Districts will determine whether consultants may be used, what materials may be purchased, whether teachers may be paid for their involvement in staff development activities, and whether substitutes may be obtained to release teachers for study or training.

Schools most often have building-level responsibility for implementation and staff flexibility to respond to their environment but not at the expense of district goals and priorities. It seems that the matter of school-district balance is not easily solvable. It represents an inherently complex dilemma between autonomy and accountability and variation and consistency.

The greatest problem faced by school districts and schools is not so much resistance to innovation but the fragmentation, overload, and incoherence resulting from the uncritical and uncoordinated acceptance of too many innovations (Fullan & Steigelbauer, 1991). The key role of district support staff is to help schools sort out and implement the right choices for each school. Many good programs are diffused at the school level simply because the schools are unclear as to the district-level priority of the program. The major function of whole-faculty study groups is to set school priorities and focus on implementing those priorities to the level that student effects are measurable. The school faculty is asked to identify the instructional initiatives and bring some coherence to what they are trying to do.

The schools that have been most successful in initiating and implementing whole-faculty study groups are those that are in districts that value schools as learning communities for the adults in their schools. Most of the initiators of the study group process are district leaders. Districts have used district funds to supplement school funds in efforts to support the study group process. Districts have recognized the schools and asked principals of schools using the study group model to speak at meetings for administrators. When districts stop showing signs of approval and support for what schools do, schools become discouraged, regardless of how well the process is going. Schools follow the lead of the district. As district interests shift, so will school interests (Murphy, 1991).

We must take very seriously the sponsorship role that districts play in change at the school level. We often forget that teachers and administrators are employed by the district, not the schools. For the vast majority of teachers, districts are unquestionably important organizations. But districts are only vaguely perceived by most teachers, especially in large districts. Districts are often perceived as unpredictable and hostile, as "they" who make ill-informed and unwelcomed decisions. If anything is to change over time in schools, we must become as concerned with the quality of district leadership and sponsorship as we are about the quality of schools.

Rosenholtz (1989) defined *stuck* and *moving* environments as learning-impoverished and learning-enriched environments for the adults and students. She found that stuck schools (i.e., learning-impoverished schools) were most often found in stuck districts; likewise, moving schools (i.e., learning-enriched schools) were most often found in moving districts. Rosenholtz went on to say that we must examine interorganizational relations, those conditions that drive schools to more or less efficient ends. She suggests that the keys to unlocking sustained commitment and the capacity for schools' continuous renewal are these:

- How districts select principals and teachers
- Whether districts offer them continuous opportunities for learning
- Whether task autonomy is delegated to schools and thereafter monitored

These three suggestions would greatly facilitate the initiation and continuation of whole-faculty study groups. It is almost impossible for schools to redesign themselves without district sponsorship. The role of the district is critical. Individual schools can become highly innovative for short periods of time without the district, but they cannot stay innovative over time without district action to establish the conditions for continuous and long-term improvement (Levine & Eubanks, 1989).

Snapshot 9 vividly illustrates the negative effects that can happen when the district or sponsoring circumstances are allowed to drift and change in a school district where successful change efforts had provided enhanced student learning. On the other hand, Snapshot 10 illustrates positive sponsorship and support of a district.

Snapshot 9   A Major Concern

At East Middle School (see Snapshots 2 and 3), the positive changes in student achievement were well documented over a period of 4 years, and those changes were directly linked to a staff development initiative. This initiative included the whole-faculty study group design and an intensive training program aimed at enabling teachers to be masters of several models of teaching. The seamless integration of these two components had proven to be successful in changing teacher and student behaviors. Because the intensity of such an effort also brought personal and professional discomfort to school and district leaders, support was not sustained. The politics of schooling was evident. Within 5 years of the staff development initiative, school and district leaders began to focus their attention and resources on other initiatives. Teachers saw a gradual disintegration of encouragement and support. They saw that school and district leaders were not displaying the same levels of sponsorship and advocacy that had initially been evident. Without sponsorship and support, individuals returned to old habits and former practices. Some continued the new approaches but apart from the whole. Without constant tending by internal and external sponsors and advocates, what was once perceived as important was no longer perceived so. Over time, at East Middle School, the administrative team changed at the school level, and new initiatives were introduced at the school that took the energy and attention of the staff. Teachers transferred to other schools. The administrative team at the district level changed, and the attention and resources that had been given to the staff development initiative at East Middle were diverted to other programs. However, the school did not lose all the ground it had gained. Fewer of the students who were served during the years the initiative was in place dropped out of school, and many of the students became leaders in the high schools they attended.

Snapshot 10 District Influence

Brushy Creek Elementary School is in a large suburban school district serving a white-collar community. The district is on the cutting edge of educational reform, making many instructional initiatives available to the schools. One Brushy Creek teacher said, "Our district leaders know what is happening nationally in education. Schools have opportunities to participate in a range of instructional initiatives with strong, supportive training programs." Like most schools in such districts, it has tried to involve itself in all the district has to offer. This has created a feeling of overload among the faculty (see the earlier section on Assimilation Capacity). The common concern was that many initiatives have been introduced through training programs, and materials were not being implemented to the depth that institutionalization was likely and student effects were measurable.

When the notion of whole-faculty study groups was shared with the faculty, there was a tremendous underground resistance at the thought of something else to put on the teachers' plates. However, the faculty supported sending a representative team (the focus team) to the summer training program that was being offered by the district. The team attended the training and was excited about the level of support the district would give the team in its plan to get the faculty interested in the potential of the whole-faculty study group approach.

When the team met with the faculty during preplanning week, the team so forcefully presented the idea that study groups could be a vehicle to do what they were already expected to do, the teachers decided to jump into the fire. The teachers acknowledged that if their colleagues would assist with the implementation of the new instructional programs, they could do in groups what they had been doing alone. Everyone dug in and made decisions about how the groups would be formed and specified the initiatives to be addressed. Once the initiatives were identified, teachers signed up for the one most critical for them.

After meeting three times, a teacher in the literacy learning group wrote:

> After our meeting this week, I had the feeling that we were experiencing a lot of discomfort. After thinking about this, I have come to the conclusion that it is not that we are uncomfortable with each other. We are insecure with our level of skill in implementing in our classrooms what we were trained to do. I know as we progress in our use of the strategies in our classrooms, we will become more comfortable. The point is this: It is not the dynamics of the group that is the problem, it is our struggle with the content of our study. Had it not been for the continued support from the consultant that the district provided, I would not have understood why we were feeling stuck.

The district, having given the school the opportunity to participate in a new approach to staff training and development, stood strong in its commitment to Brushy Creek and the other three schools that were in various stages of implementing study groups. After 3 years of encouraging schools to draw on in-house expertise, even with a change in district leadership during one of those years, the district continued to play the key role in supporting this change effort. Budget cuts have made it necessary for district leaders to be creative in supporting ways that implementers of the same initiatives can network to support each other.

The Process 6

Step-by-Step Guidelines

Process refers to a particular method of doing something, generally involving a number of steps or operations. In the context of study groups, it relates to the "how" of staff development and describes the means for the acquisition of new knowledge and skills. The whole-faculty study group approach is one process for educators to acquire and develop the knowledge and skills necessary to help enhance student performance and improve schools.

Snapshot 11 The Process

In writing its proposal to be a charter school, Addison Elementary School spent a year collecting and analyzing data, examining its curriculum, determining what assessment and instructional practices teachers were using, surveying parents, and collecting information about current instructional innovations. The Georgia State Board of Education approved Addison's application to be a charter school, one of only three in the state approved at that time. The faculty chose whole-faculty study groups as the vehicle to achieve the goals for the school and its students that were outlined in the charter. In September of Addison's first year as a charter school, the faculty began the process of determining how the groups would be organized and what the groups would do. These decisions were based on the analysis of all the information that had been collected the previous year. It was decided that the groups would focus on assessment and instructional strategies. Forming two study groups, 12 teachers chose assessment strategies. Forming seven groups, 42 teachers chose instructional strategies. Once a group was formed, the group decided on which strategy or strategies it would focus. The groups met for an hour each week for the school year. On alternating weeks on Tuesdays and Wednesdays, a team of six substitutes relieved one study group (six teachers) each hour of the school day. It took 1½ days for each of the nine groups to meet. On the weeks the substitutes were not provided, the groups met for one hour after school. This after-school study group time took the place of weekly meeting time reserved for the principal to meet with the faculty. All nine study groups were heterogeneous or cross-grade-level study groups.

The following are the condensed notes from a study group's logs for a period of 9 weeks, giving a look inside a study group that focused on assessment strategies:

Week 1: Established group norms and a leadership rotation schedule; completed an action plan, finding it difficult to be clear on intended results; we will revisit this plan as we go along.

Week 2: Examined the ITBS scores for 3rd and 5th grades; identified weaknesses in all areas and noted schoolwide patterns of weaknesses.

Week 3: Examined 4th grade ITBS, compared 3rd and 5th weaknesses to identify common schoolwide areas that need attention; identified "Language Arts: capitalization" and "Math: computation" as common areas of weakness; decided to use Daily Oral Language (DOL) to create undercap and overcap assessment; we will all use the assessment with our students.

Week 4: Discussed DOL results and realized that percentages will need to be used; shared Gwinnett County's progress reports; will all bring examples of rubrics next week; will also read "Systems and Assessment of Learners" article.

Week 5: Shared results of DOL: students perform best on DOL when sample is undercapitalized; reviewed and discussed article; set goals for next meeting.

Week 6: Examined different types of rubrics and portfolios; made copies of the rubrics for review and modification to use with our classes; discussed need to find better means of assessing and reporting students' progress to parents.

Week 7: Reviewed more rubrics in all content areas; discussed the possibility of having students practice scoring rubrics; a teacher shared conference guides; divided resource books among us.

Week 8: Created a sample of a reading rubric at each level; samples will be used by students to evaluate the responses according to the criteria of the rubric; a teacher shared a rubric she is using with her class, Author Study Presentations (the rubric was student generated); will all read Chapter 2, "Literacy Portfolios: Windows on Potential" from *Authentic Reading Assessment.*

Week 9: Set a new goal for the group: establish a rubric resource file for accessibility to entire staff; discussed how and by what date we would do this; a teacher shared a rubric for an oral book talk; another teacher shared that when she conferenced with students on report cards, she had to review the rubrics so students would see the connection between class work and grades.

Snapshot 12 Benefits and Bumps

The Jackson Elementary School faculty took from August to November to decide how the whole-faculty study group process would be implemented at Jackson. Because the school had adopted a new textbook series in mathematics the prior spring, the decision was made that study groups would focus on identified areas of study in mathematics. The 40 teachers who taught kindergarten through fifth grade formed eight cross-grade-level study groups around the following eight mathematics-related areas:

- Real-world mathematics
- Reading, writing, and mathematics
- Logic problems
- Technology
- Scope and sequence in kindergarten and first grade
- Moral reasoning (character building)

- Mathematics and science
- Meeting diverse needs in mathematics

The study groups began weekly meetings the first week of January, meeting from 2:00 to 3:00 p.m. on Wednesdays, when students were released early from school. In mid-March, after 9 weeks of weekly meetings, the groups met as a whole faculty to brainstorm perceived benefits and bumps in the study group process. The lists, unedited, that resulted from that meeting follow.

Benefits

Working together
Getting to know other levels of curriculum
Improved instruction
We have a choice of area of study
No deadlines
Were given time to work in groups
There is no right or wrong
Flexibility and we can change
Area of study matches one's need
Collaboration among professions
Sharing knowledge
Common areas of study
Shared goals
Opportunity to grow professionally
School time allocated for meeting
Learning more about mathematics in general
Becoming familiar with scope and sequence of new mathematics series
Diversity of group members and math ideas
Hope for the future
Unity within our faculty
Increased awareness of "character education"
We're all working toward a common goal
A chance to get to know each other better
Each group shares their knowledge with other groups
We did a comprehensive needs assessment
Faculty survey
There may be possible grant money
Get to work with peers
Allowed to work in an area I was interested in
We determine our own pace
Decisions reside within the group
Sense of accomplishment
Support from focus team (team trained in study group process)
Able to align with Scott Foresman
Time to talk and share between grade levels
Increase in student MEAP scores
Reflection time

Brings new ideas to school

Small groups working in parallel on different areas of math

One focus area (math) maximizes our efforts

We are all ready to use activities and resources

Bumps

Time

Knowing if materials we select are developmentally appropriate

How will we fund our ideas?

Finding time for outside research

Time to share work or findings with whole staff

Figuring out a time line

Getting started

Money

Lack of clear goal

"Just tell us" mentality

What resources are available?

Not knowing the direction the district will take

Curriculum may get in the way of our intended results

$$ for materials

Additional time needed for research

Need to narrow focus

Need to continuously revisit intended results

Fatigue at the end of the "Defining the Problem" day

Unsure about implementation ideas

How will individual be held accountable?

Identifying the group's focus within chosen area

Knowing where to go next

Trips to other schools or districts

Lack of familiarity with new math series at all grade levels

Losing clarity

Biting off more than we can chew

Communicating to the whole staff

Whole staff acceptance of our work

Isolation from other groups

Need a more definite time line

In the school's second year involving the whole-faculty study group process, the faculty is using the study group design to study and apply mathematics standards.

Process Guidelines for Study Groups

In earlier chapters, we learned that study groups may exist in the context of a school's improvement or transformation plan or in the context of a stand-alone group addressing a topic of interest to the individuals in the group. Because the aim of this book is facilitating schoolwide change and enhancing student learning through the use of study groups, we shall only look at study groups in the context of a school's improvement or transformation plan. The following 15 guidelines will provide the process structure that is required for study groups to achieve the desired results. These process guidelines are the result of Murphy's work since 1993 with over 50 schools and 500 study groups in those schools.

1. Keep the size of the group to no more than six.

The larger the study group, the more difficult it is to find common meeting times when all members can be present. Also, the larger the study group, the more likely the group will splinter into two groups. With smaller study groups, each member will participate more and take greater responsibility. The size of the groups affects how comfortable individuals feel about serving as leader. With groups of six or less, rotating leadership is comfortable. An individual does not feel the same sense of pressure with five other individuals as they would with 10 other individuals. The intimacy of a smaller group generates such a supportive relationship that when leadership is rotated, an observer of the study group often can't tell who the leader is.

2. Don't worry about the composition of the study group.

This is probably the least important concern. The homogeneity or heterogeneity of the study group is not a critical element. Study group members may have similar responsibilities (e.g., first-grade teachers, mathematics teachers, or elementary principals) or unlike responsibilities (e.g., across grade level, across subject level, or across schools or districts). The composition of a study group is most often those who want to pursue or investigate a specific student need that has been identified through an analysis of student data. The content of the study, investigation, or training generally determines who will be a member of a study group. The focus is on adult-to-adult relationships in a learning situation. What grade or subject a teacher teaches is secondary to the adult relationship forged around teaching. For example, a study group focusing on technology could be teachers of kindergartners to twelfth graders because the application of computer skills is generic.

Study groups actually form in a number of ways. Several examples follow.

At an elementary school where the faculty decided that all the study groups would address a low math achievement, a random method was used. Because there were 52 teachers, 10 study groups were formed. The principal wrote each teacher's name on an index card and stacked the cards from the lowest grade level at the school to the highest. In front of the entire faculty, the principal dealt the cards, face down, into 10 stacks. She then picked up a stack, called out the names, and groups were formed. Each group then decided what aspect of math the group would pursue.

At a large high school, the whole faculty decided that all study groups would focus on school climate, meaning that the groups would investigate issues that would advance the physical, emotional, and social health of its students. The faculty further decided that the study groups could span departments and grade levels. On a staff development day, all 152 faculty members went into the school cafeteria. On entering the room, each was given a name tag that was bordered in a color. All the members of a department (e.g., social studies) had one color. After everyone was seated, a focus team member said:

> Now, it is time to form study groups. You will note that in the middle of each table is a sheet of paper divided into sixths. You may form your own study groups by putting your name tag in one of the six squares on the sheet of paper on a table. However, there can be only one color on each sheet. You have 5 minutes to form your groups.

As recorded on video, the faculty completed the task in under 5 minutes.

At an elementary school where the faculty had identified several different student needs that were to be addressed, the method of forming study groups was more deliberate. Each of the six needs was written on a piece of chart paper, and the chart papers were taped to the wall of the media center where the faculty was meeting. Each teacher was given a Post-it note and told to write his or her name on it. Then, the teachers were asked to get up from their seats and put their Post-it notes on the chart paper that specified the student need that they wanted to address. It was immediately visible as to whether there was enough interest in all the needs or whether several study groups would need to form to address one need. Because 12 teachers wanted to address reading comprehension, two groups formed to examine the teaching of this skill. Within a very short period of time, every teacher knew the membership of the study groups and what would be the focus of each group.

In a middle school, after the whole faculty had agreed on the student needs that should be addressed, the existing teams selected a need most relevant to that team. The team had a daily common planning period. During one planning period a week when the team meets, it goes into study group mode, meaning that administrative or managerial issues are put aside and the focus is on teaching skills.

3. Establish and keep a regular schedule.

Weekly meetings, for about an hour, keep the momentum at a steady pace and give study group members ongoing learning and support systems. The study group should set the dates and times of meetings for a given period of time. It is usually assumed that a group will stay together an entire school year and would establish a set schedule, such as every Tuesday from 3:00 to 4:00 p.m. or every other Tuesday from 3:00 to 5:00. Also, it is usually better to meet more frequently for shorter periods of time than to meet infrequently for a longer block of time. More than 2 weeks between meetings is too long to sustain momentum and to get regular feedback on classroom practice. An hour is about the minimum amount of time and seems adequate to accomplish the intent of a given meeting. Many schools have found creative ways to find time in the work day for teachers to be actively engaged as collaborative learners. At the end of this chapter, a number of these ways are described.

4. Establish group norms at the first meeting of the study group.

Study group members should collectively agree on what is acceptable and unacceptable behavior in the group setting, including beginning and ending on time, taking responsibility for one's own learning, being an active participant, letting what is said in the group stay in the group, not judging others' opinions, respecting others' opinions, completing assignments, and being open to changing the status quo. These norms set the basis for the operation of the group, help to create its empowering synergy, and lead to the group's "learning team" success, as discussed in Chapter 8. Once norms are established and agreed on, members are encouraged to feel comfortable reminding each other when a norm is not being respected.

5. Agree on an action plan for the study group.

It is important that a study group develop its own action plan. If there are 10 professional study groups in the school, then there should be 10 action plans. The student needs may have been identified by a larger body, but how a study group will go about their investigation is for that group to decide. The action plan sets the common goals for the study group. A study group's action plan should include the following:

- What the general category of student needs is
- What the specific student needs are that the group will address
- What the teachers will do when the study group meets
- What evidence will confirm that the work of the study group has resulted in student change
- What the study group will use (i.e., resources) to accomplish its intended results

The action plan should be revisited at regular intervals and adjusted to be consistent with current actions. A group may initially plan to go in one direction, then once into the study or training program, see a different avenue to follow. This takes on a higher level of importance when the group does a formal evaluation of its progress toward its intended results. If the intended results for study group members and for students are not appropriate or adequate, the evaluation will indicate that the group missed its targets.

6. Complete a log after each study group meeting.

A *log* is a brief, written summary of what happened at a study group meeting and gives the study group a history. The group can go back and confirm why they decided to take a particular action. The members can see their progress in how they relate to one another, in their thinking, and in their actions. After study group meetings, a copy of the log is maintained for easy access for study group members; given to a designated person, such as the principal; and posted in a central location for others to see the status of all of the study groups. The log is not used in evaluations but as a tool for knowing what type of outside support may be helpful and to promptly address concerns or blocks that the group might be experiencing. Logs become part of the study group's portfolio or an individual teacher's portfolio. The study group log should include the following information:

- Date, time, location, and leader of the meeting
- Group members present and absent
- Classroom applications since last meeting (if appropriate)
- Brief summary of today's discussions and activities

- At the next meeting, we intend to . . .
- Concerns and recommendations

It is often not until the third or fourth meeting that the "classroom applications" section of the log is completed. It takes about that long for the study group to get organized and to do the background work to support classroom use. The study group may collect the classroom application information by taking the first 5 or 10 minutes of the meeting to go around the table and have each member share. Much of the learning about classroom practice comes from this sharing of what is and is not working in each other's classrooms. This generates concrete and precise "teacher talk" about teaching, a major function of study groups.

7. Encourage members to keep individual logs for their personal reflections.

Each log serves as an individual's map of progress toward the group's intended results. The log might include the following items:

- Date, time, and location of the study group meeting
- The meeting's accomplishments
- What the group didn't get to
- What I should do for the next meeting
- How I am feeling about what I am learning
- What I am using that I am learning

The individual log becomes a private journal of the individual's learning. Expressions of frustration, joy, new insights, and references for the future are part of one's own reflections about the process and the content of the study.

8. Establish a pattern of study group leadership.

There are two common approaches to the leadership of study groups.

Approach 1

Each member serves as the study group leader on a rotating basis. This approach is undergirded with the assumption that all teachers are leaders. The leadership rotation may occur weekly, biweekly, or monthly. Once a group forms around a student need, group members decide what the rotation will be. The schedule is noted in the study group log from the first meeting. The leader for a given meeting is responsible for confirming logistics, such as time and location, with all members; for completing the study group log after each meeting; and for communicating, as appropriate, with persons who are not members of the study group. Leadership is shared to avoid having one member become more responsible than other members for the success of the group. All members are equally responsible for obtaining resources and for keeping the study group moving toward its intended results and desired ends. Individual group members look to themselves and each other, not to a single person for direction. This sense of joint responsibility for the work of the study group builds interdependence and synergy within the group (see synergistic relationships and prerequisites in Chapter 8). When every group member feels equally responsible for the success of the group, there is a higher level of commitment. There is no one leader to blame for the failure of the group to accomplish its goals; all must share the burden of any failure and the joy of accomplishment.

There are times when one person from each study group will be required to attend a workshop or other training situation to learn a specific skill or set of skills that all members must have. At such times, any member from the study group could attend and share with the rest of the group. In such cases, the individual and the desired skill or condition could be matched. For example, the group member who has had some prior training in the topic and is excited about knowing more about it would be the logical one to attend the training session. Or the group member who is available for a summer training session would be the one to attend. The most positive feature of using the rotation approach is the important assumption that anyone from the study group can represent the group at any point in time, expanding the effective capacity for leadership at the school.

Approach 2

The leaders of the study groups are determined before groups are formed and retain leadership for an indefinite period of time. We do not recommend this approach because we believe it undermines the basic principle of shared leadership and responsibility. However, because some schools may have to take this approach, we will point out the pitfalls. If, either through volunteers or a selection process, five individuals are designated as leaders and given special training for the role, then that would limit the number of study groups to five. Depending on the number of faculty members, it may then be necessary to have more than six teachers in a study group. After the data analysis and student needs are identified, the designated leaders would indicate which student need area they would lead a group in addressing. In that context, appointed leaders may have too much influence on what the group will do.

There is another caution regarding predetermined leaders of groups. If a leader's performance is not satisfactory and is not effective, removing the person as leader may cause dissension. When one individual is the group leader over a long period of time, leadership responsibilities may take priority over the individual's role as learner. The group of designated leaders may come to be perceived as another layer of bureaucracy. Furthermore, the next guideline may be harder to attain when one person in the group is considered to have a more responsible role than the other study group members (see Table 2.1 for an elaboration of the roles and responsibilities of individuals).

9. Give all study group members equal status.

It is more productive if individuals do not feel intimidated, hesitant, or anxious about differences in job titles or certifications, experience, and degree levels among group members. No one is deferred to because of rank or other factors. Contributions from each member are encouraged and respected. The study group functions under the belief that all members have something valuable to contribute to the study group (i.e., empowerment; see Chapter 8) and then provides an opportunity for all to share fully their ideas and experiences (i.e., participative involvement; see Chapter 8). This approach provides an environment for appreciative understanding, empowers its members, and enables the group to reach a higher level of synergy and meaningful productivity. It is the shared leadership and equal-status principle and a strong content focus (see Guideline #10) that lessens the need to train groups in group dynamics. With a strong sense of individual responsibility and an action plan for accomplishing specific results, the focus is on what the group is doing and not on the characteristics of individuals. If the work of the group is substantive enough and tied to what teachers and students are doing in the classrooms, the related dynamics will hold the group together. As the individuals are progressing on the work of the group, they are developing trust and rapport with each other and learning how to work together cohesively within the context of their study.

10. Have a curriculum and instructional focus.

The content of any staff development approach should have promise for positive effects on student personal, social, and academic learning. As outlined in Chapter 4, the functions of study groups are to support the implementation of curricular and instructional innovations, integrate and give coherence to a school's instructional practices and programs, target a schoolwide instructional need, and monitor the impact of instructional changes on students. These four functions require that the individuals in the groups do not get sidetracked by administrative issues or issues that have a low instructional impact. Professional study groups take as their content curriculum materials, instructional strategies, curriculum designs, use of technologies, managing students and learning environments through effective instruction, assessment practices, and other classroom and school improvement practices and programs. The intended results may be accomplished through training, reading books and articles, viewing video tapes, demonstrating strategies to each other, visiting classrooms and schools, designing materials, viewing computer software, and developing lessons that will be taught in classrooms.

Whatever the content, it needs to be complex and substantive enough to provide a practical vision, not just rhetoric or feelings. It is the content of the study group that will hold the members together while individuals are gaining trust and rapport with each other and developing skills for working together as a cohesive group. The content takes the focus off the individual. The content supplies a foundation to the process that will lead the study group to joint, interdependent work. Through the content, colleagues can share responsibilities; support each other's initiatives; discover their unconscious assumptions; clarify their ideas, beliefs, and professional practices; and ground the group's commitment to serious, professional accomplishment.

11. Plan ahead for transitions.

A transition is needed when the study group reaches closure on what the group intended to do, when a schoolwide need has to be addressed by all groups, or when there is a break in the school calendar. Logical points for transitions to occur are in December and May for schools on a traditional calendar. Most groups stay together for at least one school year. If study groups initially begin in September, then the groups would generally stay together until May. If they begin in January, the understanding would be that the group would continue until the following December, with a formative evaluation in May.

For a group that has long-term work planned, at the end of each semester, the group assesses its progress to that point, revisits their action plan, makes appropriate adjustments to the plan, and continues. For a group that wants to stay together but has completed, to its satisfaction, the area of study or training they originally targeted, a transition would be to celebrate its success and then return to the list of student needs initially identified. If current data confirm that these student needs still exist, the group would reach consensus as to which of the student needs areas the group would address.

If 4 of the 10 study groups at a school have reached closure to their planned work and there is no consensus in those 4 groups as to what the groups should pursue next, then the 4 groups (24 individuals) could reconfigure themselves, forming new groups that are aligned with other areas of study or training. As new groups, the members would return to the schoolwide student data to determine what their work might be. It is important that everyone know that in December or in May or both, they will have new options.

If an elementary school, for example, is faced with a district initiative, such as aligning district standards in mathematics with the current mathematics curriculum and materials, it may be necessary for the principal to state in February that the current study groups should bring closure to their work by the end of May, because in September, all groups will need to address the mathematics curriculum. Under such circumstances, in September, group membership may change or stay the same, depending on how the new work will be organized. In any process, transitions can be difficult. These times especially require the support and strong sponsorship from school and district administrators. The question at transition times is not, "Do we continue having study groups?" Instead, the question is, "What changes should be made regarding what the groups do and how they are organized for continued study?"

12. Make a comprehensive list of learning resources, both material and human.

A study group designs its curriculum of study to include a comprehensive list of resources. Initially, groups should spend some time brainstorming learning resources that are easily accessible and those that are harder to obtain. Such lists might include trainers, resource people, titles of books, professional journals, videos, audio tapes, computers and software, conferences, and other sources of relevant information. The most accessible sources for materials are the files of other teachers in the building. Ask the teachers in your building to share with you their files on specific topics or general areas of study to create an enhanced, central resource file for the areas of study being pursued by the different groups.

Other sources for materials would be district offices, other schools, libraries, colleges and universities, businesses, and professional associations. Also included as learning resources are individuals who have special expertise, such as teachers, school administrators, district administrators and support staff, university professors, independent consultants, parents, and business and community leaders. The foregoing list of learning resources represents a valuable resource base for the learning that must precede the changes that the teachers hope to bring about in their classrooms.

13. Include training in the study group's agenda.

When we do not know how to do something, we can develop that skill by letting a person who is more knowledgeable in that skill area show us how. The more skillful individual may be in the study group, from the school, or from elsewhere. Attending workshops and inviting trainers to our school or study group meetings to demonstrate effective practices is necessary if skill development is required. Just reading about how to do something is usually not sufficient. Reading and discussing books and articles and studying relevant research are important because such efforts can affect attitudes, beliefs, and behaviors and can provide an expanded knowledge base for improving classroom practice. However, at some point, individuals must move from the abstract (i.e., from what is written, read, and discussed) to the concrete (i.e., to what one actually does).

Furthermore, to ensure skill development at a level that gives teachers the confidence to appropriately and effectively use the skill in the classroom, training must be well designed. A training design would include (a) the theory that explains and supports the importance of the skill and (b) opportunities for participants to observe a number of demonstrations of the skill and to practice the skill to a reasonable competency level (Joyce & Showers, 1995). The study group provides a safe environment for teachers to practice skills, design lessons together using the skill, observe each other, and feel support in figuring out why some lessons go well and others do not. The value of ongoing technical training and support of effective classroom practices can't be overemphasized.

14. Evaluate the effectiveness of the study group.

When considering what and how to evaluate the efforts of study groups, attention should be directed to

- The impact of study groups on students
- The impact of the study group on the school's culture (i.e., the school's underlying assumptions, beliefs, and behaviors, such as the school's norms of collegiality, faculty and staff learning, a change-adaptable environment, and continuous improvement)
- The effectiveness of the study group process, especially how each study group functions

Evaluation questions should be referenced to the action plan of the study group, including

- Were student needs fully or partially met? To what degree?
- Do the data indicate improvement?
- Did the teachers do what was stated in the action plan to address student needs? To what degree?
- Were intended results for students and teachers attained? To what degree?

When all of the study groups at a school address the same student needs, school-wide improvement should be the expectation. If study groups address different student needs, one cluster of classrooms may see results in one instructional area, whereas another cluster may observe results in a different area.

15. Establish a variety of communication networks and systems.

Establishing lines of communication within and outside of the school regarding the work of study groups is so important that it is a stand-alone procedural guideline.

In the whole-faculty study group design, communication among study groups is of critical importance to the individual study groups and the purpose of the overall process. If the overarching goal is to increase student success and schoolwide improvement, then it would be expected that the quality of instruction in every classroom would get better.

The term *whole-faculty study group* infers that all of the faculty will be in study groups and that everyone (the whole) will know what all groups are doing and learning. Toward these ends, the following 14 communication networks and strategies are effective:

1. Establish a means for representatives from each study group to meet every 4 to 6 weeks. Representatives briefly share the current status of their study group efforts. The representatives may set benchmarks for all groups. Concerns and recommendations that are gleaned from the study group logs that appear to be representative of the study groups are discussed. At the next round of study group meetings, the person who represented the study group shares what was discussed. At many schools, this representative group is called the *instructional council* because the representatives focus on curriculum and instruction. In schools where representative councils already exist, designated meetings are earmarked for reports from study groups. The minutes from the instructional council, or whatever name the large group has, are given to all of the faculty. Snapshot 13 is an example.

2. Have the study group logs posted in a central location so that every faculty member has access to the logs. Many post their logs over the copiers in the teachers' workrooms. If there are 10 study groups, 10 clipboards might be hung. After each study group meeting, the study group leader would clip the latest log on top of the earlier ones. This gives a cumulative look at the progress of the group.

3. Establish a "showcase" time. Whenever a study group wants to showcase what they are doing, the group would advertise the day, time, and place, and whoever wants to attend is welcome. Attendance is voluntary.

4. Use newsletters. Some focus teams do a quarterly newsletter that describes what groups are doing. In some schools, space is reserved each month for a report on the work of a study group in the school newsletter that goes to parents.

5. Create brochures. In one school, a study group designed and distributed a brochure that detailed what the group members had learned about motivating readers. The brochure outlined the facts that the group had gleaned and invited teachers not in the group to contact group members for more information.

6. Develop videos. Several groups have done videos that highlight the groups' learnings. One group, focusing on the use of technology, demonstrated its use of the digital camera, the scanner, the Internet, Windows 95, and HyperStudio.

7. Hold exhibits. One school held an exhibit for parents to share with them what study groups were doing. Each study group compiled a study group portfolio, which served as the basis for the group's exhibit. The exhibit was held in conjunction with a PTA meeting.

8. Designate a bulletin board in the faculty lounge for notes from study groups.

9. Hold a whole-faculty study group meeting every 4 to 6 weeks. This is a time when all of the study groups meet in one location. It may be for sharing or for groups to work on a common task. This joint meeting takes the place of the regular study group meeting for that week.

10. Invite district leaders to attend the whole-faculty study group meetings so they can appreciate what the groups are doing and can provide support where needed.

11. Plan special celebrations, fun times for groups to do creative things to excite others about the status of learning in the school. For example, on one of the preplanning days at the beginning of the school's second year of whole-faculty study groups, the principal of the Jackson Elementary School had "study groups" on the agenda. First, he did a brief history of the school's journey with study groups. Then, he asked the teachers to organize themselves as they were last year, take 15 minutes to make a simile representing three new learnings from their work the year before, and plan to present their creation in a maximum of 5 minutes. The groups had great fun seeing which group would be the most creative and descriptive.

This activity served several purposes. It brought the attention back to study groups, and it was a fun review of what the teachers had accomplished. Also, it was a good overview for new teachers; based on the presentations, the principal asked the new teachers to join the groups that would be most beneficial to them. In addition, this show of support and encouragement for study groups provided a wonderful indirect expression of the school's and principal's strong sponsorship of the study group approach in the school.

12. Assign liaisons to study groups. One focus team decided to assign a member to each study group to serve as a liaison to the group. The liaison would meet every few weeks with their assigned study group for about the first 5 minutes of the meeting. Then, when the focus team meets, each member shares about their liaison group.

13. Put in place deliberate strategies to communicate with the board of education, district leaders, parents, students, and the general public. These might include asking to speak to groups, using the study group concept at PTA meetings, newsletters, having a designated study group meeting when visitors are invited, and making videos of sessions when each group shares what is happening and showing them to groups external to the school.

14. Tell students what is taking place in the study groups. Teachers are encouraged to tell students that a particular strategy or activity used in classrooms with students is a strategy they learned in their study group. This type of sharing has great influence on students and on parents when students repeat this information at home. Students are especially pleased to know that their teachers are also learners and that they are colearners with their teachers.

Snapshot 13 Instructional Council Meeting

The Instructional Council at Murdock Elementary School met on April 15, 1997. Those in attendance were CH, SF, MP, SS, SD*, CH*, MN*, LB*, SSc, JL, and KH* (focus team members denoted with *).

The purpose of the Instructional Council is communication between study groups and with the focus team. Praise and applause as well as concerns and problems will make up the agenda.

Study group reports:

1. CH reported that they have read Dr. N's books and have met with him. They are investigating doing a base line for Murdock students with dyssemia. Three classes (B, G, and Z) will be involved in research by Dr. N's graduate students. Problem: Itinerant, part-time people have trouble finding time to meet.

2. SF reported that her group has done much the same as Group 1. They have read the books and are investigating ways of dealing with the students that may be identified. They have considered investigating how uniforms affect children.

3. Not represented.

4. MP reported that her group is using the Internet in investigating conferencing strategies. She stated that the group had gotten sidetracked on brain-based learning and have refocused the group to assessing and reporting. They are working toward inviting Judy J from the county office to come and address the group. They are looking at portfolio conferencing also.

5. SS reported that they have been using and becoming familiar with software. Mary T has worked with them in using "Math Keys." Problem: Lack of funds and "personal days" prevented group's attendance at technology conference in Macon this week. Look forward to making this available to group members next year.

6. SD reported that her group has been involved in the physiology of the brain but are looking at including multiple intelligences in their study. They have viewed a video on Rumanian orphanages. They are planning to discuss gender differences in the brain. They have so much material that they are taking time to digest it. Problem: Rarely has everyone been at the meeting due to the nature of the group.

7. CH reported that her group has read various articles and books about guided reading and literacy centers. They watched two Wright Group videos about guided reading and have discussed the mechanics of taking running records. They have reviewed the Rigby materials available through the media center. Problem: Lack of materials to use with students for guided reading. Each teacher needs *many* titles available to use with students.

8. MN reported that her group is investigating the connection between guided reading, writing, and assessment. They are concentrating on developing a common language. They have planned literacy-center-time visits to other classes.

9. LB reported that her group had been reading about guided readings and using running records. Problem: They are seeking answers for questions concerning time management for guided reading during literacy centers. (First grade invited this group to observe during student instructional assistance time. MN suggested that everyone read Regie Routman's new book, *Literacy at the Crossroads.*)

10. SSc reported that they have had to refocus the content of their study because there was not much research available on "family grouping." They have written a new action plan, and their focus is now cultural diversity in literature. Pam J from the county office is coming to speak.

11. JL reported that her group is looking at "inclusion" and "collaboration" and modifications and strategies for the regular classroom. They viewed a video where young children had not been nurtured and brain areas were underdeveloped. They are seeking high school students who might be interested in doing enrichment activities with designated students over the summer. Problem: Substitutes not getting to classes on time. Be sure that subs understand their schedules, especially lunch.

Focus team announcements:

Supplement meeting logs this week with "Classroom Application forms." Each person in group is to state how your learning is affecting students. Some groups may still be in the investigation period and it is appropriate to record what you have read or are doing (or both) to learn yourself.

At the end of the school year, people may elect to change and reform new groups if so desired. People who wish to continue with the same group, the same topic, or both may choose to do that.

Make corrections on schedule for study groups. *Change* May 17 to May 15. A celebration for our successes with study groups is planned for May 22. (The focus team had planned that each study group could share their "successes" with the faculty at this time, but the Instructional Council decided that this will not be necessary because we share in the Instructional Council and this information is reported back to the groups through the minutes and group reports. We will celebrate without the "formal" presentations and share informally.)

Next year, there will be 11 more schools beginning whole-faculty study groups. We are ahead on the training.

The next Instructional Council meeting is Tuesday, May 20. A different person from each group should attend each time the Council meets. Consensus of the group is that study groups are going well and the biggest "bug" is scheduling.

Finding Time

One common obstacle schools face in the study group process seems to be finding time for collegial planning and learning.

Schools have been most creative in how they have found time to make the whole-faculty study group process work in their schools, including the following approaches:

1. At Sarah Cobb Elementary School, students are released 1 day a week at 1:30 p.m. instead of the regular 3:00 p.m. dismissal time. The school had exceeded the minimum number of instructional minutes required by the state, and it was not necessary to add minutes to the other 4 days. This elementary school is one of four schools in a rural district and the only one in the district to have early dismissal on Wednesdays. For schools that exceed the minimum instructional minutes, releasing students early 1 day a week would require adding minutes to 1 or more of the other 4 days.

2. Prior to receiving a waiver from the State Board of Education for early release, the Sarah Cobb Elementary School designed a plan for using teaching assistants to release teachers for their study group meetings. A team of five teaching assistants released five teachers the first hour of the school day for the teachers to meet as a study

group. For the last hour of the day, the team of teaching assistants covered the classrooms of another five teachers. Each day, two study groups met. By Friday afternoon, all 10 of the study groups had met. Each week, the groups rotated the time of the day they met. The groups that met first hour one week would meet the last hour the next week.

3. Other schools in the process of finalizing plans for some form of shortened day once a week have used teams of parents or business partners to release teachers for the hour their study groups meet.

4. Holtville High School begins classes for students 30 minutes late on Wednesdays and teachers arrive 30 minutes early on Wednesdays. This gives the teachers 1 hour for collaborative planning and learning in their study groups.

5. Everett High School has "late start" on Wednesdays. Students report to school one hour later on Wednesday mornings. Study group logs are posted so interested parents can see how teachers use the time.

6. Several schools have used a temporary approach to finding time for study groups to meet. While the faculties are investigating other approaches, teachers are paired. Teachers from two study groups take each other's classes for the first or last 30 minutes of the day. Because teachers arrive at least 30 minutes before students arrive and stay 30 minutes after students leave, an hour block is created for study group meetings. Teachers A, B, C, and D are one study group. Teachers E, F, G, and H are another study group. Teacher A combines Teacher E's class with her class, and Teachers B and F, C and G, and D and H do the same. This allow Teachers E, F, G, and H to meet for 1 hour once a week. On another day, Teachers E, F, G, and H combine classes for Teachers A, B, C, and D to meet. In the combined classes, students have individual study, reading, and journal writing time; students work one-on-one with each other; clubs meet; and other types of student planned activities are initiated.

7. The principal at Sky View Elementary School identified a team of five substitutes that spend a day every other week at Sky View. On that day, the team releases five teachers at 9:00 a.m. to meet as a study group and continues to do this each hour of the day. The team of substitutes moves from class to class. As many as six study groups meet on that one day. Because the school has 10 study groups, the team of substitute teachers returns for part of another day so that the other four study groups may meet. On the weeks that the substitute teachers do not provide released time, the study groups meet for 1 hour after school. Murdock and Bryant Elementary Schools also use this approach to finding time for study group meetings.

8. At Deepwood Elementary School, the principal limits faculty meetings to one Wednesday a month. On the other three Wednesdays of the month, study groups meet. All teachers in the district are asked to reserve a set time every Wednesday for faculty meetings.

9. Elder Middle School teachers have a 90-minute planning period per day. On 1 day a week, the first 60 minutes of a planning period is labeled "study group" time. During that hour, the teachers meet in their study groups.

10. At Forest North Elementary School, the teachers were permitted to use the study group design for professional development to earn compensatory time for their after-school study groups. The teachers' 1-hour weekly meetings totaled what 2 full days of staff development time would equal. Therefore, on 2 days designed as staff development days on the school calendar, the teachers do not report to school.

11. In the Boyle County Schools, the first year that teachers in all of the schools were in study groups, students were dismissed 2 hours early on Wednesdays in September, October, March, and April. For November, December, January, February, and May, each school submitted a plan to the district office for how it will provide for teachers to continue their study groups. The next school year, the students were released every other Wednesday, September through May.

12. All of Woodford County's six schools dismiss 2 hours early on one Wednesday a month. On another Wednesday of the month, teachers meet after school in study groups in lieu of a faculty meeting.

13. The principal at the Addison Elementary School designed an assembly model to give teachers time to collaborate during the school day and for the enrichment of students. Special assemblies are scheduled every other week at the school. The assemblies are part of a cultural arts enrichment program that is funded by the school's PTA. Various art groups, such as the Alliance Theater; the Atlanta Opera, Symphony, and Ballet; storytellers; African dancers; and a chamber music group, present programs to the students. On assembly day, there are two assembly periods that are an hour and a half in length. Half of the classes in the school are scheduled for each assembly. Each period consists of two 45-minute performances that occur concurrently. Half of the students scheduled for an assembly period go to one of the 45-minute performances and the other half goes to the other performance; then, they switch. This creates a $1\frac{1}{2}$-hour block of time for the teachers, who attend study group meetings during the block of time their students are in the assembly. Administrators, paraprofessionals, and parents stay with the students during the two assembly periods. Classroom teachers have the responsibility of delivering and settling the students in the designated area (e.g., cafeteria or gym) and getting the students when the two performances are over. The students know that the teachers are meeting in study groups while the students are in the assemblies. When the students return to their rooms, the students share with the teacher what they have learned. Likewise, the teachers share with the students what they learned in the study group meetings. The principal has reported that on assembly day, parents show up who are not scheduled to assist and ask, "May I help?" On the alternating weeks, when the assemblies are not scheduled, the study groups meet for an hour after school.

14. At Sweetwater High School, a large faculty of 120 teachers found 1 hour in the week for heterogeneous study groups to meet. After an analysis of the number of instructional minutes in a regular school day, they determined that the school was "banking" time in terms of instructional minutes. They exceeded by 5 minutes daily the minimum number of minutes per day for instruction. To have time in the school day for 20 study groups to meet, they took the accumulated 5 minutes and combined it with the time from a staff development day to have 26 days on which they could begin classes 45 minutes later. On 1 day a week, study groups meet from 7:30 a.m. to 8:15 a.m., with classes starting at 8:20 a.m. and all periods are shortened. On the other 4 days, classes begin at 7:30. Students know that on study group day, the bell schedule is not the same as on the other 4 days.

15. The principal at Arbutus Elementary School took a holistic approach to when all of the study groups would meet. All of the times allocated on the district and school calendars for staff development and staff meetings were seen as one big block of time; this included full days, half days, and after-school time. Instead of focusing on the exact weekly clock hours the groups would meet, the faculty focused on the tasks that

were to be completed over a period of time. After looking at several data bases, the faculty made the decision that all of the eight study groups would focus on reading instruction. Another understanding was that the groups would cover the same material in the same block of time, but how they did it was up to each group. Blocks of time to cover the predetermined content was established. For example, through a whole-faculty consensus process, it was decided that from December 11 to February 12, the study groups would cover teaching vocabulary with context clues, word identification and phonics, and comprehension questioning. The groups would look at the calendar and see all of the segments of time as a whole and decide how they would organize that amount of time to cover the research and shared practice on the predetermined content.

16. Teachers at Mission Bay High School chose to select for themselves when their study group would meet once a week. Not only did the groups meet at different times, they met on different days. Several of the study groups met early in the morning; others met during lunchtime or during planning periods; still others met after school; and one met in the evening. Teachers accounted for their professional development time, and on designated staff development days, the teachers were not expected to attend meetings.

17. Ray High School initiated block scheduling the same year study groups were being considered as a viable option for earning professional development credits. The teachers who formed study groups met 1 day a week during the extended lunch period.

18. The Jackson Elementary School faculty redesigned the modified day plan that had been in place prior to the initiation of the whole-faculty study group process. The modified day, Monday, was formed by having the school start 5 minutes early and end 5 minutes later on Tuesday through Friday, making the student's day 8:40 a.m. to 3:25 p.m. 4 days a week. On Mondays, the students leave at 1:45 p.m., and the teachers leave at 4:25. Prior to study groups, teachers spent that block of time doing individual teacher preparation, meeting in committees, and participating in faculty meetings. Now, 1 hour of that block of time is for study groups to meet, beginning the second week of school through the first week in April. This leaves a few weeks of school for teachers to attend to record-keeping tasks.

19. At Whittier Elementary School the principal scheduled a weekly common planning period for teachers in the same study group.

20. Winnona Park Elementary School benefits from a team of college students that spend every Thursday at the school. The college students are participating in Eco Watch, an outward-bound environmental leadership program. They do classroom and schoolwide environmental activities with the elementary students. This frees teachers to meet in study groups on Thursdays. The college students keep a record of the hours they spend in school, and at the end of the school year, the hours are converted into dollars for college tuition.

21. A number of elementary schools in one district have 1 day per week that is modified so that students are dismissed 2 hours earlier than on the other 4 days. Generally, this time is for individual teacher preparation time, faculty meetings, and district meetings. When five elementary schools elected to initiate the whole-school study group process, those schools reconfigured the modified-day time. Four of the faculties decided to use 1 hour of the 2-hour time block for study groups. The faculty at the fifth decided that study groups would meet every other week for $1\frac{1}{2}$ hours. On study group day after the study group meetings, the whole staff meets together for half an hour to report on the progress of each group.

22. At Brushy Creek Elementary School, the principal makes allowances for the time teachers spend after school in their study groups. If teachers are expected to stay 45 minutes after students are dismissed and a group of teachers in a study group stays an hour and a half beyond dismissal time, those teachers will be allowed to leave earlier than the 45 minutes on the other days of the week. A version of this idea would be for schools where teachers, by contract, are expected to stay 45 minutes after students are dismissed, the 45 minutes being shortened to 30 minutes on 4 days, carving out an hour for all study groups at the end of 1 day a week.

23. The over 200 teachers at Round Rock High School that are in as many as 40 study groups meet for an hour once a week at whatever time the individual groups determine is best for group members. For time spent beyond regular school hours, the teachers earn staff development credits and earn hours that can substitute for traditional staff development sessions scheduled on "staff development days." This school, one of the largest high schools in Texas, encourages teachers to assume individual responsibility for designing their own learning experiences. Such efforts of teachers in a large high school will certainly demonstrate that finding time to learn is a priority for high school teachers.

24. Several schools are currently exploring how to release teachers from their teaching duties for an hour and a half each week. The students would remain at school, being dismissed at their regular times. Professionals from area universities, health care facilities, community agencies, businesses, and city and county governmental agencies are considering how volunteers can provide instruction in foreign languages, physical education, athletics, nutrition, civics, drama, music, art, environmental education, and other areas for the students during the hour and a half time. Students could be grouped differently than in the regular classes, forming larger and smaller classes across grade levels. PTAs are considering budgeting funds for this purpose where funds are required.

All of the preceding strategies for finding time for teachers to collaborate require that the time allocated be spent in serious and purposeful work, work that increases the teachers' relevant knowledge and skills. Because it might be perceived by the public that time is being taken from students, strategies must be put in place to inform the internal and external publics about how students directly benefit from the time allocated to this form of teacher development. However, the communication must be continuous and effective. As time passes, information of student gains will encourage the community to continue to support the idea that student development is directly linked to teacher development. Teachers should tell their students on a regular basis what they do and what they learn in their study groups. Right after a study group meets is a good learning opportunity for students. Teachers can often say, "Today, we are going to do something that I learned in my study group this week." From this information, many students go home and tell their parents; they then see the connection, and the idea of how students benefit when time is allocated for teacher learning is no longer an abstract concept. If the information about study groups and their effectiveness is meaningfully presented, parents and other groups can become strong advocates for this form of teacher development and school improvement.

One outcome of the whole-faculty study group structure is the realization that professional development is inclusive of various models that interact with each other to make a more dynamic whole. At the beginning of the study group process, faculties have generally seen study groups separate from the professional development days. They saw study groups and the professional development days as separate from specific whole-faculty training events at the schools. And they were likely to see all of the earlier mentioned as separate from attending conferences and doing independent activities. By the end of Year 1, the faculties were more able to see and develop professional development plans that had the various staff development strategies or models feeding each other. In these schools, what teachers did in study groups to become skillful in the classroom enabled them to see more clearly the need for a more integrated and holistic approach to professional development. When this concept becomes reality in a school, time becomes less of a problem. Teachers see, as a unified effort, the different time frames as one large block for continuous learning.

The schools highlighted in the foregoing examples and many other schools have made heroic efforts to find the time required for professional development to routinely occur within the school day. Major efforts to find time for study groups to meet take energy away from the learning process. To achieve success for all students, districts and states must shoulder the responsibility for making meaningful professional development for teachers a seamless part of the daily work life of school personnel (i.e., make learning become the norm). Setting aside days in the school calendar as staff development days does not lighten the load or eliminate the pressure that teachers feel toward further developing and fine-tuning what and how they teach. For effective schools, development and increased learning is an everyday task, and it takes time and commitment.

7 The Content

Studying What's Important

Content refers to the actual skills, attitudes, and knowledge educators need to possess or acquire to achieve the intended results.

Snapshot 14 The Content

The Fulton Health, Science, and Fitness Magnet School has nearly 600 students, in one of the largest urban areas in the country. It serves a multicultural, low-income community. The school integrates the Comer model with the whole-faculty study group process to focus on the whole child and work with the parents and community to bring about schoolwide improvement. For the 4 years that the study groups have been in place, the groups have addressed portfolios, district standards, developmental learning, literacy, and a more positive school climate.

Prior to implementing study groups, the school had 1 day per week that was modified so that students were excused at 12:15 p.m. instead of the usual dismissal time of 2:30. To offset this, the other 4 days were lengthened to ensure that the school had the required instructional minutes per week. The primary purpose of the modified day was to give teachers preparation time as well as time for staff meetings and site workshops. When the first-year study groups in this school were implemented, they met weekly for 1 hour on the early-release day. At the conclusion of the first year, the teachers found that breaking the 2 hours up into parts, study group time and individual teacher preparation time, was not productive. They decided that study groups would meet every other week for 1½ hours and that the study group meetings would be followed by a staff meeting when groups would report on their work. The study groups met in the school's media center where the members of each group sat together. Meeting in this way meant that time did not have to be allocated for movement from another place. The sharing among groups gave the staff meetings a real instructional focus.

Because the magnet was changed from academics and athletics to health, science, and fitness, the faculty focused on science instruction in the fourth year of using the whole-faculty study group design. In October of that year, a common agenda for the school's five study groups was established. The Instructional Council, with a representative from each study group, agreed that during October, each study group would read, discuss, and become aware of the science component of the Site Action Plan and how it related to the school's integrated curriculum. The questions each study group was asked to discuss were these:

- How do we evaluate? Explore current assessment strategies?
- Do we have base line data? If not, how do we establish base line data?
- What data do we need to collect?
- Do we need to establish a format for collecting and recording data? If so, how?
- Do we need a format for science journals? If so, what?
- How will we evaluate journals?

One study group developed a science rubric for the other study groups to assess for appropriateness.

The Heart of the Study Group Process

The heart of the study group process is what teachers study, what teachers investigate, and what teachers do to become more skillful in the classroom with students. Without appropriate content, the process is empty.

The process, by itself, has little power to change what teachers actually do with students. Change in what students know and do is the end result of whole-faculty study groups. If students are to become more knowledgeable and skillful, then teachers must have control of the academic content they teach and have an expansive repertoire of instructional strategies to deliver that content to students. Teachers must increase their teaching repertoires so that students will increase their learning repertoires.

The need to continuously examine and expand the tools of teaching is directly aligned with the constancy of change in the work life and workplace of teaching. Each new set of students, each new expansion of knowledge, each new set of circumstances in the teaching environment, each new set of curriculum guidelines and materials, and each new set of regulations and expectations create the need for teachers to examine what and how they teach. Change and growth most often happens on top of what is already good. To change and to grow does not mean what is currently being done is bad or of poor quality. It is not uncommon for teachers to feel that efforts to introduce them to new practices and materials is based on the remedial concept, that something is wrong and requires fixing. A more positive outlook embraces the notion that as professionals, we are always "a work in progress," always in the process of developing or becoming more effective practitioners. This is analogous to early readers. Even though some will require remediation over time, the large majority are in the developmental track.

Staff Development Content

Staff development content can broadly be identified or categorized into five aspects or dimensions of effective instruction. Generally, what study groups do will be a combination of these:

1. Academic Knowledge

This is more commonly categorized by what teachers teach or the curriculum of schools, such as mathematics, language arts, foreign language, social studies, science, health, art, music, and physical education. Academic knowledge would also include child psychology, learning principles, and learning disorders. Knowledge is not stagnant. All of the listed areas are continuously being examined for accuracy and currency. Much of what teachers learned in teacher education programs in 1995 may not be accurate or relevant in 2000, especially in the sciences. The teachers who were trained prior to the 1990s were not exposed to the technological advances of today. Other knowledge bases requiring reinforcement over time include developmental characteristics of learners, brain-based learning, learning styles, and counseling techniques.

2. Instructional Strategies

How teachers deliver the content (e.g., fractions) of their instruction is a major consideration. The degree or depth of our comprehension and ability to apply the knowledge is often determined in how the information is presented to us by another individual. A teaching strategy would be the overall design of a lesson, such as a blueprint is for building a house. The strategy is matched to the content objective. Teaching strategies are often referred to as models of teaching. A teacher's teaching repertoire would include a wide range of strategies so as to increase the chance that the needs of students can appropriately be met. Many strategies have names, such as direct instruction, cooperative learning, inductive thinking, concept attainment, mnemonics, inquiry, and simulation (Joyce & Weil, 1994).

3. Instructional Skills

Using a particular strategy involves incorporating a number of instructional skills. As stated earlier, a strategy is like a blueprint; the skills that make up that strategy would be like hammering, sawing, and measuring. Teaching skills would include giving clear directions, encouraging thinking at various levels, providing appropriate practice, making learning meaningful, involving all students, making the purpose of the lesson clear, framing questions well, providing adequate wait time after asking a question, and giving students feedback on their progress. A teacher using the concept attainment strategy to teach the concept of "land locked" would use many of the listed skills throughout the lesson.

4. Management

In classrooms, there must be strategies for managing the environment, the students, and the instructional tasks. Management of the environment would include providing for a safe and orderly learning environment. Management of instructional tasks would include how to organize materials, resources, and distribution systems for effective and timely use. If these skills are not mastered, disruptions will take time and attention from teaching and learning. Management of the students would include how limits are determined and set (e.g., class rules), how the teacher responds to positive and negative student behaviors, how choices are given, how the teacher reinforces positive behaviors, how the teacher communicates with and involves parents, how transitions are handled (e.g., moving from reading to mathematics), how negative behaviors are diffused, and the interpersonal skills of the teacher with the students.

5. Belief Systems

What we believe about students and what they can do has a powerful effect on student performance. Teachers must know the developmental needs of children and youth. If students are to succeed in a global community, teachers require the opportunity to develop knowledge, skills, and dispositions that enable them to promote learning for all students, regardless of race, gender, ethnicity, special needs, or language differences. Knowing how to involve the whole family and community in the teaching and learning process is critical for success. It is the attitudes, values, and beliefs of the adults in a school that free young people to be all that they can be or inhibit their growth. These attitudes, values, and beliefs are learned.

Not one of the preceding dimensions of effective instruction occurs in isolation. It is like conducting a symphony. The elements occur in unison, together. Teaching is an art. It is doing a lot of things at the same time and doing them well. Similarly, in development and training approaches, to give all of our attention to one of the four components to the exclusion of the others is unrealistic and superficial. A study group focusing on a new mathematics textbook series would not only examine the scope and sequence of the mathematics curriculum but would also consider what instructional strategies and skills would best match the content objectives. Teachers who are learning to use the inductive thinking model of teaching would use the inductive strategy in conjunction with mathematics, social studies, science, or any other appropriate curriculum content.

Management is integrated into every aspect of instruction. We are always alert to how students are responding and what requires tending that may be distracting learners. The point is not that the five aspects are separate elements of teaching but that the five elements become part and parcel of a natural, seamless fabric of what it means to be a professional educator (Fullan, Bennett, & Rolheister-Bennett, 1990). The National Staff Development Council (NSDC) has published *Standards for Staff Development* (NSDC, 1994). NSDC has high school, middle level, and elementary school editions of these standards. The standards include a section on staff development content standards. The content areas for which standards have been written are as follows:

- Childhood and preadolescent development
- Adolescent developmental needs
- Classroom management
- Core curriculum
- Diversity
- Interdisciplinary curriculum
- Research-based instructional strategies
- High expectations
- Family involvement

- Student performance assessment
- Guidance; advisement
- Interdisciplinary teams
- Service learning

The power in the whole-faculty study group process is in the promise that the content of the study will enable students to be more powerful learners. The hope is that teachers will become more powerful teachers, raising the students' rates of learning in the personal, social, and academic domains. It has been shown (Joyce & Calhoun, 1996) that learning rates of students can be increased in 1 or 2 years by having teachers in a school in study groups focusing on instructional strategies that

- Make the instructional environment more active
- Encourage higher order thinking skills
- Teach social skills and thereby increase the cooperative environment of the classroom and school

If the original purpose of initiating whole-faculty study groups is to change the climate of a school and create fully collegial interactions where few or none existed before, then the initiators can expect changes in student performances to take more than 2 years. This result is because the process itself will be the central feature, to break norms of privacy and isolation. However, while this is being done, as long as the work is of an instructional nature and is meaningful to individuals, the process has great value as a first step to getting teachers "around a table" on a regular basis to interact about curriculum and instructional issues. One of the guidelines given in Chapter 6 is that whole-faculty study groups be driven by efforts to improve curriculum and instruction for increased student learning. As the process becomes routine and the norms become more collaborative (i.e., more synergistic; see Chapter 7), the groups will embrace more challenging content that puts the central focus on what is best for students. Even though the initial work of some study groups may not be as student centered as we would hope, it will become stronger as teaching becomes more public and teachers become more confident with each other (i.e., as the work environment becomes more of a synergistic environment; see Chapter 8).

A Decision-Making Model

The first decision that is made by the whole faculty is whether or not the whole-faculty study group process is to be put in place at the school. Once the decision is made to do this, it is expected that all faculty members will participate in a study group. Second, it must be decided who will lead the whole faculty through an inquiry process to determine how groups will be organized and what groups will do. This may be individual(s) at the school or external to the school. This individual or group will collect and organize data for the faculty to use in making decisions that must be made. When the whole faculty works together during this initial stage of decision making, teachers begin to feel a part of the effort and, as a result, feel less coerced during the implementation stage. It is during the initiation stage when everyone is involved in the decision making that individuals see the process for what it is intended to do. Those who may not have been in favor of the process when the faculty took a vote on whether or not

The Decision-Making Cycle for Schoolwide Change through Whole-Faculty Study Groups

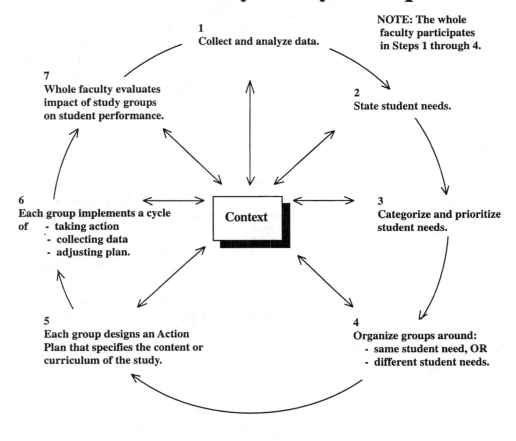

NOTE: The whole faculty participates in Steps 1 through 4.

1 Collect and analyze data.

2 State student needs.

3 Categorize and prioritize student needs.

4 Organize groups around:
- same student need, OR
- different student needs.

5 Each group designs an Action Plan that specifies the content or curriculum of the study.

6 Each group implements a cycle of
- taking action
- collecting data
- adjusting plan.

7 Whole faculty evaluates impact of study groups on student performance.

Context

The overarching contextual question asked at each step...

"Will this work here?"

Figure 7.1. A Decision-Making Cycle for Schoolwide Change Through Whole-Faculty Study Groups

Copyright © 1997 by Carlene Murphy.

the process was to be put in place at the school are most often brought more willingly into the process when their voice is heard in this developmental phase. Some teachers will still continue to feel that the process is contrived collegiality until, in their study groups, they experience total control over what they do and how they go about doing it.

The decision-making cycle (Murphy, 1997), shown in Figure 7.1 and described in the remainder of this chapter, outlines a model for the balance of the process. This model has been followed successfully in a wide variety of schools. Snapshot 15 illustrates how one faculty used this model.

Making Content Decisions
for Study Groups

The decision-making cycle described in the following pages is recommended for making decisions regarding how study groups will be organized and what study groups will do. The individuals who lead the whole faculty through the steps of the cycle must carefully think through each step. Even though the individuals leading the decision-making process may have firm opinions as to what the study groups should do, they should maintain open minds, keeping their opinions to themselves, and be totally free in letting the faculty find its own way. It is critical that the whole faculty participates in Steps 1 through 4 of the decision-making cycle. Every faculty member should have voice in how the groups are organized and what the groups will be doing. This open participation now will diminish problems after the study groups begin their work. The teachers own the process and should feel that ownership.

The Decision-Making Cycle

The decision-making cycle for school-wide change through whole-faculty study groups, shown in Figure 7.1, is a seven-step, cyclic decision-making model that will lead the faculty to what their study groups will do and how they will be formed. This model includes the following steps:

Step 1. Data analysis: Analyze a wide range of data and indicators describing the status of student learning and the condition of the learning environment. Relative to data collection, it should be noted that using at least 3 consecutive years of data for each data source will give a more accurate picture of the level of achievement or condition. Data might include several of the following:

- Examples of student work
- Standardized test results
- Performance of students on the district's content standards
- Discipline referrals and suspensions (how many and why)
- Violent behavior (incidence and types)
- Participation in art, music, and drama events
- Level of participation and complexity of science and social study fairs and projects
- Distribution of student grades by reporting periods
- Parental involvement
- Community perceptions of the effectiveness of the school or district
- Responses to questionnaires completed by parents, teachers, and students
- Promotion and retention rates by grade level
- Samples of student and teacher portfolios
- Information from community agencies (e.g., social services)
- Mobility (e.g., percentage of students in grade 12 who entered in grade 9)
- Attendance and dropout rates

- Amount of independent reading by students, including circulation reports from area libraries
- Student access in homes to computers and the Internet
- Writing by students (amount and type)
- Staff use of resources
- Reports from accrediting agencies
- Personnel resignations and transfers (how many and why)
- The school's improvement plan or other plans developed by the staff
- Percentage of graduates attending postsecondary educational institutions
- Employment rates of the graduates
- Percentage of students in advanced placement
- The status of various instructional initiatives

The last item on the preceding list means finding out the level of implementation or use of past and current instructional initiatives. The analysis of initiatives that have been introduced to the school's instructional programs (e.g., see the activity described in the Assimilation Capacity discussion in Chapter 5) will give a strong direction to what study groups will do. These instructional initiatives usually come in the form of textbooks, boxed materials or programs, manipulatives, workshops, and equipment (e.g., computers). Or they come under titles such as Reading Recovery, Writing to Read, Literacy Learning, Guided Reading, Frameworks, Higher Order Thinking Skills, Models of Teaching, and Activities for the Integration of Mathematics and Science. Whatever the initiatives are, they must be examined to confirm that the desired results are forthcoming. Also, the faculty determines whether additional training is required. If there are duplications in initiatives or if the promise for student benefits has not been realized, discarding of the initiative should be considered. This is all part of the data collection and analysis step.

Step 2. Student needs: From the data, generate a list of student needs. Examples might include the following student needs (numbers do not indicate priority order):

1. Listen actively, critically, and effectively.
2. Write effectively for a variety of purposes.
3. Speak with clarity and confidence.
4. Use various types of technology.
5. Collect, organize, and review data effectively.
6. Master and accurately apply mathematical concepts.
7. Demonstrate an increase in reading skills.
8. Interpret and appropriately apply information from maps, charts, and graphs.
9. Employ conflict management skills.
10. Understand and appreciate different cultures.

Step 3. Categorize and set priorities: Categorize student needs and prioritize the categories or clusters. When student needs are categorized, several may cluster around certain areas, such as mathematics; language development; behavior, discipline, and management of the learning environment; and technology. Give each category a name, and then set priorities for the various categories or clusters. For example, using the student needs as listed in Step 2, categories and priorities might look like this:

Student Needs	Category Name	Priority
1, 9, 10	Behavior	2
1, 2, 3, 4, 5, 7	Language Development	1
4, 5, 7, 8	Social Studies	4
4, 5	Technology	3
5, 6, 8	Mathematics	5

Step 4. Organization: Organize study groups around the prioritized student needs. As study groups are organized, the first decision required is whether or not all of the study groups at a school will focus on

- The same category of student needs (e.g., language development).
- Different categories of student needs (e.g., language development, behavior, and technology).

Once the whole faculty reaches consensus on the organizational choices, they then organize themselves to fit the choice they have made, as illustrated in the following scenarios.

Scenario 1

If the whole faculty decides to focus on *one* category of student need, such as language development, the faculty should revisit the data that verify that category of student need (e.g., students are not learning to read, write, and speak at the desired level of performance). Those data will identify the skill areas that received low scores on a standardized measure and on an analysis of student work. In such a case, study groups might be organized around the components of language skills, such as the following:

- Word attack skills
- Comprehension skills
- Vocabulary development
- Listening
- Speaking

Or study groups might be organized around language programs, such as Guided Reading, Frameworks, Literacy Learning, and the adopted reading textbook series. The district's content standards in reading and language development will give the groups direction as to the areas of language development that require attention.

Scenario 2

> If the whole faculty decides that study groups will address *different* categories of student needs, those categories would be specified. Teachers who should increase their skill in meeting the technological needs of students could form a study group. Teachers who should become more knowledgeable of behavior management strategies could form a study group. Teachers who want to examine the scope and sequence of the reading program could form a group. Teachers desirous of continuing their training in higher order thinking skills so that students will be challenged to be competent problem solvers could form a group. And so on.

In both of these scenarios, teachers have a choice of what they will pursue. As groups form, they should follow the guideline of no more than six in a group. For example, if eight teachers want to pursue technology, then there should be two study groups formed.

Each study group, regardless of its focus, should return to the data that identified the student need. This gives the group a starting point and the direction for establishing what the group should do to address the student need. The district's standards in the content area in which the group is working will keep the group focused on the desired student behaviors.

Steps 1 through 4 usually take about 10 hours to complete. If a school is beginning the process at the start of a new school year, time to accomplish Steps 1 through 4 should be scheduled for one or a part of a preplanning day and continued during other times when faculty come together. This means that study groups may not actually begin meeting until October. How long it takes to do the "front end" work will depend on where each faculty is in its understanding of schoolwide instructional needs.

Step 5. Plan of Action: Create a study group action plan. The study group action plan should include the following five steps:

1. The general category of student need, such as technology
2. Specific student needs and exactly what teachers will do in the study groups to address those needs; for example:

Data indicate that students need to	*Therefore, in the study group, teachers will*
Use software applications to facilitate learning across all curriculum areas	Determine what software is available and its appropriateness for teaching and reinforcing content knowledge
	Demonstrate competency in using the computer and for accessing information

3. The intended results of the work of the study group, specifying the evidence that will indicate that student needs have been met or lessened
4. What the study group will do in its efforts to become more skillful in the classroom in meeting the needs of students: This "what" is the content of the study, the investigation, or the training. The content is the substance of what the group will do. It includes the study group's curriculum, materials, and human resources.

Defining exactly what the group will study, investigate, or become more skillful at doing is an initial task that brings together the collective experiences of the study group members. A teacher that has attended a particular workshop or course will have ideas. A teacher that subscribes to a particular journal will have ideas. A beginning teacher just finishing college will have ideas. A teacher who attended a particular conference will have ideas. The group will decide its curriculum. If the group is focusing on students' low performance in reading, the content of the study could be how teachers teach reading more effectively and, thereby, strive to meet performance standards established by the district. The group should answer a number of key questions, such as: What exactly will be the study group's curriculum? What materials will be required? Whom should group members learn from?

Remember, however, it is the group's decision as to what it will do and how it will do it. The group might choose to

- Examine what reading skills are taught at each level
- Practice teaching strategies that encourage critical thinking
- Develop schoolwide reading goals and activities
- Examine and implement assessment procedures that enable students to have more control over their progress
- Be trained in how to use technology to support reading and writing skills

An analysis of the status of past and current reading programs or initiatives (e.g., Reading Recovery) might reveal which strategies are successful and those that are not being implemented to the level that effects on students are evident. Such analysis should suggest innovations that are candidates for the content of what the group might do.

Step 6. Implementation: Implement the study group action plan. Each study group implements its action plan. It investigates a new strategy or a new set of materials. The members use the strategy or new materials in their classrooms. The members share what happened in their classrooms. They adjust the strategies and materials based on what they learn from each other. The members plan lessons together and actually teach lessons within the group to get feedback. Group members design materials together and share what has been developed in the past. They visit each other's classrooms. They observe how students respond to the strategies and materials. They monitor the effects of the teaching strategies and materials on students by collecting information about student performance and participation. The study group action plan is revisited every 4 to 6 weeks to see if it should be amended. If a group takes an unanticipated turn, the group may have to write a new plan.

Step 7. Evaluation: Evaluate the impact of the study group effort on student performance. The effects of the work of study groups on students and the school are monitored. For example, the desired results of an instructional innovation are tracked over a period of time to see what is actually happening and what adjustments are required in the materials and the teaching and learning strategies. Did the students get better? What evidence is there that the quality of instruction improved?

Once Steps 1 through 7 have been completed, the cycle is continued by repeating Step 1 again and continuing through Steps 2 through 7.

Frequently, the process of identifying instructional problems has been accomplished when the school improvement plan or other such plan was developed for the district office, a state agency, or an accrediting association. When the work of identifying instructional problems has been done and the intended results have been established, faculties can use these plans to determine what study groups will do.

Snapshot 15 Making "What" and "How" Decisions

The focus team at Brushy Creek Elementary School attended a week of training in June with a consultant in the whole-faculty study group process. By the end of that week, the five teachers, principal, and assistant principal had developed an implementation plan for their school that was a mini version of what the focus team had experienced during the training. The team's plan included agendas for working with the whole faculty during preplanning in August and at other times as necessary after school started. On the agendas, it was specified who was responsible for leading a particular segment, how much time the individual would have, and what pages in the training handbook they would copy and use as handouts for the faculty. The team decided to call the study groups at Brushy Creek, TARGET teams. TARGET stood for Totally Aligned Realizing Growth Essential for Teachers. Their plan as it was developed is as follows.

Half Day, Preplanning Week

Setting:	Peppy music playing as teachers enter the room, posters on the walls, focus team wearing T-shirts with targets printed on them, team has question marks taped on shirts and earrings in shape of a question mark, door prizes, and at the midpoint in the presentation, they have a "dance lesson."
Opening:	TARGET for success. TARGET teams (our term for study group).
	"We know you have questions, and we're here to facilitate your finding the answers." (Judy, 10 minutes)
Exercise:	(Dee Ann, 20 minutes)
	What is your greatest fear about study groups?
	What is something you could choose to do to sabotage study groups?
	Write answers to the two questions. Do *not* put your name on the paper!
	When all finished, wad your paper up and throw it across the room. Pick up the wad nearest you.
	As responses are read, answers are put on chart paper. Tell group that everyone will review the responses at a later date to see what has come to pass.
Purpose or research:	Why are study groups needed? p. 12-14 (Kathy, 45 minutes)
	What study groups are and are not? p. 11; policies that support professional development, p. 17 (Judy, 10 minutes)
	For whom do schools exist? p. 18 (Cathy, 5 minutes)

Teachers as intellectuals, p. 16 (Judy, 5 minutes)

Study groups push you through levels of use of innovations, p. 45-46 (Dee Ann, 10 minutes)

Activity: Brainstorm and list all of the changes that have occurred at Brushy Creek over the last 5 years. Discuss stages of those innovations. Discuss current levels of use of those innovations. (Kathleen, 20 minutes)

Data review or searching for student needs: Form small groups; each group given a folder with data and asked to study data, analyzing current condition of school, and write "Student Need" statements.

Categorize problems.

Rewrite one problem for each category.

Prioritize.

Closing: (Cathy) At next meeting, we will identify the possible areas of study or the content that will address student needs.

The question that guides all decisions: What is happening differently in the classroom as a result of what you are doing and learning in your study group?

Second Meeting With the Whole Faculty

The question that guides all decisions . . .

Time for study group:

Options.

Vote.

Action plans:

Form to use.

Areas of study identified (the areas were Literacy Learning, Brain-Based Learning, Emotional IQ, Cooperative Groups, Reading Strategies, Invitations, Technology, and Mathematics Problem Solving).

Use of Post-it notes to indicate first and second choices.

Third Meeting With the Whole Faculty

The question that guides all decisions . . .

Logs:

Form and purpose.

Management, procedures, and individual logs.

Highlight questions and concerns on logs.

Review decision-making cycle.

Review action plans.

Review sample action plans.

[Note: The following meetings were added to the plan after the third meeting with the whole faculty.]

Focus Team Meeting With C. Murphy on September 5

Debrief earlier sessions.

Review areas of study identified.

Using Post-it notes of first and second choices, form groups.

Discuss role of focus team in "tending" study groups.

Discuss communication systems among study groups (e.g., the Instructional Council).

Discuss the stages of groups (e.g., orientation, dissatisfaction, resolution, and production).

First TARGET (Study) Groups Meeting, September 11

Form groups (list typed from Post-it notes).
Establish group norms.
Designate leader for each month.

Snapshot 16 Forming Study Groups

The Murdock Elementary School faculty met on staff development day in the fall of the school year to make decisions about what the study groups at Murdock would do to increase student learning and what the membership of the groups would be. The faculty had developed a School Action Improvement Plan the prior Spring. Student data had been analyzed to determine what the major instructional improvement strategies would be for the coming year. Whole-faculty study groups were to be the major vehicle for staff development. In August, a new principal was assigned to the school. To make decisions about the study groups, the focus team and the new principal decided to have the faculty review the School Action Improvement Plan and do an analysis of all of the instructional initiatives that had been introduced at the school over the past 5 years.

When the teachers arrived in the media center, they were grouped heterogeneously at tables. The groups were asked to take 10 minutes to brainstorm about all of the instructional initiatives that had been introduced to the school over the past 5 years, anything new that any teacher had been expected to do of an instructional nature with students (see the Assimilation Capacity discussion in Chapter 5). This could be materials, textbooks, instructional strategies, attitudes, equipment (e.g., computers), programs (e.g., Reading Recovery), and assessments (e.g., portfolios). The initiatives were listed on chart paper. After each group finished, the sheets of paper were put on the wall. When the lists were condensed into one list, there were 38 items on the list. Teachers were then asked to discuss with their group whether they felt each initiative was in the initiation stage, the implementation stage, or the institutionalization stage. On each table was a handout describing the characteristics of each of the three stages. There was much debate. Some teachers had never heard of an initiative, whereas another teacher assumed that all teachers had mastered the practice. The teachers saw that several "new" programs were duplicates of "old" programs. The teachers thought that only a few initiatives were in the institutionalization stage, meaning that the initiation stage was routine and integrated into other classroom practices, as appropriate.

The purpose of this activity was to use the information gleaned along with other information to determine what study groups would do. With this purpose in mind, the teachers categorized the initiatives that were in the initiation or implementation stage. The names of the categories with the initiatives in each category were as follows:

- Mathematics: calendar mathematics, AIMS, Internet, manipulatives, hands on equations, and polygons
- Discipline: positive discipline, conflict management, and dyssemia
- Technology: video microscope, satellites, computers, schoolwide network, laser discs, and electronic portfolios
- Assessment-reporting: student-grade-school-teacher portfolios, report cards, TOOLS, authentic assessments, and conferencing
- Language: frameworks, guided reading, Rigby, daily news, journaling, literacy centers, manipulatives, whole language, and spelling strategies
- Science: new science curriculum, new health curriculum, manipulatives, and AIMS
- Designs for learning: multiage family, cultural diversity, thematic and integrated teaching, cooperative learning, developmental strategies, inclusion, and coteaching
- Higher order thinking skills: Georgia's Effective Teaching Practices, TALENTS, multiple intelligences, learning styles, and brain-based learning

The 55 teachers were asked to write on a piece of paper what category and specific initiative was most critical to them. In other words, what should be the focus of your learning and training? From this question, 11 groups were formed with typically five teachers in each group. The areas of study and skill building were as follows:

Number of Groups	Category-Initiative
3	Dyssemia
1	Assessment-Reporting
1	Technology
1	Higher Order Thinking Skills
2	Guided Reading
1	Spelling Strategies
1	Integrated and Thematic Teaching
1	Inclusion

The groups turned out to be heterogeneous, not by design but by need. For example, the higher order thinking skills study group has in it the principal, the school's learning support specialist, a fifth-grade teacher, the speech teacher, the music teacher, and the TALENT (gifted) teacher. The assessment-reporting study group has three first-grade teachers, a second-grade teacher, and two fourth-grade teachers.

At the first study group meeting, the groups had to decide how they were going to address such broad areas. This discussion resulted in action plans for each group. The plans are revisited and modified every 4 weeks. Each study group's learning adventure is somewhat like a storyboard, with lots of unanticipated twists. And that is what makes the journey real for each group. Only the members of the group determine their pathway to learning. Most of the areas the faculty is addressing requires additional training, either initial or follow-up. If group members do not already have a source for the training, the members take the responsibility to do whatever is necessary to secure the support they require.

Every certified person assigned to the school is in one of the 11 study groups. The groups meet for about an hour once a week. One week, substitutes relieve the teachers in shifts during the school day, and the next week, the groups meet for an hour after school in place of a faculty meeting, thus creating an alternating schedule by weeks.

Snapshot 17 Organizing Study Groups

Washington Middle School, to overcome a severe overcrowdedness situation, was organized into four tracts and scheduled on a year-round calendar. Three of the tracts are in session and one tract is on vacation each quarter. The time for professional development was difficult to coordinate and follow up. After hearing about the whole-faculty study group concept and having a team composed of members in each tract attend training, study groups were organized within tracts. Study groups were formed by those teachers who made up the faculty of a tract. Areas of study were whole language, learning styles, cultural diversity, and student achievement data.

One additional major outcome of the study design at Washington was the decision made by the school's classified personnel. Persons serving in non-teaching, support positions also established study groups. Areas of discussion covered by these groups included the following:

- Clearer and more complete definition of the roles of the classified personnel and a better understanding of how these roles fit into the total school picture
- A sharing of job skills; what is good, what works, and how improvements can be made; what is not working and why, and problem solving each other's work
- Joint work on possible management of the dilemmas faced
- Improvement of communications with students, teachers, administrators, and parents

Classified personnel with the same or similar jobs were organized into groups and met during working hours for 1 hour per week. The results of these study groups were a classified handbook, parking lot safety procedures, patio behavior policies, and updated job descriptions.

Stuck Study Groups

Just as Rosenholtz (1989) described moving, moderately stuck, and stuck groups in her work on organizational groups, we also have moving, moderately stuck, and stuck study groups. When study groups get stuck (i.e., seem to be at an impasse), most often, the reason is not a process problem but one relating to content. Among the most important reasons why study groups may feel stuck are these 16:

1. The content of the study may not be substantive enough to keep the attention and interest of the group. If the study is shallow and the answer to the identified problem is somewhat obvious, momentum is lost. The clarity and complexity of the problem will affect the sustained energy given to the study. In such cases, group members should reconsider or revisit the following questions:

- How clear is the problem?
- Is the problem a schoolwide problem or one primarily affecting only the members of the study group?
- Is the problem a curricular or instructional problem?
- What student data verify the severity of the problem?

- How engaging is the problem for the group's members?
- In what ways will teachers and students change if the problem is solved or lessened?
- Are appropriate resources available?
- How will effects on students be measured?

2. No one is paying attention to the study group logs. If no one is reading or responding to concerns being expressed or the recommendations being made in the study group logs, study group members are going to feel disconnected and neglected. On the log, a group may ask for a specific resource or express logistics that are keeping the group dissatisfied. A designated person should read the logs within 24 hours and respond to any concern or recommendation that the group has.

3. The content may require training, both at the beginning of the study and continuing over a period of time. If a group wants to use the cooperative learning strategy in the classroom, reading about the strategy will not be sufficient. The teachers should see demonstrations in several curricular areas and have the opportunity to practice the strategy both within the study group and with their students. The teachers should share lessons and materials, observe each other trying the new strategy, and plan future applications together.

4. The content may be too passive, not requiring action. Reading articles and books, without a clear plan for converting the information to classroom practice, gets boring.

5. Sometimes, a group focuses on what others in the schools should do. The group wants to come up with guidelines or directions for others to follow. It becomes not "how I must change," but "how you must change." Or the group may get bogged down with doing surveys or inventories primarily for the benefit of the rest of the faculty. After awhile, this work gets burdensome.

6. If the problem can be solved administratively, then it should not be undertaken by a study group. For example, a common problem study groups tackle is discipline. A study group focusing on discipline often becomes a forum for formulating new rules, policies, and procedures for students to follow and not a meaningful investigation into underlying causes of disruptive behaviors and different approaches to minimizing those behaviors. There are many different perspectives on behavioral management, and many of them could be examined, synthesized, and included in a classroom or school management plan that the group designs.

7. The underlying cause of the problem the group is investigating is not being confronted. For instance, if the reason why students are disruptive is because the teachers' instructional strategies are inadequate or not appropriate, new rules are not going to improve the situation. It is natural for study groups to initially shy away from focusing on how teachers teach because of personal anxiety and discomfort. But not facing basic issues will keep the study group from moving ahead.

8. "Information overload" may describe a stuck group. Groups may have mountains of material and information and become totally frustrated over sorting out what's important to the task. If so, the group should revisit the original question or problem. Inviting a person to meet with the group that has experience or advanced information about the question could help weed out the clutter. Again, if changes in behavior are required, then someone must demonstrate the desired behaviors. If we do not know how to do something, we become more skillful at it when a person who is skillful shows

us how. Attending workshops and inviting trainers to study group meetings to demonstrate effective practices may be necessary if skill development is required.

9. A group may simply decide that the area selected for study does not hold promise for them and their students. When this happens, the group should bring to closure what they are doing and go back to the problem identification step in the problem-solving cycle. Once a group has experienced what it means to work collaboratively with their peers, they are more apt to know what will make the group more functional.

10. If one member is blocking the progress of the whole group, ask that person to provide a research-based alternative for accomplishing the same task or purpose, and consider what is offered.

11. If members are not respecting the norms that the group established, revisit the norms on a regular basis. If revisiting the norms is a part of how the group functions, it will not appear that it is being done for the benefit of one individual. As groups discuss behaviors that facilitate learning in their classrooms. For example, teachers expect students to cooperate with peers, participate in class discussions, bring what they need to class, complete assignments, and to be courteous and respectful. These are the same behaviors that keep study groups functioning effectively.

12. One or more members of the group may not be bringing to the meeting what they agreed to at the last meeting. Specify on the Study Group Log what each member is to bring to the next meeting and see that everyone gets a copy of the log after the meeting. Then, if the group does not have what it needs to do its work because a member neglects to follow through, simply state that "we can't do our work today" and put that in the log.

13. If collegiality and collaboration (i.e., synergy) are not functioning very well in the group, use the Synergy Checklist in Chapter 8 to discover the problem and learn what should be done to improve the synergy of the group.

14. Group members should remind each other of the "implementation dip" and that the energy and excitement of getting started may run low after a period of time, especially if there is a problem with the content of the study. It is helpful after groups have met four or five times to review with the whole faculty the stages of groups. This may help some groups see that what they are experiencing fits expectations. To energize the group, invite a nonmember who has expertise and experience with the area of study to share perspectives on what the group is doing. Also, changing the location of where the group typically meets helps to inject new energy.

15. As study groups spend more time together and develop trust in one another, they tend to become more open with each other. This is generally a healthy situation and helps build a powerful synergy (see the section on Synergistic Relationships in Chapter 8) within the group. Occasionally, however, it leads to conflict when the openness causes biases and beliefs to clash. Reminding members that respecting differences, operating in an "appreciative understanding" manner (a part of the synergy process; see the Appreciative Understanding section of Chapter 8), and keeping focused on the group's common goals and desired results usually keeps the conflict from being seriously disruptive.

16. It is easy for a study group to feel alone and apart from the whole. Multiple communication systems must be put in place so that at all times, all groups have a sense of what each other is doing. If two groups are pursuing a similar topic, then the two groups may want to invite a resource person to come and share with both groups together. Information and results should be constantly shared.

8 The Team

The Key to Effectiveness

Snapshot 18 Learning Teams

Before Elder Middle School used the whole-faculty study group design, the teachers worked in teams, as they still do. However, one team-planning period per week is designated study group time, when the configuration of who meets together may vary from who attends a team meeting on the other 4 days. Even when the individuals are the same, the dialogue is different. As one teacher wrote:

> A majority of our team meetings were centered around business that needed to be conducted, such as break duty schedules, student schedule changes, discipline problems, parent contacts, record keeping, and resource sharing. Before we started the study group time, most of the teachers in our team didn't read much from professional journals. To be honest, unless the teachers were taking a course that had required reading, they did very little reading to keep up to date in current educational issues. Study group time helped us stay abreast of current issues and the latest research findings, so everyone began to read more. Most important, the rapport that grew from becoming more open about our beliefs and classroom practices increased our willingness to try new methods and to share how those strategies worked with our students. For the first time, we openly shared lessons that were not effective and jointly worked on ways to make the lessons more powerful.

The longer the teams experienced the study group mind-set (of learning teams) one period per week, the other planning periods became more like the study group time. As study groups became the norm at Elder Middle School, the dialogue in the faculty lounge, in faculty meetings, and in department meetings were also noticeably different. Teachers talked about instruction. When the school was designated for the third time as one of Georgia's Schools of Excellence, interviews with teachers reflected the attitude: We are a community of learners. The cumulative effect of this dynamic was also validated in the student data.

Team Building

Effective study groups are effective teams! No study group will be effective if it does not have real teamwork. Teamwork is what differentiates an effective study group from a typical committee or other work group. The following is an insightful story of the four people named Everybody, Somebody, Anybody, and Nobody, which very nicely helps us understand what teamwork and team building are not:

> There was an important job to be done and Everybody was sure that Somebody would do it. Anybody could have done it, but Nobody did it. Somebody got angry about that because it was Everybody's job. Everybody thought Anybody could do it, but Nobody realized Everybody wouldn't do it. It ended up that Everybody blamed Somebody when Nobody did what Anybody could have done.

On the other hand, the great automobile industry leader, Henry Ford, gives us a sense of the meaning of teamwork: "Coming together is a beginning; keeping together is progress; and working together is success."

As Pat Riley (1994) describes in *The Winner Within,* a group of friends went down the Colorado River in an inflatable raft. After 2 days, "the river became a great equalizer. People accustomed to being pampered and indulged had become a team, working together to cope with the unpredictable twists and turns of the river."

The twists and turns that study groups encounter are as real and personally as scary as those in the raging river. Consequently, study groups cannot make it as just a collection of individuals but instead, can work together cooperatively and have tremendous success as an effective team.

Teamwork is the ability of people to work together in a genuinely cooperative manner (i.e., interdependently) toward a common vision. Teamwork is joint work and joint responsibility. Teamwork is a vehicle that allows common people to attain uncommon results.

Good examples of teamwork are the California's giant sequoia trees. Their roots are barely below the surface of the ground. The sequoias grow in groves, and their roots intertwine. When strong winds blow, the intertwining (i.e., interdependent) roots of the sequoias help hold them all up.

Another impressive illustration of teamwork happened in the 1980 Winter Olympic Games at Lake Placid, New York. Rather than just trying to find the top players, the ice hockey coach selected individuals who could function in a team setting and respond effectively under pressure.

The U.S. team began ranked seventh in a field of eight. But, when the closing seconds ticked away, the final score read U.S.A., 4, and U.S.S.R., 3. The U.S. team maybe didn't have the best players on the ice, but they did have the best team! They were a synergistic team, collectively striving for a common vision, interdependently playing and empowering each other, and functioning as the best ice hockey team in the world.

The preceding illustrations and Snapshot 18 provide a good overview of teamwork and team building. However, they don't give us the specifics we require to help us understand the fundamental basis of teams, teamwork and team building, and the creation of effective study group teams. Snapshot 19 and the remaining sections of this chapter discuss and illustrate in detail these fundamentals.

Snapshot 19 Study Group Synergy

The science department at Mission Bay High School decided that six science teachers at the school would be a study group. Except for the school's art teachers, the other 15 study groups were formed across departments. One physics teacher wrote:

> Avoiding the development day doldrums wasn't the only benefit to the study group process. Our group's foremost benefit was that I got to know the teachers in my department much better than I had in 7 previous years. I grew to understand the priorities of my fellow teachers, to see the way their teaching flowed from their view of science and education. As I spoke with them week after week, I appreciated their personalities more and found strengths and abilities I hadn't suspected were there.
>
> Of course, there were other, more tangible benefits. We invented some new labs to use in our physical science classes. We researched and made acceptable progress in designing a new curriculum in marine science. We worked together to calibrate recalcitrant old equipment, we learned of treasure we could borrow from each other's hoards, and we even plotted how best to fit our sequence together to get maximum mileage from our lab supplies and demonstration devices. And we laughed a lot at ourselves, at each other, and at life in this big city high school with an enrollment of over 1,700 students.
>
> I appreciate the conversations I have with the other teachers in my department; I'm grateful that I know them better now—that's the best thing about the study group idea. I got to talk with people whom I found interesting and admirable, and whose company was welcome after the burden of the day's teaching. (Our group met 1 hour a week after school.)
>
> Naturally, not all our meetings were productive. But they were *our* meetings, and the responsibility for making them productive or frustrating, enlightening or confounding, was our responsibility. It left us with the lingering, seductive taste of "freedom."

True teamwork is called synergy; it is when the teamwork of a group allows it to get the maximum results from the available resources. Effective study groups are synergistic, self-directed, learning teams.

In the remaining sections of this chapter, we describe and discuss the specifics and details of this type of teamwork, synergy, including its prerequisites, the process for attaining it, and its development in study groups.

Synergistic Relationships

In a group or team, relationships are established that make the group more productive or less so. If a group collectively is less productive than the sum of what the individuals would produce, we say we have a *self-destructive relationship* in the group. This, unfortunately, happens frequently and comes about in a group because of such things as poor communications or miscommunications, lack of trust, blaming, defensiveness, self-centeredness, backbiting, and internal competition.

In groups with self-destructive relationships, the group uses up so much energy in nonproductive ways that it has little additional energy to be creative and to generate new ideas and more effective processes. No doubt, you have seen groups composed of bright, capable individuals that couldn't seem to accomplish much of anything, and it made you wonder: How could such a strong group of individuals be so ineffective? Unfortunately, the individuals were most capable, but the relationship in the group was self-destructive, keeping the group from effectively using the many talents of the group.

Typically, self-destructive groups or teams are self-defeating and negative in a school setting, making it even harder to accomplish school goals. These are the groups that generally function at the level of the lowest common denominator of the group and accomplish less than if the members worked alone. Peter Senge (1990), in his book, *The Fifth Discipline,* describes destructive teams in what he calls the "myth of teamwork: Most teams operate below the level of the lowest IQ in the group. The result is 'skilled incompetence,' in which people in groups grow incredibly efficient at keeping themselves from learning" (pp. 9-10).

Another type of relationship exists in a group or team when the group produces the same as would be produced by the members individually. In this case, we say we have a *static relationship* in the group. Static relationships exist because of some of the same types of negative, nonproductive features described earlier for self-destructive groups. Static relationships produce enough energy to get by but nothing extra for doing new and creative things beyond what the individual group members could have produced. In static relationship situations, hopes are generated for groups and teams, but little is gained by having people working together.

A third type of relationship in a group, the desired one, is the *synergistic relationship.* In a synergistic relationship, the members of a group or team work together to produce a total result that is greater than the sum of the efforts of the individual members. Saying it another way, the *synergy* of a group or team is the combined cooperative action in the group or team that generates additional energy beyond that consumed by the group and produces a total outcome beyond what could be obtained by the individual members. In a truly synergistic group, people energize and inspire each other, and the diversity of ideas and openness to them provide the basis for new creative ideas and approaches.

The power of synergy or synergistic relationships is nicely illustrated by the following physical example. If you take an 8-foot 2 by 4 (i.e., a piece of wood 2 inches by 4 inches and 8 feet long) and place it on blocks at the ends of the 2 by 4, the 2 by 4 will hold 100 pounds of weight before it breaks. If, however, you take two 8-foot 2 by 4s and you glue them together, the pair will hold a staggering 800 pounds! Why? The glue bonds the two boards together, creating a synergistic relationship between them so that when the fibers in one board run in different directions to those of the other, one gives strength at the places where the other might be weak. This significantly enhances the total strength or weight capacity of the combination. The expected or intuited increase in strength in this situation would have been twofold; instead, the synergy or synergistic relationship in this situation gave an eightfold increase in strength.

In the U.S. hockey team example of the previous section, the coach said that he didn't necessarily have the best players, but he did have the best Olympic hockey team that year. Why? Because they functioned as a synergistic team. They were striving together for a common vision, playing in an interdependent manner (i.e., genuinely cooperative) and significantly empowering each other for the collective best of the team. As a result, they functioned that year as the best Olympic hockey team in the world. Another good real-world example of synergy is that found in a healthy marriage. In a healthy marriage, the spouses develop a caring support system in which they genuinely and openly cooperate with each other and provide creative sharing, assistance, and encouragement toward the couple's common goals.

Communication is an important part of effective, synergistic teams. In his book, *The 7 Habits of Highly Effective People,* Covey (1990) says about communicating synergistically: "You are simply opening your mind and heart and expressions to new possibilities, new alternatives, new options." And he adds about synergistic groups, "You begin with the belief that the parties involved will gain more insight, and that the excitement of that mutual learning and insight will create a momentum toward more and more insights, learnings, and growth" (p. 264).

The characteristics that Covey describes are among the critical factors for turning groups or teams into effective, synergistic groups or teams. But what exactly are the vital prerequisites for synergistic groups, and how do we generate them? In the next two sections, we discuss the four prerequisites for synergistic groups and teams and the four-step process for developing them.

Synergy Prerequisites

Just how important is synergy in our work with study groups? Daryl Conner (1993), one of the world's top experts in change and effectively dealing with change, says that *synergy* is the "soul of a successful change project" (p. 188). Our efforts with study groups are aimed at change projects that, ultimately, will help enhance student learning and improve our schools. So synergy and synergistic study groups will be critical to our success; they will be key vehicles to increasing both quality and productivity in our schools.

When we talk about the *capacity* of a group to do something, we find that we must take into consideration two factors, the group's willingness and its ability. To be effective, a group must both be willing and have ability. If either of these factors is missing, then the group has a lesser capacity. The same is true when we consider the potential capacity for synergy. That is, for a group to be synergistic, it must be willing to do what is required to bring about synergy, and it must also have the ability to do so. Most groups fail to be synergistic because they really are not willing to do what is required, or they do not have the ability or circumstances for them to be synergistic, or both.

In his more than 20 years of research and experience with change, Conner (1993) found that the key fundamentals for the development of synergy in a group were (a) willingness, arising from the sharing of common goals and interdependence (i.e., mutual dependence and genuine cooperation), and (b) ability, growing from member and group empowerment and participative involvement.

Snapshot 20 A Synergistic Team Effort

The focus team from a large high school that has 230 faculty members took a full year and a half to prepare the school's faculty for whole-faculty study groups. An assistant principal and four teachers (foreign language, science, social studies, and language arts) made up the focus team. This was a team of professionals who accepted the challenge of investigating a new approach to staff development and the responsibility to share that knowledge with the whole faculty. The team knew it had a mountain to climb.

The five-member team attended a week of training one summer. During that week, the team realized how different the study group model was from the traditional approach to staff development. These high school teachers typically had an initial 4 days of staff development, usually with all speakers. For the team, the challenge became one of figuring out how to change the traditional system and how to get their colleagues to buy in to the notion of whole-faculty study groups. It was clear that it would take 100% from each team member.

During the first month of school, the team took the time to speak informally, one-to-one, with a large number of teachers, particularly those in their departments. In October, the team issued an invitation to all of the teachers at the school to attend a Saturday seminar on whole-faculty study groups, stating that lunch and baby sitters would be provided. Fifteen teachers attended the full-day seminar led by the focus team. The team took full responsibility for the day, dividing the many tasks that would make the attending teachers feel glad they had taken a Saturday to learn a new approach to meeting the needs of the school and its 3,000 plus students.

After the seminar, there was a total of 20 teachers at the school who believed that heterogeneous study groups focused on schoolwide needs would benefit the whole school. These 20 teachers formed three study groups that met for the remainder of the school year. Two members of the focus team were on each of the three study groups. Through experiencing the process, the teachers became committed to it. An additional five teachers joined the original focus team, bringing the membership of the team to 10.

The following summer, the focus team met for 3 full days. The purpose was to design a plan, based on their own experiences, for orienting the remainder of the faculty to the possibilities of study groups. The team worked out an agenda for a half-day orientation to the whole faculty that was scheduled for a preplanning day in August. The focus team decided to divide the 230-member faculty into 10 groups, meaning each focus team member would meet with about 25 colleagues. The team developed a presentation script that each would follow to ensure consistency in the information presented. They developed sets of overheads and prepared handouts. On the day of the orientation, teachers were given a list that indicated to which classroom they were to report for the orientation. At the end of the 3-hour sessions, each group voted as to whether they wanted to continue the traditional model of professional development or if they wanted to participate in the whole-faculty study group design. Ninety-three percent of all the teachers voted for the study groups. Over the next 2 weeks, 41 study groups were formed, all focused on instructional issues.

The logistics of how the focus team conducted the orientation and did the initial organizational work is secondary to the synergy that was created by the joint work of the team. The team felt that they had the power to influence the future of the school and the condition of its students. Five interdependent individuals became 10 interdependent individuals. The momentum generated by their collaborative efforts made the mountain easier to climb.

As discussed, the four prerequisites for synergistic study groups are

Willingness	*Ability*
1. Common goals	3. Empowerment
2. Interdependence	4. Participative Involvement

As we have seen from the examples of this chapter, synergistic relationships are both powerful and productive. However, most groups don't function synergistically; they don't understand the fundamentals of synergy or don't apply them very well. Why? Because developing and maintaining synergy in a group, though vitally important, is not an easy task.

One of the key things to remember when working with people and trying to develop synergistic relationships is insightfully expressed in the following quotation by an unknown author:

> People are very tender, very sensitive inside. I don't believe age or experience makes much difference. Inside, even within the most toughened and callused exteriors, are the tender feelings and emotions of the heart. That's why in relationships, the little things are the big things.

Willingness: Common Goals and Interdependence

The first step in creating a synergistic group is the development of a common goal or common goals for the group. This gives a clear-cut focus for the group and can be an inspiring incentive to keep the group on track. Unfortunately, most groups don't initially take the time and make the effort to clarify or create the common goals that the group is working together to accomplish.

A common goal for a study group, for example, in the context of enhancing student learning and improving the effectiveness of their school, might be to understand a new learning process and successfully implement it in their school, or to do research on a new student evaluation system, understand the new system, and successfully integrate it into the learning processes of their school.

Willingness to seek, create, and continue to focus on a common goal or goals for a group is critical to the full success of the group. The same can be said for the group's willingness to function interdependently—that is, for the members of the group to operate in a genuinely cooperative and mutually dependent fashion.

People in a group do not have to agree on everything to have synergy. In fact, having differing ideas and bringing diverse information, opinions, and approaches to the group are part of the building blocks for successful synergistic groups. However, to be synergistic and effective, groups must agree on and focus on common goals and must function interdependently.

For example, consider two soldiers in a foxhole in a battle. Their common goal is survival. One has the ammunition and the other has the machine gun. They are genuinely dependent on each other, one to provide the ammunition and the other to fire the gun. It doesn't matter whether they like each other or care about the same things in the other parts of their lives. What matters now is that they clearly know what their common goal is (survival) and that they work interdependently (feeding the ammunition into the gun and effectively firing the gun). This kind of willingness, a clearly defined common goal and effective interdependence, we refer to as a *foxhole mentality.*

A foxhole mentality is when people who have different backgrounds and viewpoints accept that they have the same intent and are willing to genuinely cooperate. For study groups to be effective, they must develop a foxhole-type mentality, where diverse members are willing to set and accept common goals and to work in a genuinely cooperative and mutually dependent manner with each other. They must determine that their differences are less important than their need to work together.

Often, foxhole mentalities, having common goals and functioning interdependently, happen as the consequence of special opportunities that would not be realized without synergistic teamwork. The key for successful study groups is either to exploit naturally formed foxholes (e.g., groups that spontaneously and sincerely come together around a common intent and openly and freely work together as a team) or build new foxholes that have the potential for successful teamwork.

When study group members feel that they are in a foxhole situation with each member working with them and that success depends on working together, then synergy can occur. If those in the study group have a feeling that they are the ones metaphorically carrying the ammunition or firing the gun, it boosts their sense of self-worth and team worth. They each feel that the study group "needs me," I "need the study group," and we "must work together" to accomplish our important goals. Such relationships motivate team members to be willing to do what is required for having a synergistic and successful study group.

Ability: Empowerment and Participative Involvement

Common goals and interdependence motivate and are necessary for people to work together synergistically, but more than these are required for teams to be fully effective and synergistic. For study groups to operate at or near their maximum effectiveness, their members must feel empowered, and they must participate completely in the activities and work of the study group. That is, empowerment and participative involvement are key abilities that study group members must have to function synergistically with other team members and increase team synergy.

Empowerment is not the same as delegation. Someone may give you the authority to take responsibility for or make the final decision in a particular matter. That is not empowerment but delegation. Empowerment is quite different. You have a sense of empowerment or are empowered when you believe that you have something valuable to contribute to the situation, and what you offer might have a bearing on the outcome. In other words, the circumstances are such that you feel you have something of value to contribute, and what you contribute may affect the decisions being considered.

With empowered study group members, each person is more willing to share their part of the diversity of the group, increasing the potential for new and possibly valuable information, knowledge, and ideas to be added to the work of the group.

In a study group, if members feel comfortable saying what they feel about each matter under consideration, they are empowered by the group and circumstances and can be important contributors to the success of the study group. Study groups have their best chance for success when their members feel empowered and want to openly and fully express their views and ideas throughout the work of the study group.

However, empowering study group members is not always an easy task. The circumstances of the study group and how other members of the study group behave are critical. For members to feel empowered, they must be willing to overcome their inhibitions and feel a sense of personal security that others will respect what they say, not judge them, and will consider their input seriously.

Feeling a sense of empowerment is necessary for an ability to function synergistically but not enough by itself. You must not only be empowered but also must have the opportunity to share your knowledge and ideas. Members of a study group have participative involvement when they are encouraged and free to openly and fully share their skills, knowledge, and ideas in the study group.

Participative involvement is both a philosophy and a method of operating study groups. Philosophically, participative involvement focuses on the belief that all study group members have a genuine interest in the success of the study group and each member has something valuable to contribute. Participative involvement is also a method for managing human resources, whereby circumstances are created so that study group members are respected and their contributions are encouraged, valued, and used. Like empowerment, participative involvement does not come easily. It requires conscious concern and deliberate action for how the study group will operate. The leader and the members of the study group must understand the concept and importance of participative involvement and then together, collectively and individually, work toward its becoming a reality for the operation of their study group. To do so will mean that strong egos and aggressive personalities must be kept in check and that the normal competitive interplay among study group members gives way to an open and balanced approach in the discussion and consideration of matters before the study group. Everyone must have and feel comfortable with their opportunity for full participation in the business of the study group.

The ability of a study group to operate synergistically requires both member empowerment and participative involvement. This approach offers potential for substantially increasing the effectiveness of the study group and involves members freely and fully sharing knowledge and ideas and functioning as an entity, a team, to learn together, plan initiatives, make decisions, solve problems, and evaluate results. When study groups operate synergistically in this fashion, the productivity and quality of their efforts are increased significantly.

Synergy Process

The prerequisites for synergistic study groups are the willingness to establish common goals for the group's initiative and develop a genuine interdependence among its members and the ability to create circumstances that provide empowerment for members, giving them a sense of importance and freeing them to participate, and that offer participative involvement so that members interact openly and fully in the work of the study group.

Now that we know and understand the fundamental prerequisites for synergistic study groups, the question becomes: What is the process for creating these prerequisites and synergistic study groups?

To answer this question, we turn once again to the master of change dynamics, Daryl Conner (1993) and the early work of Henry Nelson Wieman (1990). Their research and writings tell us that an effective four-step process for building synergy in study groups is

1. Interaction
2. Appreciative understanding
3. Integration
4. Implementation

Interaction

The dictionary (Webster's, 1986) defines interaction as "action on one another or reciprocal action or effect." The first step in the process says that if study groups are to be synergistic, they must be interacting—that is, they must have members acting on one another or reciprocating.

Most of us have been in groups where some of the members don't say anything. Clearly, in this situation, those individuals are not interacting. As a result, the group will have a difficult time being as effective as they might have been, because those noninteracting individuals are not helping to enrich the group's mix of knowledge and ideas. In fact, they are often a deficit to the group, because they are filling positions that more contributing, interacting persons might have taken. By the same token, those who interact too much (e.g., members who monopolize the discussions) also have the potential for diminishing the study group's effectiveness.

The three elements of interaction that reduce related group problems (e.g., misunderstandings, alienation, and confusion) and enhance group potential are (a) effective communication, (b) active listening, and (c) creating trust.

In the development and operation of synergistic study groups, effective communication among members is essential. *Effective communication* means direct communication in a well-understood language, covering relevant and thoughtful material and reflecting a nondistorted sense of what the communicator believes.

In most groups, the typical approach of members is the competitive one, where each person is an advocate for certain ideas, makes that case at each opportunity, and listens with an ear attuned to information for countering contrary ideas rather than trying to see the merits in others' ideas. Such approaches are usually destructive and seriously hamper the prospects for study group synergy.

Instead, study group members must become active listeners. Active listening means that a study group member will eliminate, as best possible, their competitive aggressiveness and listen intently to understand, appreciate, and search for value and application in the communications of others.

To be synergistic, study group members don't have to be friends or even like each other, but they must generate relationships among themselves that create trust and credibility. Trust is fundamental to the development of synergy in a study group.

If the members of a study group communicate effectively with one another and listen actively to their colleagues, over time, the relationship that develops has the potential to be one of trust and credibility. People begin to let down their guard with each other and allow themselves to become vulnerable within the group. When this level of trust occurs, the group has an opportunity for genuine sharing and use of the valuable diversity that each person in the group brings to the discussions.

Appreciative Understanding

As we work to develop synergy in our study group, we find that meaningful interaction (i.e., effective communications, active listening, and trust) is a necessary element of synergy but is not sufficient to guarantee it. Something more is generally required. In the earlier section on synergistic prerequisites, we presented a quotation that reminded us that: "People are very tender, very sensitive inside. That's why in relationships, the little things are the big things." One of the keys to help people deal with these sensitivities is the operational concept of *appreciative understanding*.

Appreciative understanding is the capacity to value and use diversity. For the members of a study group to achieve appreciative understanding, each must understand why others see things differently than they do and work to appreciate the differences.

Covey (1990) reminds us that we cannot achieve win-win ends with win-lose or lose-win means. If we want to have the team success of synergy, win-win ends, in our study group, then we must have genuinely effective means, win-win means, in our group relationships.

The four methods for building appreciative understanding (i.e., win-win means and relationships) are to (a) create an open climate, (b) delay negative judgment, (c) empathize with others, and (d) value diversity.

The effective communication, active listening, and trust generated by genuine interaction by members of a study group lay a foundation for appreciative understanding to develop. In particular, even with the inevitable differences of opinion and perspectives of the members, the conflicts, and the possible misunderstandings, the members realize that all of this is fundamental to surfacing important issues, understanding different frames of reference, seeing things in a new light, and generating the basic building blocks for new and potentially better solutions.

An *open climate* in an environment is where study group members allow and encourage constructive discussion, conflict, and differences to take place, fostering win-win relationships and helping its members understand relevant issues and gain new insights. By creating an open climate, study group members learn to appreciate conflict and differences and use them to broaden their basis of understanding toward the development of potentially more valuable answers and solutions.

Have you ever been in a group discussion where someone offers a thought that seems silly or out-and-out stupid, and yet from that idea came a cascade of ideas that led to new insight and a better solution for the original problem? If, on the other hand, someone had intervened earlier in that sequence of ideas and said something like, "That's a dumb idea," then that discussion would have no doubt been cut short, the innovative cascade of new ideas would not have taken place, and the better solution might very well have never been discovered. Events comparable to this latter situation happen all the time, creating win-lose relationships and effectively inhibiting real synergy in the group.

Most new and creative ideas or perspectives come from sensitive people and are extremely vulnerable to attacks by others. At the same time, they frequently are the ideas and perspectives that have the highest potential for leading to innovative solutions and productive synergy. Consequently, study groups function best and have greatest potential for synergy when team members have the discipline to *delay forming negative judgments* about the ideas and perspectives of other members.

The dictionary (Webster's, 1986) defines *empathy* as "the projection of one's own personality into the personality of another in order to understand him better" or "ability to share in another's emotions or feelings." When we empathize with other study group members, we are allowing ourselves the opportunity of knowing what the others are experiencing and feeling and being emotionally sensitive to these.

Although showing empathy to other team members' ideas and perspectives does not necessarily mean agreeing with them, it does provide a good position from which to understand others' ideas and perspectives, why they feel about them as they do, and how their ideas might fit into the overall discussion and possibly become part of the desired solution. When study group members empathize with other members of their team, they increase the group's chances of generating greater team synergy and building meaningful solutions.

Whether we want to admit it or not, we are all sensitive about our ideas and perspectives, especially those that are personal to us. As a result, we tend to hold them back and only slowly let them come out as we test the water to see how others will respond to them. Yet these ideas and perspectives in a study group are the very diversity that gives the group its unique strength.

By genuinely *valuing diversity* in a study group, members are showing their respect for each other and their ideas and perspectives, increasing trust, enhancing cohesiveness, and searching for the most appropriate input and building blocks. In such situations, study group members are committed to finding positive aspects in the input of others, each member is motivated to freely and fully share their diversity, and the team and each member have an improved basis for generating synergy and the best solutions.

Integration

Synergistic interaction (i.e., communicating effectively, listening actively, and creating trust) and appreciative understanding (i.e., having an open climate, being nonjudgmental, showing empathy, and valuing diversity) provide a strong foundation for effective study group teams. With these effective relationships and mechanisms in place, a study group is in an excellent position to take on the difficult task of *integration:* considering all of the input from the group, evaluating its value and usability, and synergistically pulling together the appropriate ideas and perspectives to generate the best available solution or outcome. Experience has shown that the effectiveness of the integration process is often enhanced by tolerating ambiguity and being persistent, being flexible, being creative, and being selective (Conner, 1993).

Many of the problems facing study groups will be extremely complex and will lead to ambiguous information, ideas, perspectives, and circumstances. Like most people, study groups have a tendency to seek a quick, easy solution. Frequently, this approach proves to be nonproductive or leads us down a path to a less valuable result. Consequently, study groups must shift from the more typical quick-fix approaches to problem solving and be more persistent with the ambiguity of the input and circumstances as they bring together and flexibly, creatively, and selectively integrate their relevant ideas and perspectives and move synergistically toward the best available solutions.

Implementation

The first three steps of the process to generate synergy—interaction, appreciative understanding, and integration—provide the study group with their desired outcome. Thus, the remaining step in the synergy process is to implement and manage the various parts of the desired outcome effectively in the school. The four key elements of successful *implementation* are to (a) strategize, (b) monitor and reinforce, (c) remain team focused, and (d) update.

To increase the likelihood that the study group outcomes will be implemented and managed effectively, the group must *strategize,* creating a plan for the implementation that sets its direction, manages the resources, determines priorities, and ensures that the various implementation steps are compatible.

Once a strategy and plan have been developed and the implementation process begun, it is critical that the process be *monitored and reinforced* to ensure that appropriate behavior and progress are sustained.

In the implementation process, there will be potential for some members of the study group and others involved in the implementation to move ahead more rapidly than their colleagues. Doing this has the potential for getting people out of step with each other and reducing the synergy of the total effort. Consequently, it is important and valuable to *remain team focused,* respecting the team's common goals and interdependence and continuing to function as a unified, integrated work team.

During the implementation process, circumstances and environments may very well change. When this happens, there accordingly should be an *updating* of the study group's implementation and action plans. Teams have a tendency to fall in love with their plans and become resistant to change them. However, the implementation process is most effective when its action plan is continuously and appropriately updated.

Synergy Development

Creating strong, effective study groups means doing those things necessary to build synergistic teams. Developing synergistic teams requires a substantial commitment and effort, but the cost for not operating in this manner is high, and the potential for producing meaningful results is reduced dramatically. The synergistic process is an extremely powerful approach for increasing the effectiveness, productivity, and quality of the work of study group teams.

As you attempt to apply the concepts, principles, and approaches discussed in this chapter to create synergistic study groups, it will be beneficial to stop from time to time and monitor how your efforts are going. The Synergy Checklist to follow should be helpful in identifying what elements of the synergy development process are working well and which ones require improving.

Synergy Checklist

The following eight question sets provide a practical synergy checklist for assessing the synergistic effectiveness of a group and identifying how to make the group more synergistic:

1. *Common goals.* Has your study group discussed, agreed on, and written a clearly and precisely stated goal or goals for its work?

2. *Interdependence.* Has the discussion, interaction, and sharing of your study group been interdependent (i.e., mutually dependent and genuinely cooperative)?

3. *Empowerment.* Do the members of your study group feel a sense of empowerment? That is, does each member feel that what he or she has to offer is important and valuable and may have an effect on the outcome of decisions?

4. *Participative involvement.* Do the members of your study group feel that they can and do openly and freely participate in the discussions and activities of the study group?

5. *Interaction.* Do the members of your study group, individually and collectively, interact effectively? That is, do they communicate effectively and actively listen to each other, and has a sense of trust and credibility been created in the group?

6. *Appreciative understanding.* Do the members of your study group show appreciative understanding of each other and to each other's ideas? That is, does the group have an open climate and value diversity and does each member delay judgment and empathize with the ideas of the others?

7. *Integration.* As your study group works to consider all of the input, evaluate its value and usability, and pull it together to generate the best decision or outcome, do they show persistence in their deliberations and tolerate its ambiguity and are they flexible, creative, and selective as they consider the issues and transition toward their final result?

8. *Implementation.* Once your study group arrives at the desired outcome to be completed, are they effectively initiating and managing the implementation process for a successful conclusion? That is, did your study group create a plan for the implementation that sets its direction, manages the resources, determines priorities, and ensures that the various steps are completed; that ensures that appropriate behavior and progress are sustained; that remains team, not individual, focused; and that continuously and appropriately updates the action plan for the implementation?

Study Group Action Plans

Study Group Action Plans are designed to give the study group members a plan of action. What the group is to do is directly aligned with student needs. Before the groups form, the faculty reviews student data, states the student needs, and prioritizes the student needs. If all of the study groups will address one category of student need, each study group will design an Action Plan that addresses that one category of student need, e.g., reading. Each study group will decide how the group will address the need. Even though the student need is the same, what a group will do and how they will do it is a group decision. If it is decided that study groups will address different student needs, the Action Plans will reflect those differences.

The Action Plan has five parts.

1. The general area of need. The need comes from the student data.
2. The specific areas of need within that category. Teachers would identify these needs from their work with their students.
3. The specific actions the teachers will take when the study group meets.
4. The sources of the evidence that change occurs.
5. A list of what and who will be the resources of the group.

The Action Plan should be revisited often. If the group changes direction or decides that the plan no longer represents their work, they should modify or rewrite the plan.

Under the section of the Action Plan that is entitled "THEREFORE, IN THIS STUDY GROUP TEACHERS WILL:," group members specify verbs that give the reader a visual of what the group will actually do when it meets. The Action Plan should reflect hands-on learning. The following verbs infer strong action.

> Practice	> Demonstrate	> Explore
> Collect	> Share	> Investigate
> Construct	> Critique	> Design
> Train	> Model	> Role play
> Share	> Read	> Examine

SCHOOL:_____ GROUP:_____ DATE:_____

<u>STUDY GROUP ACTION PLAN</u>

GENERAL CATEGORY OF STUDENT NEEDS:

DATA INDICATE THAT STUDENTS NEED TO:	THEREFORE, IN THIS STUDY GROUP TEACHERS WILL:

WHAT ARE THE INTENDED RESULTS OF THE WORK OF THE STUDY GROUP? The evidence that the level of proficiency has increased in the above student needs will be documented on/by/in:

WHAT WILL BE THE CONTENT OR CURRICULUM OF THE STUDY? To accomplish the above, the study group will use the following materials and other resources (e.g., individuals):

STUDY GROUP ACTION PLAN

GENERAL CATEGORY OF STUDENT NEEDS:

Spelling

DATA INDICATE THAT STUDENTS NEED TO:	THEREFORE, IN THIS STUDY GROUP TEACHERS WILL:
1. spell correctly in all written work	*1. design appropriate lessons that develop spelling skills*
	2. identify most common misspelled words
2. use the dictionary routinely	*3. plan and implement activities that encourage students to proofread and edit their work*
3. use reference books in all subject areas	*4. share strategies for teaching dictionary and reference book skills*
4. demonstrate responsibility for an assignment's final product	*5. plan school-wide activities and programs that encourage students to share their written work*

WHAT ARE THE INTENDED RESULTS OF THE WORK OF THE STUDY GROUP? The evidence that the level of proficiency has increased in the student needs listed above will be documented on/by/in:

- all written work   - teacher evaluation   - student portfolios

WHAT WILL BE THE CONTENT OR CURRICULUM OF THE STUDY? To accomplish the above, the study group will use the following materials and other resources (e.g., individuals):

- *Student work*
- *Age appropriate word lists*
- *Activities to strengthen phonetic and structural analysis skills*
- *Effective teaching strategies*
- *Computer software, e.g., Spell-It 3, Children's Writing and Publishing Center*
- *Franklin's Reading World*
- *Kid Phonics*
- *Surveys from teachers that identify current practices in teaching spelling*

STUDY GROUP ACTION PLAN

GENERAL CATEGORY OF STUDENT NEEDS:

Assessment practices

DATA INDICATE THAT STUDENTS NEED TO:	THEREFORE, IN THIS STUDY GROUP TEACHERS WILL:
1. demonstrate improved self-esteem by taking more responsibility for quality "final product" of work	*1. use assessment results to plan lessons*
2. demonstrate increased ownership in evaluation of their work and in self-evaluation	*2. model techniques for conferencing with parents and for involving students*
3. participate in parent-teacher conferences	*3. design multiple assessment tools for evaluating student work*
4. demonstrate confidence in multiple types of evaluation	*4. practice how to effectively examine and discuss student work with colleagues*

WHAT ARE THE INTENDED RESULTS OF THE WORK OF THE STUDY GROUP? The evidence that the level of proficiency has increased in the above student needs will be documented on/by/in:

- demonstrated understanding of assessment of student work   - how students talk about their own progress with others   - suggestions students make regarding evaluation of their work   - comments from parents

WHAT WILL BE THE CONTENT OR CURRICULUM OF THE STUDY? To accomplish the above, the study group will use the following materials and other resources (e.g., individuals):

- Student work
- Assessing Student Performance, an Inquiry Kit by ASCD
- <u>Best Practices</u>, chapter on evaluation
- Develop rubrics together for all subject areas
- <u>Together Is Better</u> (book on 3 way conferences)
- <u>Redesigning Assessment</u> (3 videos) by ASCD
- Attend IRA Conference
- <u>Writing and Reading Conferences</u> by Donald Graves
- Judy (district coordinator for assessment)
- Observe and discuss "writing circle" techniques

STUDY GROUP ACTION PLAN

GENERAL CATEGORY OF STUDENT NEEDS:

Composition

DATA INDICATE THAT STUDENTS NEED TO:	THEREFORE, IN THIS STUDY GROUP TEACHERS WILL:
1. demonstrate ability to use mechanics of writing	*1. determine if current practice is consistent with district standards and align practice with standards*
2. demonstrate ability to use correct grammar	*2. develop strategies for encouraging all teachers to use common vocabulary in teaching basic writing skills*
3. construct paragraphs with a main idea and at least three supporting detail sentences	*3. review and use computer software that develops and reinforces writing skills*
	4. share strategies that each has found to be effective and examples of what has been tried with success
4. demonstrate ability to write narratives that have a beginning, middle, and ending	*5. design opportunities for students to make their writings public*
	6. examine student work
5. express ideas clearly	

WHAT ARE THE INTENDED RESULTS OF THE WORK OF THE STUDY GROUP? The evidence that the level of proficiency has increased in the above student needs will be documented on/by/in:

- *meeting district standards*   - *writing samples*   - *checklists*
- *collections of writings overtime*   - *"on demand" writings*

WHAT WILL BE THE CONTENT OR CURRICULUM OF THE STUDY? To accomplish the above, the study group will use the following materials and other resources (e.g., individuals):

- *Student work*
- *Inspiration software*
- *Survey of teachers*
- *Tennessee Writing Assessment rubric*
- *District standards*
- *Workshops, conferences, university courses*
- *Teachers who have attended training workshops*
- *District curriculum staff*

STUDY GROUP ACTION PLAN

GENERAL CATEGORY OF STUDENT NEEDS:
  Behavior Management

DATA INDICATE THAT STUDENTS NEED TO:	THEREFORE, IN THIS STUDY GROUP TEACHERS WILL:
1. respect and appreciate diversity	*1. plan and implement lessons and opportunities for students to learn about other cultures*
2. employ conflict management skills	*2. share and research procedures that instill respect and assistance for special-needs students*
3. feel good about themselves (self-esteem)	*3. demonstrate how to resolve conflict between and among students*
4. involve parents in their school work and school programs	*4. share strategies that work and do not work so that recommendations can be made to the whole faculty*
	5. identify strategies for recognizing and giving positive feedback to students who demonstrate respect for themselves and others
	6. develop strategies for involving parents in the daily work of the school

WHAT ARE THE INTENDED RESULTS OF THE WORK OF THE STUDY GROUP? **The evidence that the level of proficiency has increased in the above student needs will be demonstrated on/by/in:**

- fewer referrals to the office   - fewer suspensions - more parental involvement - changes in student behavior patterns   - surveys of parents, students, and teachers indicate a higher level of satisfaction with the school

WHAT WILL BE THE CONTENT OR CURRICULUM OF THE STUDY? **To accomplish the above, the study group will use the following materials and other resources (e.g., individuals):**

- Materials on "character education"   - Workshop on conflict management
- Multicultural Education, video tape with guide by ASCD
- The Dreamkeepers: Successful Teachers of African American Children by Gloria Ladson-Billings (Jossey Bass, publisher)
- Effective teaching strategies that actively engage students in the learning task, e.g., higher order thinking skills, models of teaching

STUDY GROUP ACTION PLAN

GENERAL CATEGORY OF STUDENT NEEDS:
Technology

DATA INDICATE THAT STUDENTS NEED TO:	THEREFORE, IN THIS STUDY GROUP TEACHERS WILL:
1. use software applications to facilitate learning across all content areas.	*1. determine what software is available for students to use and decide how to make that software accessible to all students*
2. select and apply appropriate equipment	*2. preview available software; have discussions regarding appropriate applications; and, plan for integrating software with print materials.*
3. use the Internet for accessing information in all subject areas	*3. demonstrate competency in using equipment, i.e., digital camera, scanner*
	4. plan student opportunities for using technology for team projects
	5. practice how to use the Internet for instructional purposes

WHAT ARE THE INTENDED RESULTS OF THE WORK OF THE STUDY GROUP? The evidence that the level of proficiency has increased in the above student needs will be documented on/by/in:

- *teacher observation* - *"check-out" records* - *written/oral reports*
- *team projects* - *demonstrated ability to access information*

WHAT WILL BE THE CONTENT OR CURRICULUM OF THE STUDY? To accomplish the above, the study group will use the following materials and other resources (e.g., individuals).

- *Student work*
- *Software in all curriculum areas*
- *The Research on Technology for Learning (ASCD, publisher)*
- *Teaching and Learning with the Internet (ASCD, publisher)*
- *Training programs offered by the district and area colleges*
- *District technology standards*
- *School media specialist and district technology specialists*

STUDY GROUP ACTION PLAN

GENERAL CATEGORY OF STUDENT NEEDS:

Math writing

DATA INDICATE THAT STUDENTS NEED TO:	THEREFORE, IN THIS STUDY GROUP TEACHERS WILL:
1. write what they are thinking when doing computations	*1. read <u>First Step</u> books on recounts, explanations, and procedures*
2. increase math vocabulary	*2. examine student work*
3. have a complete understanding of math concepts	*3. compare grade levels/classes of math writing*
4. have a complete understanding of math processes	*4. examine samples of Benchmark I and II example tests*
5. know strategies to solve problems	*5. determine how the standards are applied to math writing in the tests*
6. know how to sequence math events	*6. share ideas for getting students to do #11 in "Try It" and the results*
7. know specific math vocabulary	*7. develop math rubrics*
	8. design pre and post tests and identify a test that grades 5 and 6 haven't done
	9. create vocabulary quizzes and context sentences for math vocabulary

WHAT ARE THE INTENDED RESULTS OF THE WORK OF THE STUDY GROUP? The evidence that the level of proficiency has increased in the above student needs will be documented on/by/in:

- *improved results on the benchmark I and II tests*
- *better use of math vocabulary in writing samples*

WHAT WILL BE THE CONTENT OR CURRICULUM OF THE STUDY? To accomplish the above, the study group will use the following materials and other resources (e.g., individuals):

- *Student work*
- *Assessment rubrics in the math series*
- *"Try It" #11*
- *Mark Jewell*
- *Standards book with ideas and samples*
- *Benchmark I test practice book*
- *Fourth grade teachers*
- *The work of the teachers in this study group*

STUDY GROUP ACTION PLAN

GENERAL CATEGORY OF STUDENT NEEDS:

Parental involvement

DATA INDICATE THAT STUDENTS NEED TO:	**THEREFORE, IN THIS STUDY GROUP TEACHERS WILL:**
1. know that parents and teachers are working together for their benefit	*1. gather information on effective conferencing skills*
	2. determine the criteria for conducting effective conferences with parents
	3. create a conference checklist
	4. model and role play conferencing situations
	5. critique a conference after one has been held
	6. interview parents

WHAT ARE THE INTENDED RESULTS OF THE WORK OF THE STUDY GROUP? **The evidence that the level of proficiency has increased in the above student needs will be documented on/by/in:**

- *fewer referrals to office*   - *more students completing assignments*
- *increase in number of parents that attend scheduled conferences*
- *improved teaching and learning environment as evidenced on teacher, parent, and student surveys*

WHAT WILL BE THE CONTENT OR CURRICULUM OF THE STUDY? **To accomplish the above, the study group will use the following materials and other resources (e.g., individuals):**

- *District and school policies and procedures*
- *Student handbook*
- *Resources from the Teaching and Learning Academy*
- *Resource persons and materials from the district's parenting center*
- *Articles, videos, books from professional associations*

STUDY GROUP ACTION PLAN

GENERAL CATEGORY OF STUDENT NEEDS:

Reading Comprehension

DATA INDICATE THAT STUDENTS NEED TO:	THEREFORE, IN THIS STUDY GROUP TEACHERS WILL:
1. improve self-monitoring	*1. identify what skills are taught and when the skills are taught*
2. develop and improve decoding and phonics skills	*2. identify materials and resources and share effective classroom use*
3. improve ability to identify story elements	*3. formulate a set of open-ended questions for reading to use with students*
4. develop and improve story telling and summarizing skills	*4. develop and implement a set of assessments for each skill area*
5. improve critical thinking skills	*5. demonstrate effective teaching strategies*

WHAT ARE THE INTENDED RESULTS OF THE WORK OF THE STUDY GROUP? **The evidence that the level of proficiency has increased in the above student needs will be documented on/by/in:**

- running records   - standardized tests   - checklists using district standards   - informal inventories   - amounts of independent reading

WHAT WILL BE THE CONTENT OR CURRICULUM OF THE STUDY? **To accomplish the above, the study group will use the following materials and other resources (e.g., individuals):**

- *Courses and workshops offered by district and area colleges*
- *Teachers' manuals*
- *Supplementary reading materials that accompany the text*
- *Articles and books to be determined*
- *District reading specialist*
- *Jan Bennett*
- *Surveys from teachers to determine when and how skills are taught*
- *District reading standards and curriculum guides*

STUDY GROUP ACTION PLAN

GENERAL CATEGORY OF STUDENT NEEDS:
Reading

DATA INDICATE THAT STUDENTS NEED TO:	THEREFORE, IN THIS STUDY GROUP TEACHERS WILL:
1. demonstrate ability to decode new words by using structural and phonetic clues *2. increase vocabulary and the number of sight words* *3. read for understanding and use multiple comprehension strategies* *4. apply reading skills in content areas* *5. increase the amount of free or independent reading*	*1. clarify what skills are taught and when the skills are taught* *2. discuss strategies to insure consistency across grade levels* *3. review all the reading packages, materials, and programs being used in the school to identify: where additional training is needed; where inconsistencies are; where duplications are; and where additional resources are needed* *4. identify the vocabulary that needs to be taught in the content areas* *5. design a school-wide incentive program for independent reading* *6. demonstrate effective strategies*

WHAT ARE THE INTENDED RESULTS OF THE WORK OF THE STUDY GROUP? The evidence that the level of proficiency has increased in the above student needs will be documented on/by/in:

- ITBS   - teacher observation in all subject areas - writing samples
- informal reading inventories - amounts and types of free reading

WHAT WILL BE THE CONTENT OR CURRICULUM OF THE STUDY? To accomplish the above, the study group will use the following materials and other resources (e.g., individuals):

- Student work
- Language arts materials used at all grade levels in school
- Invite district level coordinator to meet with group
- Differentiating Instruction for Mixed-Ability Classrooms (ASCD, publisher)
- Best Practice, chapter 2
- Survey teachers to get ideas for reading incentive program
- Examine teaching strategies used for teaching reading skills
- Computer software programs

STUDY GROUP LOGS

The set of Study Group Logs on the following pages is from one study group in a school where all certified personnel are members of study groups. The school is Addison Elementary School in the Cobb County (GA) School District. The following logs were collected during the school's second year to have all faculty in study groups. There are a total 54 teachers and administrators in ten study groups. At the beginning of the school year, the whole faculty had met together several times to review the latest reports on the status of student learning. The one area of student need that was given highest priority was the use of technology to support learning in the content areas. The other student need priorities were assessment strategies, science, literacy, and problem centered classrooms. Twenty-three teachers wanted to pursue technology. Following the procedural guideline that suggests that groups be no larger than six, those twenty-three teachers formed four (4) "technology" study groups, each taking an aspect of technology that was needful to them. Twelve teachers formed two study groups addressing assessment needs, six teachers wanted to explore the new science textbooks, six teachers who were involved in a new language arts program formed a "literacy" group, and five teachers interested in developing a more problem centered classroom came together. The principal and assistant principal invited four district level leaders to join their group, looking at effective strategies for implementing change. All of the ten study groups met for the first time on October 7. All of the groups met weekly, except for holiday weeks, for about an hour. May 13 was the last study group meeting for the school year. Each group met twenty-five (25) times. The study groups alternated meeting during the school day and after school. Every other week a team of six substitutes released six teachers each hour. The six teachers released at the same time were members of the same study group. The schedule was developed in such a way that if a study group was released from 8:00 to 9:00 one week, those teachers would be released from 9:00 to 10:00 on the next release time day. The after school study group meetings lessened the need to have more than one faculty meeting a month. In this district, one afternoon a week is reserved for school and/or district meetings. The following set of logs is the logs from one of the study groups that chose technology. First is their Action Plan and last is their evaluation of their work.

It is strongly recommended that study groups complete a log during or immediately after each meeting. The logs are a map of the group's journey, the group's history. A log completed in November may be needed in March to remind the group of why it decided to take a particular action. The logs become the body of work of the group. The logs record the substance of the relationship of the adults in the group. The "classroom application" section of the log represents the purpose of study groups. It is what teachers do differently in classrooms that cause students to perform differently. It is this "differentness" that is change. It is the change in how teachers teach that creates change in student learning; change that is measurable in higher levels of achievement. It is often not until the third or fourth study group meeting that the classroom application section of the log is completed. It takes about that long for the study groups to get organized and to do the background work to support classroom use. The study group may collect the information about classroom application by taking the first five or ten minutes of the study group meeting to go around the table and have each member share. Much of the learning about classroom practice comes from this sharing of what is working and what is not working in each other's classrooms. This discussion generates concrete and precise "talk" about teaching. It is the classroom application discussions that motivate group members to continue. Teachers generate excitement and willingness to try new practices or materials as they hear their colleagues describe a teaching situation. At first, the talk may be somewhat awkward. That awkwardness soon gives way to a sense of celebration and support for each other's work.

The logs indicate that the leaders change weekly so that leadership rotates among study group members. The rotation may be weekly, every two weeks, or monthly. Once the group forms around a student need that was identified through an analysis of data, group members decide what the leadership rotation will be. The leader at any given time is responsible for attending to the logistics of the meeting and seeing that the log is copied and given to the appropriate person. All members are equally responsible for the work of the group. This approach to leadership is based on the assumption that all teachers are leaders and that leadership is fluid throughout the school. It also seems to lessen the chance that the leadership of a study group will become a burden to one individual, distracting from the individual's role as learner. Keeping groups small (4 to 6 members) makes the rotation system more feasible. When one person in a group needs to be trained on a specific process or content piece that all members of the group need to know, any group member can represent the study group.

Readers should remember that the logs were not done for the reader. The purpose of the log is to give the group a recorded history, what they did and why. Study Group Logs are made public for two primary reasons. One, so that technical assistance can be provided as needed. And, secondly, so study groups can learn from each other. Logs are generally done while the group is working, meaning that neatness and word usage is of minor importance. Members of the group take turns doing the log. One person rewrote the following logs after it was determined that the logs would be used in this publication. The logs were rewritten because the originals were too light to make readable copies.

Readers of the logs are reminded that the learners are adults. It does not matter that the adults are elementary teachers. The focus here is on adult to adult relationships in a learning situation. What grade a teacher teaches is secondary to the adult relationships forged around teaching. In a study group focusing on technology, the teachers could range from teachers of kindergartners to teachers of twelfth graders. The application of skills is generic. Readers should focus on the substance of the learning.

School *Addison*　　　Study Group　*5*　　　Date *10-14*

STUDY GROUP ACTION PLAN

GENERAL CATEGORY OF STUDENT NEEDS:

Technology

STUDENTS NEED TO:	THEREFORE, IN STUDY GROUPS TEACHERS NEED TO:
1. Use software in all content areas, as appropriate	1. Determine what software is available
2. Produce own stories with illustrations, using computer programs	2. Practice various applications of the software
3. Use other equipment that will facilitate their work	3. Be trained on appropriate use of software and computer "attachments"

INTENDED RESULT OF THE STUDY GROUP: To increase the level of proficiency in the student needs listed above, as evidenced on/by/in:

- Records of teacher use - Records of student use
- Ease with which students manipulate the computer; the software programs, and attachments
- Quality of writing

WHAT WILL BE THE CONTENT OR CURRICULUM OF THE STUDY? This would be the materials and other resources the group will use.

1. Wiggle Works
2. Digital Camera
3. LCD panel
4. tVator
5. Laptop
6. Kid Pix
7. Internet
8. MECC Programs
9. Storybook Weaver
10. Windows 95
11. MacMillan Dictionary
12. Hyper Studio
13. The Learning Company
14. Photography on disk
15. First Connections
16. Terri
17. John Carter
18. district office
19. Kennesaw College

Study Group: _# 5_____ (name/number)

STUDY GROUP LOG # _1_

DATE: _10-7_____ LEADER: _Judy_____

TIME: _3:00_ to _4:00_ LOCATION: _Judy's room_____

GROUP MEMBERS	Pre.	Ab.		Pre.	Ab.
1. Lori : 1st Grade	✓		4. Lorraine : Kin	✓	
2. Anne : 4th Grade	✓		5. Laura : 4th Grade		✓
3. Judy : 2nd Grade	✓		6. Charlene : Sp. Ed.		✓

Next scheduled meeting:
DATE _10-14_ TIME _11:30_ LOCATION _Conf. Rm_ LEADER _Lori_

DISCUSSIONS AND ACTIVITIES FOCUSED ON:

- Worked on Action Plan
- Brainstormed the software that we think
   will be available to us. Our list :
     • Wiggle Works   • Internet
     • Kid Pix   • MacMillan Dictionary
     • Storybook Weaver   • Hyper Studio
     • Windows '95   • The Learning Co
         • First Connections

- Agreed on the leadership rotation : weekly in the
                         following order :

FOR NEXT MEETING, WE NEED TO:
   - Agree on group norms
   - Recommend equipment to review

1. Judy
2. Lori
3. Laura
4. Anne
5. Charlene
6. Lorraine

CONCERNS/RECOMMENDATIONS:
    It will be several weeks before we
   will complete "Classroom App." - OK ?

CLASSROOM APPLICATIONS SINCE LAST MEETING
Group Members:

Study Group: _# 5_ (name/number)

STUDY GROUP LOG # _2_

DATE: _10-14_   **LEADER:** _Lori_

TIME: _11:30_ to _12:30_   **LOCATION:** _Conf. Rm_

GROUP MEMBERS

	Pre.	Ab.			Pre.	Ab.
1. Lori	✓		4. Lorraine		✓	
2. Anne	✓		5. Laura			✓
3. Judy	✓		6. Charlene		✓	

Next scheduled meeting:
DATE _10-21_ **TIME** _3:00_ **LOCATION** _Laura's Rm_ **LEADER** _Laura_

DISCUSSIONS AND ACTIVITIES FOCUSED ON:

- Completed our Action Plan
- Discussed how we'll measure our results
- Discussed what training opportunities will support our work
- Agreed on group norms
  - Begin, end on time
  - No fault
  - Respect all
  - Do what we agree to do
  - Stay focused
  - Implement what we learn

FOR NEXT MEETING, WE NEED TO:

Begin!

CONCERNS/RECOMMENDATIONS:

CLASSROOM APPLICATIONS SINCE LAST MEETING
Group Members:

Study Group: _____5_____ (name/number)

STUDY GROUP LOG # 3

DATE: 10-21 _____ **LEADER:** Laura _____

TIME: 3:00 to 4:00 **LOCATION:** Laura's Rm _____

GROUP MEMBERS	Pre.	Ab.			Pre.	Ab.
1. Anne	✓		4. Charlene		✓	
2. Laura	✓		5. Lorraine		✓	
3. Lori	✓		6. Judy		✓	

Next scheduled meeting:
DATE 10-28 **TIME** 1:30 **LOCATION** Conf. Rm **LEADER** Anne

DISCUSSIONS AND ACTIVITIES FOCUSED ON:

- Explored laptop computers; learned
  basic procedures; discussed use
- Lorraine introduced us to Windows '95

FOR NEXT MEETING, WE NEED TO:
Be ready to work with a writing program

CONCERNS/RECOMMENDATIONS/ note → Laura will represent
us tomorrow at the
Instructional Council (IC)
meeting.

CLASSROOM APPLICATIONS SINCE LAST MEETING
Group Members:

Study Group: _____5_____ (name/number)

STUDY GROUP LOG # _4_

DATE: _10-28_ LEADER: _Anne_

TIME: _1:30_ to _2:30_ LOCATION: _Conf. Rm_

GROUP MEMBERS	Pre.	Ab.		Pre.	Ab.
1. Judy	✓		4. Anne	✓	
2. Lorraine	✓		5. Laura	✓	
3. Charlene	✓		6. Lori		✓

Next scheduled meeting:
DATE _11-4_ TIME _3:00_ LOCATION _Charlene's Rm_ LEADER _Charlene_

DISCUSSIONS AND ACTIVITIES FOCUSED ON:

- Loaded a site licensed writing program (learned how to)
- Discussed possible applications
- Reviewed course offerings at Kennesaw College and benefits to the group if one of us enrolls in a computer course. Lorraine will!
- Laura reported on IC meeting

FOR NEXT MEETING, WE NEED TO:

Be ready to review Print Shop Deluxe

CONCERNS/RECOMMENDATIONS:

CLASSROOM APPLICATIONS SINCE LAST MEETING
Group Members:

Study Group: ____5____ (name/number)

STUDY GROUP LOG # 5

DATE: _11-4_   LEADER: _Charlene_

TIME: _3:00_ to _4:00_ LOCATION: _Charlene's Rm_

GROUP MEMBERS	Pre.	Ab.		GROUP MEMBERS	Pre.	Ab.
1. Laura	✓		4. Lorraine	✓	
2. Anne	✓		5. Lori	✓	
3. Judy	✓		6. Charlene	✓	

Next scheduled meeting:
DATE _11-11_ TIME _8:30_ LOCATION _Conf. Rm._ LEADER _Lorraine_

DISCUSSIONS AND ACTIVITIES FOCUSED ON:

- Learning how to use Print Shop
- Mrs. Elmore demonstrated how to use LCD panel
- Judy ① shared her record keeping system for computer use and gave us a copy of the forms; ② showed us how to hook up the LCD panel; ③ showed us how to use Print Shop Deluxe for class lists, cards, labels

FOR NEXT MEETING, WE NEED TO:
Expect Terri to train us on the LCD panel

CONCERNS/RECOMMENDATIONS:

CLASSROOM APPLICATIONS SINCE LAST MEETING
Group Members:

Study Group: ___5___ (name/number)

STUDY GROUP LOG # _6_

DATE: _11-11_ LEADER: _Lorraine_

TIME: _8:30_ to _9:30_ LOCATION: _Conf. Rm_

GROUP MEMBERS

	Pre.	Ab.			Pre.	Ab.
1. Laura	✓		4. Lorraine		✓	
2. Anne	✓		5. Lori		✓	
3. Judy	✓		6. Charlene		✓	

Next scheduled meeting:

DATE _11-18_ TIME _3:00_ LOCATION _Judy's Rm_ LEADER _Judy_

DISCUSSIONS AND ACTIVITIES FOCUSED ON:

- Charlene guided us through getting onto the Internet using Mindspring and Wide Web
- John Carter showed us the Addison Homesite: http://www.mindspring.com/r ADDISON
- Explored Santa links
- Received more information about how to send/get E-Mail

FOR NEXT MEETING, WE NEED TO:

Bring examples of how we could use the Internet and E-Mail in our classrooms.

CONCERNS/RECOMMENDATIONS:

Judy will show us how she uses LCD panel in her room.

CLASSROOM APPLICATIONS SINCE LAST MEETING

Group Members:

Study Group: _____5_____ (name/number)

STUDY GROUP LOG # _7_

DATE: _11-18_____ LEADER: _Judy_____

TIME: _3:00_ to _4:00_ LOCATION: _Judy's Rm_____

GROUP MEMBERS	Pre.	Ab.		GROUP MEMBERS	Pre.	Ab.
1. Laura	✓		4. Lorraine	✓	
2. Anne	✓		5. Lori	✓	
3. Judy	✓		6. Charlene	✓	

Next scheduled meeting:
DATE _12-2_ TIME _9:30_ LOCATION _Conf. Rm_ LEADER _Lori_____

DISCUSSIONS AND ACTIVITIES FOCUSED ON:

- Shared examples of how we can use the Internet
- Terri demonstrated : • LCD panel
                         • Writing Pad
                         • Digital Camera
- Judy demonstrated how she uses LCD panel

FOR NEXT MEETING, WE NEED TO:

CONCERNS/RECOMMENDATIONS: Need long cable from computer to panel

CLASSROOM APPLICATIONS SINCE LAST MEETING
Group Members:
Anne - did class story on Student Writing Center on LCD panel then printed it.
Lorraine - did class story on Wiggle Works on LCD panel
Lori - used encyclopedia program for class to do research

Study Group: _____5_____ (name/number)

STUDY GROUP LOG # _8_

DATE: _12-2_____ LEADER: _Lori_____

TIME: _9:30_ to _10:30___ LOCATION: _Conf. Rm_____

GROUP MEMBERS	Pre.	Ab.			Pre.	Ab.
1. Lorraine	✓		4. Anne			✓
2. Lori	✓		5. Charlene		✓	
3. Laura	✓		6. Judy		✓	

Next scheduled meeting:
DATE _1-7_____ TIME _3:00_ LOCATION _Lauri's Rm_ LEADER _Laura_____

DISCUSSIONS AND ACTIVITIES FOCUSED ON:

- Learned how to set up LCD panel
- Explored (pen) use with LCD panel
- Explored Wiggle Works and the Student Writing Center (Anne & Lorraine shared more about their use of these programs)
- Celebrated our accomplishments! We all feel great about what we are learning to _actually_ do!
  Great hands-on Cooperative effort!

FOR NEXT MEETING, WE NEED TO:

CONCERNS/RECOMMENDATIONS:

CLASSROOM APPLICATIONS SINCE LAST MEETING
Group Members:

Lorraine - HyperStudio book
Lori - installed Windows '95
Charlene - set up centers for/with Student Writing Center
Judy - Made notes for students on Print Shop, with pictures
Laura - used Student Writing Center

Study Group: _____5_____ (name/number)

STUDY GROUP LOG # 9

DATE: 1-7   LEADER: Laura

TIME: 3:00 to 4:00   LOCATION: Laura's Rm

GROUP MEMBERS	Pre.	Ab.	GROUP MEMBERS	Pre.	Ab.
1. Lorraine	✓		4. Anne	✓	
2. Lori	✓		5. Charlene	✓	
3. Laura	✓		6. Judy	✓	

Next scheduled meeting:
DATE 1-14 TIME 10:30 LOCATION Conf. Rm LEADER Anne

DISCUSSIONS AND ACTIVITIES FOCUSED ON:

- Began to write detailed instructions for using LCD panel. We plan to make a booklet that we will share with all the faculty.

- How we will collect samples of student work and data from our classrooms

FOR NEXT MEETING, WE NEED TO:
Practice setting up LCD panel according to the instructions we wrote. Bring examples of student work.

CONCERNS/RECOMMENDATIONS:
Judy wants to attend the Macon conference

CLASSROOM APPLICATIONS SINCE LAST MEETING
Group Members:

Laura - Used Student Writing Center, printed and saved on disc

Judy - introduced dictionary to class

Charlene - demonstrated how to print and save on disc

Lori - used LCD panel to write class story to introduce new Wiggle Works features

Anne - took class to Media Center and showed class different encyclopedias on CD Rom and how to print from that

Lorraine - used LCD panel to introduce Wiggle Works program

Study Group: _____5_____ **(name/number)**

STUDY GROUP LOG # _10_

DATE: _1-14_   LEADER: _Anne_

TIME: _10:30_ to _11:30_   LOCATION: _Conf. Rm_

GROUP MEMBERS	Pre.	Ab.		GROUP MEMBERS	Pre.	Ab.
1. Lorraine	✓			4. Laura	✓	
2. Judy	✓			5. Charlene	✓	
3. Lori	✓			6. Anne	✓	

Next scheduled meeting:
DATE _1-21_   TIME _9:00_   LOCATION _Media Center_   LEADER _Whole Faculty Sharing_

DISCUSSIONS AND ACTIVITIES FOCUSED ON:

- Made an outline of what we want to share with the faculty

- Will select samples of student work to use when we share with faculty — (the student work we brought today will be used)

FOR NEXT MEETING, WE NEED TO:
Be prepared to share with faculty

CONCERNS/RECOMMENDATIONS: / note → Anne will represent us at IC meeting tomorrow.

CLASSROOM APPLICATIONS SINCE LAST MEETING
Group Members:

All of us are using the writing programs and are collecting samples of student work

Study Group: _____5_____ (name/number)

STUDY GROUP LOG # _11_

DATE: _1-21_   LEADER: _Whole Faculty Sharing_

TIME: _9:00_ to _12:00_   LOCATION: _Media Center_

GROUP MEMBERS	Pre.	Ab.			Pre.	Ab.
1.			4.		
2.			5.		
3.			6.		

Next scheduled meeting:
DATE _1-28_ TIME _12:30_ LOCATION _Conf. Rm_ LEADER _Charlene_

DISCUSSIONS AND ACTIVITIES FOCUSED ON:

Staff Development Day —
Each study group shared. Lots
of interaction!

FOR NEXT MEETING, WE NEED TO:
Be prepared to look at Hyper Studio

CONCERNS/RECOMMENDATIONS:
Anne and Laura want to register for "Thematic
Teaching with Technology" at Kennesaw College.
Any help with
tuition?

CLASSROOM APPLICATIONS SINCE LAST MEETING
Group Members:

Didn't have time to share individually
with each other.

Study Group: _____5_____ **(name/number)**

STUDY GROUP LOG # 12

DATE: 1-28   LEADER: Charlene

TIME: 12:30 to 1:30   LOCATION: Conf. Rm

GROUP MEMBERS	Pre.	Ab.		Pre.	Ab.
1. Laura	✓		4. Lorraine	✓	
2. Anne	✓		5. Lori	✓	
3. Judy	✓		6. Charlene	✓	

Next scheduled meeting:
DATE 2-4   TIME 3:00   LOCATION Judy's Rm   LEADER Judy

DISCUSSIONS AND ACTIVITIES FOCUSED ON:

- Discussed HyperStudio and Kid Pix; Terri demonstrated features of each
- Introduced to PowerPoint
- Reviewed LCD panel instructions; got feedback from Terri and made changes
- Learned how to clean print cardridge
- Anne reported on IC meeting she attended on 1-15

FOR NEXT MEETING, WE NEED TO:
Use LCD panel while following our directions

CONCERNS/RECOMMENDATIONS:

CLASSROOM APPLICATIONS SINCE LAST MEETING
Group Members:
Laura - used Student Writing Center (SWC)
Anne - " " " "
Judy - taught individual students on SWC; made several versions of class newsletter
Lorraine - taught Wiggle Works writing features with LCD panel
Lori - used SWC to type poems for the class; class used writing feature on Wiggle Works
Charlene - produced fact sheets with students for explorer exhibits in Dixie's class; searched on Web for Roscoe's class - looking for governors for state reports

Study Group: _____5_____ (name/number)

STUDY GROUP LOG # _13_

DATE: _2-4_   LEADER: _Judy_

TIME: _3:00_ to _4:00_   LOCATION: _Judy's Rm_

GROUP MEMBERS	Pre.	Ab.			Pre.	Ab.
1. Laura	✓		4. Lorraine		✓	
2. Anne	✓		5. Lori		✓	
3. Judy	✓		6. Charlene		✓	

Next scheduled meeting:
DATE _2-11_ TIME _8:00_ LOCATION _Conf. Rm_ LEADER _Lori_

DISCUSSIONS AND ACTIVITIES FOCUSED ON:

- Practiced hooking up the LCD panel with our step-by-step directions
- Practiced using our directions with Study Group #9 to see if they could do as directed
- Revised our directions
- Reviewed the Kids Learning Pack program
- Judy showed us the MacMillan Dictionary
- Terri showed us award winning software: "One Small Square", "Ballyard", "With Open Eyes"

FOR NEXT MEETING, WE NEED TO:

Read: "Do Computers Help Children Learn?"

CONCERNS/RECOMMENDATIONS:

CLASSROOM APPLICATIONS SINCE LAST MEETING
Group Members:

Lorraine - Continuing Wiggle Works "Write It"

Laura - students are using SWC and saving on disc

Anne - students were taught MECC - Fractions & Decimals using LCD panel in classroom; students are using program on their own during center time.

Judy - used LCD panel during Spelling with MacMillan Dictionary to show students how to locate words; used LCD panel to model some Wiggle Works activities

Lori - continued to use Wiggle Works magnetic board

Charlene - students working in Centers and saving their work on disc and printing

Study Group: _____5_____ (name/number)

STUDY GROUP LOG # 14

DATE: 2-11   LEADER: Lori

TIME: 8:00 to 9:00   LOCATION: Conf. Rm

GROUP MEMBERS	Pre.	Ab.		Pre.	Ab.
1. Laura	✓		4. Lori	✓	
2. Lorraine	✓		5. Anne	✓	
3. Judy	✓		6. Charlene	✓	

Next scheduled meeting:
DATE 2-18   TIME 3:00   LOCATION Charlene's Rm   LEADER Charlene

DISCUSSIONS AND ACTIVITIES FOCUSED ON:

- Discussed Article, "Do Computers Help Children Learn?"

- Judy demonstrated how to use Hyper Studio and shared student work

- Terri demonstrated the scanner

FOR NEXT MEETING, WE NEED TO: Use Hyper Studio and bring pictures to scan

CONCERNS/RECOMMENDATIONS: ① We need to contact Scholastic. Problem: Wiggle Work's Priority Word List can't be carried over from one book to another (I'm unclear about this!) ② We need more scanners, Hyper Studio programs, & LCD panels

CLASSROOM APPLICATIONS SINCE LAST MEETING
Group Members:

Laura - students have been typing biographies, saving on disc & printing; using Science disc with textbook
Anne - using MECC Fractions + Decimals
Lori - used First Connections encyclopedia to research animals; students used Wiggle Works to respond to story using the writing & drawing feature
Charlene - helped students with explorer report on Student Writing Center
Lorraine - used Print Shop Deluxe to do kindergarten calendar for students
Judy - put priority words identified by teacher assessment so students could use the words they need to practice during Wiggle Works writing

Study Group: _____5_____ (name/number)

STUDY GROUP LOG # 15

DATE: 2-18 _____ LEADER: Charlene _____

TIME: 3:00 to 4:00 LOCATION: Charlene's Rm

GROUP MEMBERS	Pre.	Ab.		Pre.	Ab.
1. Laura	✓		4. Lorraine	✓	
2. Anne		✓	5. Charlene	✓	
3. Lori	✓		6. Judy	✓	

Next scheduled meeting:
DATE 2-25 TIME 9:00 LOCATION Conf. Rm LEADER Laura

DISCUSSIONS AND ACTIVITIES FOCUSED ON:

- We all brought pictures and drawings (from students) to scan with Hyper Studio. After scanning we saved on disc. Will see if we can transfer our pictures onto the Learning Company
- Shared our use of Hyper Studio
- Shared ideas for using photographs with student writing

FOR NEXT MEETING, WE NEED TO:

CONCERNS/RECOMMENDATIONS:
When will other CD Roms be available?

CLASSROOM APPLICATIONS SINCE LAST MEETING
Group Members:

Anne - students continue using Decimals & Fractions during centers

Lorraine - students are writing words & stories with Wiggle Works Write Your Own Story and illustrating their work with Computer Graphics

Judy - exposing more students to Spell Check, editing, and other features of The Learning Company. A few are printing Completed Stories (2nd graders)

Lori - Students are accessing their own information using First Connection. Introduced new WW program. Students are writing, illustrating, printing on their own!

Charlene - Using CD Roms on: Explorations, Ancient Cities, Mayan Culture, Oregon Trail

Laura - Using science games. Students can write, save, exit, + bring back up.

Study Group: _____5_____ **(name/number)**

STUDY GROUP LOG # _16_

DATE: _2-25_   LEADER: _Laura_

TIME: _9:00_ to _10:00_   LOCATION: _Conf. Rm_

GROUP MEMBERS	Pre.	Ab.			Pre.	Ab.
1. Laura	✓		4. Lorraine		✓	
2. Anne	✓		5. Lori		✓	
3. Judy	✓		6. Charlene		✓	

Next scheduled meeting:
DATE _3-4_   TIME _3:00_   LOCATION _Media Center_   LEADER _Whole Faculty Sharing_

DISCUSSIONS AND ACTIVITIES FOCUSED ON:

- Discussed problems with bringing up graphics on room computers
- Looked at various electronic portfolios
- Reviewed how to use scanner
- Reviewed & typed directions for using scanner — we'll also share this with the faculty

FOR NEXT MEETING, WE NEED TO:
Share our work with faculty. Judy will prepare a one page hand-out listing what we have covered

CONCERNS/RECOMMENDATIONS:

CLASSROOM APPLICATIONS SINCE LAST MEETING
Group Members:

Judy - installed cable to allow another computer to print; worked with Learning Co to edit & print.
Anne - worked with individual students to write, edit, cut, paste, etc on Martin Luther King stories
Lori - students used First Connections to locate info on polar animals
Laura - students typed biographies; saved on disks; illustrating with graphics
Lorraine - continuing with Wiggle Works; students are typing stories
Charlene - still working with Mayan culture, Indians, and Ancient Cities on CDROM

Study Group: ___5___ (name/number)

STUDY GROUP LOG # _17_

DATE: _3-4_   LEADER: _Whole Faculty Sharing_

TIME: _3:00_ to _4:00_   LOCATION: _Media Center_

GROUP MEMBERS	Pre.	Ab.		GROUP MEMBERS	Pre.	Ab.
1. Laura	✓			4. Lorraine	✓	
2. Anne	✓			5. Lori	✓	
3. Judy	✓			6. Charlene	✓	

Next scheduled meeting:
DATE _3-11_ TIME _10:00_ LOCATION _Conf. Rm_ LEADER _Anne_

DISCUSSIONS AND ACTIVITIES FOCUSED ON:

> Each group shared a hand-out on its work

> The faculty decided that each group would do a "study group portfolio" to share its work. It can be in any format. We will exhibit the portfolios at the April 8 PTA meeting

> Last study group meeting will be 5-13 so bring closure to this year's work by that date

FOR NEXT MEETING, WE NEED TO:
Discuss what our portfolio will be.

CONCERNS/RECOMMENDATIONS:

We have so much left we want to do!

CLASSROOM APPLICATIONS SINCE LAST MEETING
Group Members:

Study Group: _____5_____ (name/number)

STUDY GROUP LOG # 18

DATE: _3-11_ LEADER: _Anne_

TIME: _10:00_ to _11:00_ LOCATION: _Conf. Rm_

GROUP MEMBERS	Pre.	Ab.			Pre.	Ab.
1. Laura	✓		4. Judy			✓
2. Lori	✓		5. Lorraine		✓	
3. Anne		✓	6. Charlene		✓	

Next scheduled meeting:
DATE _3-18_ TIME _3:00_ LOCATION _Judy's Rm_ LEADER _Judy_

DISCUSSIONS AND ACTIVITIES FOCUSED ON:

- Charlene shared information for the course she attended. She recommends: "Inspiration" and "Kids Work"
- Experimented with digital camera and how to put a picture in the computer
- Discussed what we will do for a portfolio. We are going to do ours on a computer.

FOR NEXT MEETING, WE NEED TO:

Demonstrate our use of Windows 95

CONCERNS/RECOMMENDATIONS:

CLASSROOM APPLICATIONS SINCE LAST MEETING
Group Members:

Laura – worked with laptop to look up QCC for 3rd grade

Charlene – attended Technology workshop at Kennesaw College

Lori – used LCD panel to introduce Math Keys to students

Lorraine – continuing to use Wiggle Works, students are writing and illustrating

Study Group: _____5_____ (name/number)

STUDY GROUP LOG # 19

DATE: 3-18 _____ LEADER: Judy

TIME: 3:00 to 4:00 LOCATION: Judy's Rm

GROUP MEMBERS	Pre.	Ab.		Pre.	Ab.
1. Laura	✓		4. Lorraine	✓	
2. Anne	✓		5. Lori	✓	
3. Judy	✓		6. Charlene		✓

Next scheduled meeting:
DATE 4-1 TIME 11:00 LOCATION Conf. Rm LEADER Lorraine

DISCUSSIONS AND ACTIVITIES FOCUSED ON:

- Reviewed scanner instructions, made corrections
- Lorraine demonstrated the use of microphones with Wiggle Works
- Discussed our portfolio
  · outlined what we will do
  · assigned responsibilities

FOR NEXT MEETING, WE NEED TO:

Next week is spring holidays

CONCERNS/RECOMMENDATIONS/ Note → Judy goes to the IC meeting tomorrow

CLASSROOM APPLICATIONS SINCE LAST MEETING
Group Members:

Lori - introduced new Wiggle Works story

Anne - students are writing letters on Student Write using proper form

Judy - continued to introduce The Learning Co. students are writing, editing, printing

Laura - typing sentences for "book cube" book report. Whole class is keyboarding in lab

Lorraine - Used the scanner with our directions; introduced microphones with Wiggle Works

Study Group: _____5_____ (name/number)

STUDY GROUP LOG # 20

DATE: 4-1　　　　　LEADER: *Lorraine*

TIME: 11:00 to 12:00　　LOCATION: *Conf. Rm*

GROUP MEMBERS	Pre.	Ab.		GROUP MEMBERS	Pre.	Ab.
1. Laura	✓		4. Lorraine	✓	
2. Anne	✓		5. Lori	✓	
3. Judy	✓		6. Charlene	✓	

Next scheduled meeting:
DATE 4-8　TIME_____　LOCATION *Media Center*　LEADER *PTA Exhibit*

DISCUSSIONS AND ACTIVITIES FOCUSED ON:

- Worked on our portfolio. This gave us a chance to reflect on the group's work. We are going to spotlight:
  - Hyper Space
  - Internet
  - Windows '95
  - Scanner
  - Digital Camera

- Planned how we will video demonstrations

- Judy reported on IC meeting. Wish we could be in every group - great ideas!

FOR NEXT MEETING, WE NEED TO:

Prepare for PTA Exhibit on Apr. 8, 7:00PM

CONCERNS/RECOMMENDATIONS:

CLASSROOM APPLICATIONS SINCE LAST MEETING
Group Members:

All of us worked on getting examples of student work to include in our study group portfolio.

Study Group: ___5___ (name/number)

STUDY GROUP LOG # 21

DATE: _4-15_   LEADER: _Lori_

TIME: _3:00_ to _4:00_   LOCATION: _Lori's Rm_

GROUP MEMBERS	Pre.	Ab.		Pre.	Ab.
1. Laura	✓		4. Lorraine	✓	
2. Anne	✓		5. Lori	✓	
3. Judy	✓		6. Charlene	✓	

Next scheduled meeting:
DATE _4-22_ TIME _12:00_ LOCATION _Charlene Rm_ LEADER _Charlene_

DISCUSSIONS AND ACTIVITIES FOCUSED ON:

- Celebrated the response we got from parents and faculty on our work
- shared software programs we've used effectively in our classrooms that we haven't had an opportunity (time) to do in this group
- Terri shared with us First-Aid for Windows
- Redid scanner directions for faculty use

FOR NEXT MEETING, WE NEED TO:

Bring examples of pictures/work we have scanned. Also need update from Anne + Laura on course.

CONCERNS/RECOMMENDATIONS:

How can we buy software for personal use?

CLASSROOM APPLICATIONS SINCE LAST MEETING
Group Members:

Lorraine - used Wiggle Works writing + illustrations to share with parents at conferences

Lori - using microphone; students reading, recording Wiggle Works books

Laura - using programs from class at Kennesaw

Charlene - typing, editing for Little House on the Prairie stories

Anne - using programs from class at Kennesaw

Judy - using microphone to read + record Wiggle Works. All students are using printer to print short stories on Learning Co.

Study Group: _____5_____ (name/number)

STUDY GROUP LOG #22

DATE: _4-22_____ LEADER: _Charlene_____

TIME: _12:00_ to _1:00_____ LOCATION: _Charlene's Rm_____

GROUP MEMBERS	Pre.	Ab.		Pre.	Ab.
1. Charlene	✓		4. Laura	✓	
2. Lori	✓		5. Lorraine	✓	
3. Anne	✓		6. Judy	✓	

Next scheduled meeting:
DATE _4-29_ TIME _3:00_ LOCATION _Laura's Rm_ LEADER _Laura_

DISCUSSIONS AND ACTIVITIES FOCUSED ON:

- Scanned pictures to review our directions

- Anne and Laura reported on what they are doing in the technology course at Kennesaw. They shared 8 programs with us.

FOR NEXT MEETING, WE NEED TO:
Look at Kid Pix

CONCERNS/RECOMMENDATIONS:
Lots of conflicts coming up!

CLASSROOM APPLICATIONS SINCE LAST MEETING
Group Members:

Charlene - used SWC to publish "Jack's Story" and "My Dream"

Anne - continued with SWC; used Brain Quest

Lorraine - preparing for Hyper Studio workshop that she will be doing for teachers not in our group

Lori - students used First Connections to find cat facts; using all the features of WW

Judy - using the LCD panel to explore Kid Pix

Laura - using programs from technology course; she will summarize for us

Study Group: _____5_____ (name/number)

STUDY GROUP LOG #23

DATE: _4-29_____ LEADER: _Laura_____

TIME: _3:00_ to _4:00_ LOCATION: _Laura's Rm_____

GROUP MEMBERS	Pre.	Ab.		Pre.	Ab.
1. Laura		✓	4. Lorraine		✓
2. Lori	✓		5. Anne	✓	
3. Judy	✓		6. Charlene	✓	

Next scheduled meeting:
DATE _5-6_ TIME _1:00_ LOCATION _Conf. Rm_ LEADER _Anne_

DISCUSSIONS AND ACTIVITIES FOCUSED ON:

- Laura demonstrated Kid Pix – we looked at various components
- Lori shared the reports her students have done
- Reviewed the many possibilities of Hyper Studio
- Judy shared the workshop she did with other teachers

FOR NEXT MEETING, WE NEED TO:
Use Kid Pix and plan to share

CONCERNS/RECOMMENDATIONS:
The lunch schedule is getting crazy –

CLASSROOM APPLICATIONS SINCE LAST MEETING
Group Members:

Anne – using Decimals program in Math Keys

Lori – using microphone feature in WW; used The Learning Co. to type poems

Charlene – used SLC to attempt to correct Grant's spatial difficulties

Judy – taught 6 children how to write their own version of WW story and print it

Study Group: _____5_____ (name/number)

STUDY GROUP LOG #24

DATE: 5-6   LEADER: Anne

TIME: 1:00 to 2:00   LOCATION: Conf. Rm

GROUP MEMBERS	Pre.	Ab.		GROUP MEMBERS	Pre.	Ab.
1. Judy	✓			4. Anne	✓	
2. Laura	✓			5. Lorraine	✓	
3. Lori	✓			6. Charlene		✓

Next scheduled meeting:
DATE 5-13 TIME 3:00 LOCATION Lori's Rm LEADER Lori

DISCUSSIONS AND ACTIVITIES FOCUSED ON:

- We reviewed our Action Plan
- We did the 3 things we said we would do
- We reflected on how we have worked together as a group
- We have evidence that
  - We are better!
  - Our students are better!

FOR NEXT MEETING, WE NEED TO:

CONCERNS (RECOMMENDATIONS):

1. Every classroom needs a tVater. It would be more economical than LCD panel

2. We want to keep same group next year. We still have lots to do together!!

CLASSROOM APPLICATIONS SINCE LAST MEETING
Group Members:

Judy - continued small group instruction with Amazing Writing Machine

Laura - students used School Mom for division; MacMillan Science games coincide with texts

Anne - students used Googal Math during center time

Lorraine - attended district workshop on Kid Works + Kid Pix Studio

Lori - introduced Spell-It; students learned how to use my story feature on Wiggle Works

Study Group: _____5_____ (name/number)

STUDY GROUP LOG #25

DATE: _5-13_   LEADER: _Lori_

TIME: _3:00_ to _4:00_   LOCATION: _Lori's Rm_

GROUP MEMBERS	Pre.	Ab.		Pre.	Ab.
1. Anne	✓		4. Lorraine	✓	
2. Laura	✓		5. Lori	✓	
3. Judy	✓		6. Charlene	✓	

Next scheduled meeting:
DATE_____ TIME_____ LOCATION_____ LEADER_____

DISCUSSIONS AND ACTIVITIES FOCUSED ON:

- Completed the Study Group Reflective Exercise

- Reflected on
  - the process: how we did as a group
  - the content: what we learned and implemented
  - the context: how our work will have an impact on whole school

FOR NEXT ~~MEETING~~ YEAR, WE NEED TO:
Stay together!

CONCERNS/RECOMMENDATIONS:
Let's have whole school celebration on May 20

CLASSROOM APPLICATIONS SINCE LAST MEETING
Group Members:

Study Group #5
Technology
May 13, 1997

Study Group
Reflective Exercise

Focus of your study group's school improvement effort:

Reflection	Inquiry
• What was intended? • What did you do? • What happened? • What results occurred? • How might what you did have contributed to your results (positively/negatively)?	What evidence is there that a sense of community is being formed among staff at your school?

> We intended to get more confident & competent with using computer in classrooms — and for our student to become more confident & competent.

> We did that — recognizing we still have lots to learn.

> The major success factor for us was that we had a very concrete focus: computers & software & attachments

We depend on each other. We look forward to learning from each other. Our talk – in the lunchroom & faculty lounge – is what we are learning.

What evidence is there that the quality of instruction is improving at your school?

Records we kept indicate we integrated computer technology in all subject areas – going deeper into concepts than we could have done on our own.

What evidence is there that student achievement is improving at your school?

- Writing is more advanced on state writing tests

- Reading scores on ITBS continue to increase

- More students are receiving district/state recognition

Resource C

Assessing Progress of Study Groups

It is important that formative and summative assessments of the work of study groups are in place.

The definition of *whole-faculty study groups* is "small groups of individuals joining together to increase their capacities through new learning to meet the needs of students." Therefore, the work of the study groups is based on analyzing student needs and examining the work of the study group to ensure that the two are consistent.

Each faculty and each study group has the following forms from which to choose to keep the focus of the new learning on what is most beneficial to the students.

The study group action plan remains the basic document that is used as a reference point for connecting student needs to what teachers do in study groups.

Assessing Progress Using The Study Group Action Plan

INSTRUCTIONS:

As a study group, members discuss the items below. Each member will need to have a copy of the latest version of the group's Study Group Action Plan. One member records the group's consensus response (for each item) <u>directly on the Action Plan.</u>   The marked Action Plan is to be given to the principal or to his or her designee by May 8.

1. Look at the section entitled "DATA INDICATE THAT STUDENTS NEED TO:" On the Action Plan in the left margin beside the student needs, list the data sources that the group used to varify the student needs, e.g., teacher grades, referrals to the office, Iowa Test of Basic Skills.

2. Look at the section entitled "THEREFORE, IN THIS STUDY GROUP TEACHERS WILL:" On the Action Plan:
   - ➤ Circle each action word.
   - ➤ Beside each statement that states what the group will do, write a number (0 to 5) that indicates the degree to which the study group did what the group said it would do. Use the scale "0" to mean "no action" to a "5" to mean "to the fullest."

3. Look at the next section of the Action Plan where the group listed the documents that the group <u>thought</u> would provide evidence of changes in student behavior, attitude, and/or academic achievement. On the Plan:
   - ➤ Circle the sources that can currently be used as evidence that change has occurred.
   - ➤ With a red pen, add sources that were not listed when the group wrote the Action Plan but can currently be used as evidence that change has occurred.

Note: A list of possible data sources is attached.

4. Look at the last section of the Action Plan.   It is a list of the resources that the study group intended to use.   How beneficial the resources have been will be assessed with "Assessing Progress Using Study Group Logs."

5. At the bottom of the Action Plan, write a number that represents the total number of hours that the study group met from Sept. through May.

Make sure the school and the study group is identified at the top of the Action Plan.

CHECK-LIST of DATA SOURCES

Study groups are encouraged to use this check-list to remind the group of the data sources that are available to guide all decisions. The study group would "check" the sources that are used in the planning stages. As additional data are used during the year, those sources are identified with a "check". Overtime, it is the expectation that the sources checked will be the documents that will provide evidence of changes in student learning, behavior, and attitude.

Prior to doing Action Plan		Since doing Action Plan
_____	Student work	_____
_____	Student grades	_____
_____	Standardized tests	_____
_____	Attendance reports	_____
_____	Drop-out records	_____
_____	Discipline referrals	_____
_____	Suspensions from class	_____
_____	Suspensions from school	_____
_____	Student/staff surveys	_____
_____	Violent incidences	_____
_____	Vandalism reports	_____
_____	Parent conference attendance	_____
_____	Parent participation in school functions	_____
_____	Promotion and retention	_____
_____	Completion of in-class work	_____
_____	Participation in out-of-class assignments/projects	_____
_____	Student portfolios	_____
_____	Independent reading	_____
_____	Courses selected	_____
_____	District assessments	_____
_____	State assessments	_____
_____	Guidance referrals	_____
_____	Community agencies	_____
_____	Staff perceptions	_____
_____	Teacher observations	_____
_____	Computer expertise	_____
_____	_____	_____
_____	_____	_____
_____	_____	_____

SCHOOL:_____**STUDY GROUP #___**

Assessing Progress Using Study Group Logs

As a study group, use the Study Group Logs to list the activities of the study group and indicate how beneficial the activity was. This would include, by name: articles read, books read, software reviewed, equipment used, instructional materials used, district publications used, and invited guests. Also indicate benefits of specific demonstrations and sharing of classroom practices by group members (not by name of individual). This review of study group activities is to be given to the principal after the last study group meeting. The information will be used to guide next year's study groups as activities and resources are selected.

ACTIVITY:	LITTLE BENEFIT			GREAT BENEFIT	
	1	2	3	4	5
_____	1	2	3	4	5
_____	1	2	3	4	5
_____	1	2	3	4	5
_____	1	2	3	4	5
_____	1	2	3	4	5
_____	1	2	3	4	5
_____	1	2	3	4	5
_____	1	2	3	4	5
_____	1	2	3	4	5
_____	1	2	3	4	5
_____	1	2	3	4	5

Use another copy of this form to continue listing, if needed.

Assessing Progress Through Personal Perceptions

Study groups have been meeting for about two months. Let's reflect on our work up to this point. As a study group, consider each of the questions below and have each member share their personal reactions.

1. What did you hope to achieve through whole faculty study groups?

2. List the verbs that best describe what your group has been doing.

3. What is happening differently in the classroom as a result of what you are doing in the study group?

4. What <u>internal</u> resources are you using that have been most helpful?

5. What <u>external</u> resources are you using that have been most helpful?

6. What else do you need from both internal and external sources?

7. What internal structures or procedures need to be adjusted to help you to accomplish what you need to do?

8. What would be your advice to a study group just beginning?

Assessing Progress Using Open-Ended Questions

As a group, respond to the following items. One member is to record the responses of group members.

1. We started

2. As far as cultural changes, we see

3. As far as student changes, we see

4. We feel progress is being made in

5. We project

6. Next year, we hope

Assessing Progress Through Reflection and Analysis

All members of the study group participate in the discussion and completion of the following.

Reflection on the process	Examination of the inquiry
Share perceptions of how the following facilitated/impeded the group process. • Group size and composition • Leadership • Group norms • Equality • C & I focus • Results orientation	What **evidence** is there that a sense of community is deeper among the staff? What **evidence** is there that the quality of instruction is improving? What **evidence** is there that student achievement is improving?

Assessing Progress Through Individual Assessment

Please complete the following items as you personally reflect on the study group process. It is not necessary to indicate your name. Return the form to the school office by May 15. The information will be summarized and the information used to plan for next school year.

1. Do you have an increased knowledge of:
   a. subject matter content? ___Y ___N If yes, please elaborate.

   b. students (e.g., levels of maturity, levels of achievement, quality of work)?
   ___Y ___ N If yes, please elaborate.

2. Have you modified:
   a. planning or organizing for instruction? ___ Y ___ N If yes, how?

   b. teaching practice? ___ Y ___N If yes, how?

   c. evaluating student learning? ___Y ___N If yes, how?

   d. teacher to teacher, teacher to student, student to student relationships?
   ___ Y ___N If yes, how?

3. What do you perceive to be the strengths of the whole faculty study group process?

4. What do you perceive to be the weaknesses of the whole faculty study group process?

5. What suggestions do you have for improving the whole faculty study group process?

6. How do you rate the overall effectiveness of your study group? (Effectiveness is measured in terms of whether or not the group accomplished what it intended to do as stated on the group's Action Plan.)

PLEASE CIRCLE

LOW 1 2 3 4 5 HIGH

Sharing Progress

Each teacher completes the following. When each has finished writing, each teacher shares their responses.

1. In my study group, the student need we are addressing
is_____

2. In my study group, we have spent most of our time
    - ___ focusing on how to implement an instructional initiative
    - ___ integrating materials and strategies
    - ___ targeting a school-wide need
    - ___ studying the research, reading the literature
    - ___ monitoring the effects of an initiative on students
(The five bulleted items are the five functions of study groups.)

3. Through today, my group has met for a total of ____ hours (approx.).

4. In my study group, the verbs circled below are the verbs that best describe what we **do (the actions we take)** when our group meets.

develop	use	read	create
search	make	discuss	share
explore	construct	investigate	demonstrate
collect	plan	design	practice

5. Go back to # 4. Under the verbs circled, write <u>one</u> word that tells "WHAT".   **For example: WHAT is being developed;   WHAT is being practiced; WHAT is being explored. Continue in this way with all the verbs that are circled.**

6. In my study group, I believe for us to fulfill our purpose, increase student performance, we will need to do more: (refer to above action words)

7. As a result of what we have done in my study group, the greatest impact on **my** work with **my** students in **my** classroom has been:

Sweetwater Union High School

Study Group Focus Team

The Study Group Focus Team was formed in July 1993. The Focus Team is comprised of a group of seven teachers and two administrators from Sweetwater High School who attend training sessions on the Study Group Process. These training sessions are provided by San Diego Unified School District and the San Diego County Office of Education. Training sessions and materials are developed by Carlene Murphy, a staff development specialist from Augusta, Georgia.

In addition to attending training sessions on the Study Group Process, the Focus Team will: meet as a Study Group on each of the scheduled Study Group meeting dates, meet with the Representative Council on their scheduled meeting dates, and meet once weekly beginning in January 1994 to assure the success of the overall implementation of Study Groups on our campus.

Should you have any questions or concerns regarding Study Groups, you might contact one of the members of the Focus Team.

Study Group Focus Team

Patti Clark	Laura Charles	Ben Curatolo
Ellen Hall	Barb Hombs	Carl Moon
Ralph Mora	Louise Phipps	Sheri Peltier

Study Group Representative Council

The Study Group Representative Council is comprised of one member from each of the Study Groups. It is recommended that the appointment of this representative be rotated monthly to facilitate shared leadership among the members of each study group team. The Representative Council's main function is to serve as a communication bridge between all of the Study Groups on campus, and to provide feedback to the Study Group Focus Team. The imput from this Council will have a direct impact on the planning of future staff development.

Representative Council Meeting Dates
1993 - 1994 School Year

Meeting Dates	Time and Place
Wednesday, January 12, 1994	After School 2:30-3:30p.m. / Room 710
Wednesday, February 2, 1994	After School 2:30-3:30p.m./ Room 710
Wednesday, April 6, 1994	After School 2:30-3:30p.m./ Room 710
Wednesday, May 4, 1994	After School 2:30-3:30p.m./ Room 710

Sweetwater High School / Study Group Notebook

SOURCE: Reprinted by permission from Sweetwater Union High School, National City, California.

Date: March 8, 1994

MEETING REMINDER:

PLEASE NOTE:
MEETING TIME
CORRECTED ON
THIS AGENDA

To: Study Group Focus Team Members:
From: Patti Clark, Group Leader-March 1994
RE: Planning Meeting

An important planning meeting has been scheduled for the Study Group Focus
Team Members on Thursday, March 10th from **1:00p.m. -4:00p.m.** in the SUHI
Library. The agenda will be as follows:

Thursday, March 10th / 1:00p.m. - 4:00p.m. Agenda Items	Discussion Leader	# of Minutes (approx.)
Focus Team Concerns	Carl Moon	5 -10
Revisit Group Norms	Patti Clark	5-10
Determine Leadership May-June-July	Patti Clark	5-10
Set remainder of 1993-1994 meeting dates	Patti Clark	30-45
Review/Analyze Study Group logs	Patti Clark	30-45
Set Representative Council Agenda for April	Patti Clark	30-45
Long Range Planning for 1994-1995 school year	Patti Clark	45-60

Note:
**If you were unable to attend the session with Carlene et al. on Tuesday, March 1st at
the Dana Center, please review the information on the left side of your folder before
coming to our meeting on Thursday, March 10.**

SOURCE: Reprinted by permission from Sweetwater Union High School, National City, California.

STUDY GROUPS

1995-1996

Group #1
Student Incentives

FA 1	Dorothy Cable
SpEd 2	Vicki Cowart
Eng 3	Beverly Follendorf
Coun 4	Linda Gillespie
SS 5	MariJane Moon
Sci 6	George Varga

Group #2
Staff Morale

SS 1	Bob Alcock
SpEd 2	Susan Lang
ROTC3	Russ Hanthorn
Sci 4	Steve Jensen
Coun 5	Lee Romero
6	

Group #3
U.S. Citizenship

SS 1	Maria Elena Gallaher
Math 2	Mario Haro
Bus 3	Arturo Lopez
For L 4	Antonio Peraza
SS 5	Joe Lara
Lib 6	Vicki Urias

Group #4
Mobile Multimedia

IA 1	Eileen Giorgetta
LC 2	Paula Goleta
Math 3	Jorge Ley
SS 4	Yolanda Rocha
SpEd 5	Alma Stults
Sci 6	Geri O'Brien

Group #5
Reading Lists

SS 1	Jim Geddes
Eng 2	Nancy Hokenson
For L 3	Maria Mauck
Eng 4	Donna Mulrean
Eng 5	Debbie Rosenbach
Eng 6	Sue Zimmer

Group #6
Bilingual Education

IA 1	Maria Cordero
Sci 2	Eduardo Gonzalez
SS 3	Ralph Inzunza
ESL 4	Hilda Paul
Eng 5	Diane Rider
Bus 6	Juanita Taubner
Bus 7	Ethel Floyd
For L 8	Marina Corrales

Total # of teachers: 105

Group #7
InterNET /Curriculum

SpEd 1	Gordon Gungle
LC 2	Rick Kessler
IA 3	Gabby Ley
Sci 4	Jim Merzbacher
Sci 5	Jill Shapira
IA 6	Sonia Tanner
IA 7	Dan Quigley

Group #8
ELP/Block Schedule

SS 1	Ivy Callaway
SS 2	Ken Callaway
LC 3	Ron Gipson
PE 4	Mike Morey
Adm 5	Marieanne Perrault
Eng 6	Nancy Wise

Group #9
Staff Incentives

Eng 1	Virginia Cordova
SpEd 2	Mary Gardner
FA 3	Gail Mitchell
Nurse 4	Karen Neal
LC 5	Andy Sanchez
Eng 6	Joe Vogel

Group #10
Self-Esteem

PE 1	Gene Alim
FA 2	Tommy Bryant
FA 3	LeRoy Lane
Math 4	Diem Nghiem
Math 5	John White
SS 6	Carl Yamashiro

Group #11
A-Team

ESL 1	Cristeta Dumaran
Sci 2	Carmen Gutierrez
Coun 3	Frank Tarantino
FA 4	Tracey Toler
SS 5	Marlene Wagman

Group #12
Student Panel

Adm 1	Bob Aguilar
Coun 2	Olivia Beltram
LC 3	Mike Challis
PE 4	Tim Latham
Coun 5	Elaine Leano
Coun 6	Maria Elena Ochoa
SS 7	Tony Valdez

SOURCE: Reprinted by permission from Sweetwater Union High School, National City, California.

Group #13
New Math Adopt

Math 1	Bill Bokesch
Math 2	Scott Grover
Math 3	Blanca Lacanilao
Math 4	Joe Pistone
Math 5	Karen Waddell
SpEd 6	Michelle Brunkow

Group #14
Health Services

Adm1	Bettina Bautista
Eng 2	Cindy Espinosa
Eng 3	Kristin Kok-Page
SpEd 4	Salome Riingen
SS 5	Rudy Wiess
SpEd 6	Paula Fialkoff

Group #15
Focus Team

LC 1	Patti Clark
FA 2	Laura Charles
Eng 3	Ellen Hall
For L 4	Debbie Hansen-Arce
SS 5	Carl Moon
Adm 6	Louise Phipps
Eng 7	Crystal ReVeal
Math 8	Sheri Soldau
SS 9	David Ybarra

Group #16
Tech Prep

Eng 1	Michelle Challis
Math 2	Larry Fernandez
Bus 3	Jo Hazard
SS 4	Cyndi Lusink
Bus 5	Michele Tyler
Sci 6	Maureen Rymer

SOURCE: Reprinted by permission from Sweetwater Union High School, National City, California.

FOCUS

Volume 1, Issue 2   **November 1, 1995**

Study Groups In Focus

Faxtttt   Communication?

Determining what is important to focus on to improve student achievement is the goal of Sweetwater High School's Study Groups. Sixteen teams research issues such as: Incentives, Morale, Citizenship, Multimedia, TESA, Tech Prep, InterNet, ELP, Block Schedule, Self-Esteem, and Health Services.

The projected outcome of Study Groups is to research professional priorities that promote a better education for Sweetwater High School students.

The teams are not required to re-invent the wheel or implement a high-tech, "school-wide" educational product. Rather, they focus on research and professional trends that impact student achievement.

This is not to say that the study groups have not implemented their findings! Block scheduling is a reflection of the Study Group process at Sweetwater High.

REP Council Meets November 7

Every other month, Rep. Council meetings are held in Room 509 to update progress of each study group. A team-selected member attends Rep Council every other month. The November 7 representatives will present the evaluation phase of their Route Map. The council focus will be on the degree of progress each team has made, pertinent to their research goals. To promote school-wide communication, Rep. council members share meeting minutes with their study group at the next scheduled team meeting.

Focus

On April 23, 1996, Sweetwater High School celebrates three years of whole school study groups. Congruent to their vision, Sweetwater High School staff, via study groups, have collaboratively implemented research to enhance students' holistic endeavors as life-long learners. Group 15, focused on career paths, generated a prodigious 'Tech-Prep' surge into school climate. Group 10, concentrated on the school as a simulation of a community, stressing the significance of a safe, clean and esthetic environment. Group 16 through effective communication channels, endeavored to center whole school study groups on improving student achievement; hence, the 'Focus Team'. Empathetic to the demands of traditional and technological literacy, professional teams 4 and 7 pioneered parallel investigations to clarify demands for their students. Group 4 researched the contrivance of mobile multimedia technology in the classroom; while, team 7 assiduously pursued the role and access of the InterNet through Sweetwater's state-of-the-art library/ media center.

Life-long learning, mirrored by study groups 5 and 12 amplified Sweetwater High School's understanding of the challenges of complex global educational demands facing graduates. Group 5's investigation strengthened academic literature bridges for successful high school-to-college transitions; which, parallels team 12's holistic perspective of the Sweetwater student as a lifelong learner. Dialog and research have exposed social, contractual and administrative influences that impact overall logistics and accountability that belongs corporately to parents, community and school, as fellows. Empowered by sensitive camaraderie, study groups 3 and 6 have synthesized cultural diversity into an enriching climate urging sensitivity and tolerance for all. One facet team 3 has highlighted asserts cultural pluralism as a cornerstone in building improved student achievement. Group 6 investigated the planning and development of National Hispanic University in San Diego as a coextension of cultural plurality.

Believing in their own self worth as a team members, study group 1 considered the frequently overlooked 'ordinary heroes' and implemented incentives to honor them, inspiring others to enroll in a lifelong personal growth continuum. Responsible for their own study groups' quests, teams 2, 14, 9 and 11 as pundits, refract character that is indicative of effective citizenship in a world community. Group 2, highlighting responsible forerunners (SUHI staff), improved schoolwide communication and esteem by publicity and recognition. Group 14 extended the demand for personal responsibility by establishing a youth health promotion initiative. One of group 9's discernments on attendance meliorated a sense of personal responsibility for better attendance schoolwide. Group 11, alias the 'A-Team', projected the outcomes of personal and academic responsibility through a photographic profile of pupils with straight-A report cards.

SOURCE: Reprinted by permission from Sweetwater Union High School, National City, California.

Study Group Meeting Log
(Please write in pen)

Date:	Group # Room #

Group Representative:

Next Month's Group Rep:

Members Present:
(Please put a checkmark √ next to those present)

Laura Charles	Patti Clark
Ellen Hall	Sarita Hathaway
Carl Moon	Ralph Mora
Crystal ReVeal	David Ybarra

Our Study Group's focus: Changing the Role of the Teacher

Summary of Today's Content:
Today our group discussed the concept of constructivist teaching and what it meant to each of us. Although we realize that in order for learning to take place in schools, teachers must provide a learning environment where students search for meaning, appreciate uncertainty, and inquire responsibility, how does this look in our classrooms? How are lessons developed using the constructivist approach? We decided that we must begin to make a difference in how our students learn by encouraging student-to-student interaction initiating lessons that foster cooperative learning, and provide opportunities for students to be exposed to interdisciplinary curriculum.

Focus Team Assistance Requested:
Do you know of any published works on the Constructivist approach to teaching?

Next Steps:
- Read article on Constructivist approach that Crystal shared.
- Bring one idea of a lesson utilizing the constructivist approach to share.

Are we staying on target?
Our time together today was well spent. We accomplished what we had set out to do from our last meeting's log...as far as next steps. Enthusiasm is building with regard to trying some new things in our classrooms.

SOURCE: Reprinted by permission from Sweetwater Union High School, National City, California.

KEEPING IN TOUCH

with

Study Group #_____

I received your study group log, dated _____. Thank you!

_____

_____

_____

_____

_____

Focus Team Liason

KEEPING IN TOUCH

with

Study Group #_____

I didn't receive your study group log, dated _____. I anticipate responding to your concerns as soon as I receive your group's log! Thank you!_____

_____

_____

_____

Focus Team Liason

KEEPING IN TOUCH

with

Study Group #_____

I received your study group log, dated _____. Thank you!

_____

_____

_____

_____

_____

Focus Team Liason

SOURCE: Reprinted by permission from Sweetwater Union High School, National City, California.

Whole Faculty Study Groups
Third Anniversary Celebration
Thinksheet/Group Reflection Activity
Tuesday, April 23, 1996

You've done an honorable job and we'd like you to reflect upon your successes.

Study Group Name: Group Number:
Group Members:

1.   5.
2.   6.
3.   7.
4.   8.

Group Reflection Thinksheet Directions:
Discuss possible responses to the following queries and come to consensus on a response for each item.
Record your group's responses and return your completed Thinksheet to the front table in exchange for a goodie bag.

Provide a brief summary of your group's focus:

How has your group positively affected student achievement at SUHI?

What will your group do to maintain the relationships you have developed in order to continue to impact student achievement and strengthen the culture of the personal and professional development at our school?

SOURCE: Reprinted by permission from Sweetwater Union High School, National City, California.

COBB COUNTY (GA) SCHOOLS

ADDISON ELEMENTARY SCHOOL
STUDY GROUPS

1. Assessment

Jan Bernard/2nd
Ann Evans/1st
*Pat Evans/4th
*Vickie Roscoe/3rd
Virgie Blakney/K

2. Assessment

Marie Crawford/4th
Laura Lee/4th
Vickie Matacotta/3rd
*Pam Roach/K

3. District Issues

*C. Jurick/Principal
*J. Timmons/Asst. Principal
J. Jones/District Coord. of Evaluation
K. Claybar/Asst. Superintendent
B. Bush/District Dir. of SD
P. Rooks/Dir. of Elem. Educa.

INSTRUCTIONAL STRATEGIES

5. Listening

Chuck Black/PE
*Sandra Ergle/LSS
Sheri Kress/K
Linda Lambert/3rd
Pam Carson/2nd
Susan Mullis/5th

7. Centers

Terri Browne/Speech
Margaret Caudle/4th
*Jan Clos/3rd
Anna Garretson/Music
Charlene Kennedy/SpEd
Lori LeVan/1st
Sandra Middleton/S/A

6. Spelling

Lori Bagwell/3rd
Terry Elmore/Tech
Dionne Lipscomb/SNK
*Judy Mize/2nd
Nancy Northern/1st
Karen Ricketts/5th

4. Computer Software

Nicole Cassara/SpEd
Lorry de la Croix/Med.Sp
*Jan Fogarty/1st
Adrienne McAuley/4th
Veronica Stubbs/2nd
Wanze Walston/K

9. Listening

*Pat Chadwick/2nd
Pam Britton/Counselor
Jayne Hebert/Art
Martha Stamps/5th
Anne Voyles/4th
Robin Wallman/1st

8. Centers/Multiple Intel.

Susan Blunk/Speech
Janey Gill/Counselor
*Cheryl Harvey/Target
Kim Hughes/1st
Alana Reynolds/5th
Carol Surber/Preschool
Pat Tillery/3rd

10. Critical Thinking

Kristie Lewis/SpEd
Mary Lynn Gaughan/2nd
Carolyn Johnson/PE
Amy Koenning/S/A
Lorraine Long/K
*Dixie Minor/5th

* Focus Team member

SOURCE: Diligent work by the certified staff of Addison Elementary School, Marietta Georgia; reprinted by permission.

Bryant Elementary School
SURVEY

Teachers:
Please help us evaluate the current status of the study group process.
Thank you.
The Study Group Focus Team

1. Are you seeing any change in your classrooms as a result of what you are doing in your study groups?

   ____ too early to tell
   ____ I am trying some of the ideas
   ____ I can see that my new learnings are impacting the students

2. How do you rate the overall effectiveness of study groups for professional development?

   Low   1   2   3   4   5   High

3. After reviewing the stages of high performing teams/groups, where do you think your group is?

   ____ orientation ___ dissatisfaction ____ resolution ____ performing

4. What suggestions do you have for improving the study group process?

PLEASE RETURN THIS TO SHEILA JONES BY NOVEMBER 1.

SOURCE: Reprinted by permission from Bryant Elementary School, Mableton, Georgia.

BROCHURE (ONE SIDE) ONE STUDY GROUP
DID TO SHARE WITH WHOLE
FACULTY WHAT THEY HAD LEARNED.

MOTIVATING LITERACY AT BRYANT

The following pamphlet is an outgrowth of Bryant Elementary School's program, Participating Actively with Study Groups. It is intended to be an aid for teachers at Bryant and other schools who wish to create literate environments in the classrooms.

Included in this pamphlet are ideas to promote and foster literacy by motivating students in a variety of ways. Also included are assessment tools and a list of literacy materials available at Bryant.

The members of the study group are Tracey Orenstein (5th Grade), Mike Porterfield (4th Grade), Laura Powers (3rd Grade), Diane Brannen (1st Grade), Marleen Ensley (SIA), and Will Rumbaugh (Assistant Principal). For further information, call (770) 732-5697.

Bryant Elementary School
6800 Factory Shoals Road
Mableton, GA 30059

Assessment

Assessment is an integral part of an effective literacy program. It should be a continuous process in which the teacher observes and interacts with the students in a variety of ways. These interactions should include both formal and informal measures that are authentic and relevant to the classroom learning. Assessment of reading behaviors, reading strategies, and reading comprehension include, but are not limited to, the following:

- Observational Checklists;
- Anecdotal Record Keeping;
- Portfolio Assessment;
- Informal Reading Inventories;
- Running Records;
- Criterion-Referenced Standardized Tests;
- Student Self-Assessments.

More information on these types of assessments can be found in the Professional Library located in the school Media Center.

Reading Resources

The following is a current list of literacy materials available at Bryant

- Literature Anthologies (Houghton Mifflin): Primary & Intermediate;
- SIA Reading Materials: Primary;
- Rigby Reading Materials (Literacy 2000): Primary & Intermediate;
- Sunshine Books (Wright Group): Primary;
- Class Sets of Novels and Varied Literature: Primary & Intermediate;
- Reading Center Materials (Provided by Teachers): Primary & Intermediate;
- Multi-Media Reading Materials (Media Center): Primary & Intermediate;
- Phonics Materials (School Zone/Frank Schaffer): Primary;
- Literature/Reading Teaching Kits (Media Center): Primary & Intermediate
- Letter People (Alpha I): Primary.
- Letter Island Kit (Sullivan & Associates): Primary;
- Guided Reading by Fountas/Pinnell (Media Center): Primary & Intermediate;
- Holistic Reading Strategies by Racinski/Podeic: Primary & Intermediate.

Expository Text Motivation

Instructional strategies for ensuring student comprehension of expository texts must incorporate understanding about readers' interactions with the text, the teacher, and with each other.

GUIDELINES FOR EFFECTIVE INSTRUCTION:
- Activate and engage the readers' backgrounds before reading begins;
- Encourage text predictions;
- Assist students with evaluations of their own efforts;
- Foster cooperative involvement and joint problem solving.

PRE-READING ACTIVITIES:
- Word Sorts;
- Brainstorming;
- Anticipation Guides;
- K-W-L;
- Jackdaws;
- Experiments;
- Demonstrations;
- Media/Audio-Visual presentations.

READING STRATEGIES:
- Directed Reading-Thinking Activity;
- Dialectic/Double-Entry Journal;
- Save the Last Word for Me.

POST-READING ACTIVITIES:
- Distinctive Features Activity;
- Herringbone;
- Guided Reading;
- Writing in a Learning Log;
- Preparing a class newspaper/magazine;
- Preparing artistic representations such as murals, pictures, sculptures, or dioramas;
- Participating in skits or role-playing activities.

SOURCE: Reprinted by permission from Bryant Elementary School, Mableton, Georgia.

Bryant Elementary School
May 5, 1996

The following information is the result of the discussions teachers had in the study groups last week. Study groups were asked to discuss the groups' preferences for the organization of study groups for next school year. Since Bryant is completing its first year of having all faculty in study groups, it is unclear how to proceed into a new year. Groups were asked to indicate one of the following:

1. Stay together as a group and continue present work
2. Stay together as a group and address another student need
3. Disband forming new groups

The results are as follows:

Study Group	Choice
1. Instructional practices	2
2. Brain-based learning	1
3. Reading	3
4. Project Outreach	1
5. Discipline	3
6. Interactive writing	1
7. Reading motivation	3
8. Teaching strategies	1
9. Curriculum compacting	1

Three (3) groups want to disband and form new groups. This means that there are, at this time, eighteen (18) teachers that will regroup. In August, those teachers will meet and decide how they will group themselves into no less than three (3) groups. Each group will decide the student need that the group will address.

The Instructional Council will review the Study Group Reflective Exercise that each group completed. The Council will also use the comments and suggestions that were made on the individual evaluation forms to consider adjustments that need to be made to make next year even more successful than this year.

Whole Faculty Study Group Schedule
March 20 - May 17, 1997
Murdock Elementary

March 20, 1997 - To follow brief staff meeting   1.

March 27, 1997 *Group #*   March 28, 1997 *Group #*   2.
```
7:30-8:30  -   8                     7:30-8:30  -  10
8:40-9:40  -   6                     8:40-9:40  -   2
9:50-10:50 -  11                     9:50-10:50 -   4
                                    11:00-12:00 -   9
                                    12:10-1:10  -   5
                                     1:20-2:20  -   3 & 7
```

Group 1 will meet on Thursday as previously scheduled.

April 3, 1997 - To follow brief staff meeting   3.

April 16, 1997 *Group #*   April 17, 1997 *Group #*   4.
```
7:30-8:30  -   3 & 7                 7:30-8:30  -  11
8:40-9:40  -  10                     8:40-9:40  -   8
9:50-10:50 -   2                     9:50-10:50 -   6
11:00-12:00 -   4
12:10-1:10  -   9
1:20-2:20  -   5
```

Group 1 will meet on Thursday as previously scheduled.

April 24, 1997 *Group #*   April 25, 1997 *Group #*   5.
```
7:30-8:30  -   5                     7:30-8:30  -   6
8:40-9:40  -   3 & 7                 8:40-9:40  -   8
9:50-10:50 -  10                     9:50-10:50 -  11
11:00-12:00 -   2
12:10-1:10  -   4
1:20-2:20  -   9
```

Group 1 will meet as previously scheduled.

May 1, 1997 - To follow brief staff meeting   6.

May 7, 1997 *Group #*   May 8, 1997 *Group #*   7.
```
7:30-8:30  -   9                     7:30-8:30  -  11
8:40-9:40  -   5                     8:40-9:40  -   6
9:50-10:50 -   3 & 7                 9:50-10:50 -   8
11:00-12:00 -  10
12:10-1:10  -   2
1:20-2:20  -   4
```

Group 1 will meet as previously scheduled.

May 17, 1997 - To follow brief staff meeting   8.
```
              Last meeting for 1996-1997 school year
              Study Groups will begin September, 1997
```

SKY VIEW ELEMENTARY SCHOOL

TO: All Sky View Certified Staff

FROM: Susan and Carolyn

RE: Tentative Schedule for Study Groups

Study groups will be formed and ready to go by the end of January 1997. By then, all of our preliminary work for organizing groups and identifying student needs will be completed. The following dates are scheduled for weekly study group meetings and include a combination of staff meetings (SM) from 2:45-4:00 p.m. and one-hour release time (RT) during which substitutes will be provided. On the days your study group meets during the one-hour release time, the time of day will rotate so that groups are not out of the same classroom period each time. If we have eight (8) study groups, we will need to schedule them over a 1 ½ day period.

The dates were scheduled with consideration to "This Year At A Glance" calendar in the staff lounge, therefore, taking into consideration any scheduled field trips, etc. If you know of conflicts that have not been posted, please see Susan ASAP to see if a schedule change can be worked out.

DAY	DATE	TYPE	TIME
Tuesday/Wednesday	January 28/29	RT	TBA
Thursday	February 6	SM	3:00-4:00
Wednesday/Thursday	February 12/13	RT	TBA
Thursday	February 20	SM	3:00-4:00
Thursday/Friday	February 27/28	RT	TBA
Thursday	March 6	SM	3:00-4:00
CONFERENCE WEEK	March 10-14	NO STUDY GROUPS	
Monday/Tuesday	March 17/18	RT	TBA
Thursday	March 27	SM	3:00-4:00
Thursday	April 3	SM	3:00-4:00
SPRING BREAK	April 7	NO STUDY GROUPS	
Thursday	April 17	SM	3:00-4:00
Tuesday/Wednesday	April 22/23	RT	TBA
Thursday	May 1	SM	3:00-4:00
Wednesday/Thursday	May 7/8	RT	TBA
Thursday	May 15	SM	3:00-4:00

SOURCE: Reprinted by permission from Sky View Elementary School.

ROUND ROCK HIGH SCHOOL
Round Rock, Texas
Dr. Lynn Russell, Principal

On August 7, 1997 the faculty of Round Rock High School made a decision that will impact faculty and students at RRHS for years to come. With a 93% majority, the 216 teachers and administrators voted for study groups to be the primary staff development model here at RRHS. This means that there will be at least 34 study groups that will meet every two weeks for the 1997-98 school year. Each of the study groups has tentatively selected an area of focus. The following list is the areas that have been identified. The Study Group Action Plans that are due by October 1 will more clearly specify the student needs that each group will address.

1. Research-based instructional strategies
2. Classroom management: "The Effective Teacher" by Harry Wong
3. Brain-based learning strategies
4. Creative teaching strategies or how to made school fun
5. Cooperative learning strategies (both intradisciplinary and interdisciplinary)
6. Youth Empowering Systems
7. Building self-esteem
8. How to get students to pursue their educational priorities on a daily basis; student accountability and responsibility; intrinsic motivation
9. Increase student morale, school spirit, and participation in school activities
10. Helping 9th graders be more successful
11. High expectations
12. Respect for diversity, possibly using the book Poverty
13. Skills and techniques for working with athletics to keep them academically eligible to participate
14. Adolescent development and learning
15. Guidance/mentoring/advising students
16. ZAP (zeros are not permitted)
17. Career development, school to work transition, community modeling in classes
18. Connecting classroom learning to the real world
19. Increase family-community involvement in the classroom
20. Time management of block scheduling (what to do with 90 minutes)
21. Increase vocabulary in all subjects
22. How to integrate core subjects
23. How can non-core subjects help the core subjects
24. Cross curriculum mini-writing projects
25. Motivation of at risk and low level students
26. Motivation of "the average" or middle of the road student
27. Appropriate communication in all classrooms
28. Reading programs
29. Using current events in the classroom

SOURCE: Reprinted by permission from Round Rock High School, Round Rock, Texas.

30. Technology: Integrating into the curriculum
31. Technology: Graphing and programmable calculators
32. Technology: The internet as a research tool
33. Improving test scores: AP, TAAS, SAT, end of year exams

34. + Content specific groups indicated interest in

  - dealing with the new TEKS
  - making manipulatives and activities
  - incorporating a new textbook and supplementary materials

Teachers in the following content areas want to form groups.

  - Chemistry
  - A+ / credit plus
  - Spanish
  - Algebra I and II
  - Business law
  - Physics
  - Special Ed. English
  - Government

The Focus Team will keep everyone informed of the work of all the study groups. Be on the lookout for a newsletter that will FOCUS on study groups. Share your ideas with us!

Focus Team Members:

Barbara Baker, Social Studies department
Ginny Jones, Spanish department
Sandy Kinn-Burks, Science department
Elizabeth McGonigal, English department
Gordon Perez, Administration

September 15, 1997

SOURCE: Reprinted by permission from Round Rock High School, Round Rock, Texas.

Target Groups
Newsletter

On Target

Round Rock High
School Faculty

Volume 1, Issue 1

December 1997

Teachers comment on Target Groups

For many teachers, Target Groups furnish a way to do what we do anyway, but in a cooperative work setting. Here are a few comments from the Surveys.

* Working together to plan activities and discuss teaching methods has been a GIFT....the best use of my inservice time....Absolutely [beneficial]! It relates directly to what we are doing on a day to day basis.

* ...good way to integrate new teachers....five new ideas for lab or demonstrations already.

* What our group is trying to resolve requires that we communicate and come to agreement with each other, and we are effective at doing this....We are getting rid of "old" stuff or inappropriate material and upgrading our subject matter. Our new material is more current and meaningful to our students, and they will benefit from our efforts.

* All Algebra I and II students have functions and graphing. We are developing materials/activities for all teachers to use.

* It is a great opportunity to learn from my colleagues. The perfect form of professional development....

* Working on C++ programming and curriculum is the most important thing computer science teachers can do. Most workshops do not apply to my classroom.

* I really enjoy my group! We discuss and find ways to improvement [Harry Wong's] policies into our classrooms.

* As a first-year teacher, I am learning bunches from the experienced teachers in the Target Group.

* All four of us communicate openly and honestly to compile curriculum that will suit the needs of our students. They (the students) are our focal point for creating/updating the chemistry curriculum.

* This is a great opportunity for a first-year teacher to get some helpful hints on presentation of materials/curriculum while implementing the new TEKS and RRISD's standards in science.

* The chemistry curriculum target group prepares me, as an educator, to give each student an opportunity to be successful in chemistry, and this spills over into the biology standards and expectations.

* I love the update on technology! I am more efficient with letting my students know their grades. We've been using the slide show for presentations—awesome!

* We get to work on what we feel we need to work on.

TARGET GROUP
SURVEY

Sandy Kinn-Burks reports that the Target Group Survey, distributed the last week in October, indicates general satisfaction with the new staff development program. On a scale of 1-5, five means greatest satisfaction; the results of the survey are from the responses of 59 teachers.

1. The dialogue with my colleagues is effective.
Average Score: 4.44

2. The subject or content of my target group is worthwhile.
Average Score: 4.68

3. I feel my target group study will be beneficial to the students in my classroom.
Average Score: 4.46

From Edna Harris, Staff Development

On October 16, Carlene Murphy, a nationally known consultant in the area of target groups, was on campus to meet with this campus core team. Several members of the core team have worked closely with Carlene for the last two years.

In addition to Round Rock ISD, Carlene's work currently takes her to Seattle, Washington: Boston, Massachusetts; San Diego, California; Philadelphia, Pennsylvania; and several school districts across the nation. Although Carlene consults with campuses serving a wide variety of student populations, she has taken a special interest in Round Rock High School.

This is the largest high school implementing this "grass roots" staff development effort. She always comments on the professionalism exhibited by the Round Rock High School staff as they work together to refine their classroom instructional skills.

Look for Round Rock High School to appear in Carlene's soon to be published articles and book.

Note: At RRHS "study groups" are called "target groups."

REPORTS FROM GROUPS WORKING ON TARGET

Here are just a few of the interesting projects underway in Target Groups. Information on other groups will appear in later newsletters.

Physics Homework Generator
-Steve Watson, Skip Richardson, Ted Hervey

We are looking at ways to integrate UT physics into homework assistance by computer or touch-tone telephone and eventually having exams on line so they may be accessed 24 hours a day for a specific time period and with immediate feedback on scores.

Chemistry Curriculum
-Debby Reddig, Carl Ingraham, Kelly Wedding, Jane Coburn

We are integrating current updated labs and classroom activities into the chemistry curriculum to conform to new chemistry TEKS.

Parent/Student Commitment to AP
-Jan Redden, Sharon Langerhans, Jill Wetzig, Randall Frizzell, Jenny Esler, Denise George

We want to cut down on schedule changes and get stronger commitments from students and parents. So far we have done the following:

1. Researched criteria requirements for AP classes.
2. Written content-specific AP contracts and course descriptions.
3. Worked on a required meeting for AP teachers, parents, and students at the end of January or the beginning of February.
4. Met Nov. 3 with counselors and Registrar and all AP teachers (Agenda: scheduling of AP classes and criteria requirements.)
5. Discussed changes in AP booklet that is given to students/parents.

Student Motivation
-Susie Baird, Tracy Mandeville, Peggy Grow, JoLea Telotta, Barbara Cromwell, Cindy Teich

Our target group is studying methods of helping students become self-motivated. We are reading/studying Stephen Covey's book The 7 Habits of Highly Effective People. We are truly enjoying the study (even the donuts!) It is sometimes hard to get together, but it has always been worth the effort.

News or announcements for your Target Groups?

Drop a note, article, or update in Elizabeth McGonigal's or Patrick Schmidt's mailbox.

TARGET GROUPS COVER DIVERSE FIELDS

Our Target Groups follow logically into five areas, with a fairly even distribution of groups in each of the following areas.

✳**Using Technology**
-Computer Applications/Integration
-Physics Homework Generator
-Utilizing Graphic Calculators
-Researching on the Internet and Application
-Introduction to C++

✳**Student/Parent Involvement**
-Student Morale (3)
-Student Motivation
-Increase Family/Community Involvement
-Parent/Student Commitment to AP
-YES Program

✳**Students/Jobs**
-School to Work (Career, Tech & Special Ed.)
-School to Work (Coop Teachers)
-School to Work (Real World Transition)

✳**Curriculum Writing**
-TAAS Scores
-Social Studies Curriculum
-Spanish Curriculum
-Chemistry Curriculum
-Physical Science Target Group
-Content Specific Curriculum
-Algebra I and II
-Special Ed. English

✳**Teaching Strategies**
-Portfolio Assessment
-Vertical Coordination Between 9th & 10th Pre-AP English
-Higher Expectations
-"The Effective Teacher" (2)
-Creative Teaching Strategies
-Integration of AUEN
-Identify Educational Priorities

✳ Special thanks:

To Sylvia Williams, junior, and Jason Smith, junior, for excellent help with the On Target masthead and newsletter layout/design.

SOURCE: Used by permission from Round Rock High School, Round Rock, Texas

Brushy Creek Crier

Published by the Brushy Creek Elementary School PTA   October, 1997

From the Assistant Principal

Dear Brushy Creek Parents,

What a pleasure this school year has been thus far! We have thoroughly enjoyed having the students and staff of Great Oaks Elementary with us and we have received very positive feedback from both parents and staff regarding how smoothly the two schools have run on one campus! A great deal of the credit for this goes to you, our parents, who have been so co-operative and willing to work with us. Thank you for your terrific support!

School is moving right along and Brushy Creek continues to be a community of learners. As one would expect, the children are studying and learning daily, but did you know that our staff members are students, too? Last year we were trained in the Whole-Faculty Study Group process and as a result implemented faculty study groups to address topics relevant to children, learning, education, teaching, etc.

This year we have chosen as the primary focus for our study groups the following topics: Math, Technology and Literacy. Staff members will form small groups focusing on subtopics of these main categories. Those interested in pursuing the area of mathematics might combine, for example, into various groups to research math assessment, math labs, the use of math in the real world, problem solving or the integration of math, science and technology. The topics are endless and the enthusiasm for learning is high!

Study groups meet every other Thursday afternoon and share their findings, successes and questions with one another and then also spend time addressing strategies for achieving the

(continued on next page)

From the PTA President

Dear Parents, Students and Teachers,

What a terrific beginning. September came and went and our PTA is already going strong with several exciting activities. This past month was our Membership Drive, however if you have not joined and would like to, it's never too late. Your membership dues to the PTA are of great value in supporting Brushy Creek Elementary by giving us the ability to provide many programs and materials for the school. For example, we are able to sponsor Odyssey of the Mind, Reflections, the Child Identification Program, Clothes Closet and Cultural Arts programs. In addition we provide educational software, TAAS enrichment materials and books to name a few. September also ended our Innisbrook fundraising project which was a great success! Your support is greatly appreciated by all the students and staff of Brushy Creek Elementary.

October marks the month to focus on Community Involvement. El Chico night proved to be a great way to bring our families and community together and we will continue this type of involvement with a Putt-Putt night on October 10th. This month is also Crime Prevention Month. As parents, our children's safety is always a major concern. To address these concerns, the Texas PTA in partnership with Texas High School Coach's Association is implementing a Child Identification Program. A kit can be purchased through the PTA. The program is for children ages three and up. Further information will be included in the Tuesday folders. Remember....we are the ones who make a difference in the lives of our children.

I would like to mention a few of the activities that are cur-

(continued on next page)

SOURCE: Used by permission from Brushy Creek Elementary School, Round Rock, Texas.

(continued from previous page, Assistant Principal)

goals they formulated as a group. Research on Whole Faculty Study Groups indicates that six is the maximum number of participants a group should have to be effective, therefore no group exceeds that number.

Our study groups met with great success last year and we anticipate another year of new learning for our staff, and ultimately improved achievement and an increased desire of learning for our students. As educators we are keenly aware of the importance of being life-long learners and we welcome the opportunity for continued professional growth.

I am very excited about this school year and all the possibilities it brings. Feel free to let me know if I can be of assistance to you or your child in any way. I am eagerly looking forward to working with you.

Sincerely,
Lane Mason

VOLUNTEER OPPORTUNITIES

THANKS A MILLION to our CAFETERIA MONITORS. Vicki Wells, Georgia Miller, Karen Sherer and Marie Piña have been assisting with monitoring during our very busy lunch periods. Monitors are still needed, however, and you may be able to help. Monitors assist younger students in opening food packages (milk cartons, juice boxes, ketchup packets, etc.), exhibiting correct behavior and entering/exiting the cafeteria. This is a fabulous way to become acquainted with all our students. Call Michelle Garcia to volunteer (255-8476).

UPCOMING OPPORTUNITY!! Volunteer NOW to help in the Brushy Creek PTA concession booth at the Celtic Festival, October 11-12, 1997. Selling popcorn/lemonade at this Saturday/Sunday festival offers working parents an opportunity to get involved outside of regular school hours. Call Michelle if you'd like to help with this FUN FAMILY event!

THANKS TO ALL OUR PARENT AND COMMUNITY VOLUNTEERS!! YOU TRULY MAKE BRUSHY CREEK A WONDERFUL SCHOOL EXPERIENCE!!

(continued from previous page, PTA President)

rently going on at school: Ice Cream is now being sold, Odyssey of the Mind is beginning and the School Directory will be completed soon. If you have any questions regarding PTA, please feel free to contact me at home by calling 255-6360.

I would like to thank all of the parents for helping to maintain a safe environment while dropping students off before school and picking up after school. The lines may be long, but our children and their safety are worth the wait.

Finally, a special thanks to all the volunteers for contributing their time and energy for our school. We are better together.

Sincerely,
Margaret Bomkamp

Cultural Arts

Welcome back to school students, staff and parents. We hope you all had a great and relaxing summer. Your PTA will again strive to bring you diverse and educational experiences through Cultural Arts Programming. Your support of PTA makes this possible — thank you to all members.

We thank Martha Walsh, Kindergarten Teacher, who arranged for the Celtic musical demonstration in September. Students enjoyed this program and got a preview of what can be enjoyed at the 1st Annual Celtic Festival, October 11th and 12th. PTA will have a booth selling popcorn and lemonade. We hope to see you all there for a day of family fun and sharing where you can enjoy traditional Irish and Scottish music, dance, arts and crafts, and music and language workshops. Again, thank you Mrs. Walsh for a wonderful preview of this upcoming festival.

MR. WIZARD'S *"EVERYDAY ENERGY IN ACTION"*
October 28, 1997, 8:15 and 9:15 a.m.

What is Energy? How do you use energy in your home? What can you do every day to save energy? Through experiments and volunteer audience participation, Mr. Wizard's assistant will show us the answers to these questions and more in this month's program.

Remember: Your "extra mile" courtesy will shine out in next month's newsletter if your class thanks our special guests by way of letter and/or drawings. Be a pacesetter and join the "Extra Mile" club where Blue Jay manners and courtesy always stand out!

Lynn Morozink
Cultural Arts, PTA

SOURCE: Used by permission from Brushy Creek Elementary School, Round Rock, Texas.

JACKSON ELEMENTARY SCHOOL
2002 25th Street
Greeley, CO 80634
970-352-3757
Fax: 970-395-7468

END OF SCHOOL YEAR CELEBRATION!

March 17, 1997

Dr. Carlene Murphy
961 Heard Avenue
Augusta, GA 30904

Dear Carlene:

Well, we've made it to spring break. The year has gone by very quickly. It seems like our meeting in Atlanta was a long time ago.

I thought I might take this opportunity to fill you in on our Whole Faculty Study Group progress, and where we (Jackson School) are headed.

First, I will be sending you a videotape that shows our progress through December 9, 1996. I think you will be pleasantly surprised.

On April 7, we will hold our final sharing session. This will mark the end of the first phase of our WFSG process. At the end of this session, we will no longer have eight heterogeneous study groups focusing on areas within mathematics.

Here's what we think the afternoon of April 7 will look like, sound like, and be like:

[Played to the theme song of Dragnet]

Key Question:

> If you, as a study group, were under investigation for connecting effectively (or having the capacity to) with students, to increase student achievement in mathematics, what would three newspaper headlines read like (to be written on picture of magnifying glass)?

This question will be furnished to study groups Monday, March 24.

SOURCE: Reprinted by permission from Jackson Elementary School, Greeley, Colorado.

Dr. Carlene Murphy
Page 2
March 17, 1997

To begin the afternoon, RoeAnn Wallin has purchased a few hundred red jaw breakers (hard candy). These jaw breakers represent school districts in Colorado. Into this mix will be one different colored piece of hard candy. This piece will represent Jackson School. The point we'll try to make is that we (Jackson), and a few other schools around the country are involved in a unique and significant innovation.

Each study group will then share their headlines and progress with the entire staff. We feel the headlines are important so that each study group can bring value to what they've learned. [Note: This idea was given to us by Dr. Sharon Carson, our District's Professional Developer.]

After each study group has presented, they will be given one last task. Each group will be given two very large jigsaw puzzle pieces. Study groups will be asked to answer the following questions:

> When you think about Colorado, what makes it unique? The group will then use their response to answer this stem: **Study groups is like** _____ **because.....**

> What's the group's favorite fruit or vegetable? The group will then use their response to answer this stem: **Participating in Study Groups is like** _____ **because** .....

After each group presents their answers, we'll put the jigsaw puzzle together, turn it over, and look at something that captures the essence of our work. We haven't thought of what that might be, yet!

We'll end the afternoon with refreshments, and a magnifying glass for everyone as a token of our appreciation.

As always, we'll videotape this session, and send it to you. We'll keep in touch and let you know of our progress.

Thanks for all your help.

Sincerely,
Barry and The Focus Team

p.s. - Is the 1997 Rendezvous being planned?

■

SOURCE: Reprinted by permission from Jackson Elementary School, Greeley, Colorado.

Lyons, Kansas

Information for Whole-Faculty Study Groups:

Stages of Innovations

	Extended Opportunity to Learn	Instructional Delivery Strategies	Organizational Changes	Early Interventions	Climate of High Expectations	Coalitions & Partnerships
Extended Day	⊗				⊗	
Summer School	⊗		⊗		⊗	
Parents as Teachers	☒			☒		☒
All Day Kindergarten	☒		☒	☒		
Reading Recovery				☒	☒	
Accelerated Reader		☒				
Alignment of Curriculum and Instruction		⊗	⊗		⊗	
LEEP (At-Risk Kids)	☒	☒		☒	☒	
Ten Sigma Model			⊗		⊗	
Pre-School	⊗		⊗	⊗		
TESA		△			△	
Teaming		△	△			
Block Schedule		△	△			
CCC Lab	⊗	⊗		⊗	⊗	
Inquiry Method		△				
Inductive Reasoning		⊗				
Brain Research		△				
Integrated thematic Units		△				
Everyday Math		⊗				
Whole Language & Phonics		⊗				
6 Trait Writing		☒				
Reading in Content Area		☒				
Learning Center	⊗		⊗			⊗
CBE—Community Based Education	☒					☒
Plato Lab	⊗	⊗			⊗	
Goals 2000 Project			⊗		⊗	
5 Minute Daily Math		☒				
Hands on Science		⊗				
Cooperative Learning		⊗				
Local Assessments	△	⊗			⊗	
ITBS			☒	☒		
Kansas Assessments		⊗	⊗		⊗	

△ = RESEARCHING   ⊗ = DEVELOPING   ☒ = FULL IMPLEMENTATION

SARAH COBB NEWSPAPER

A Community of Learners - An Environment for Success

November 22, 1993   *1901 Valley Drive*   *924-4888*

Invent America Winner

Sarah Cobb School is very proud of Nichole Berger, 3rd grade TAG student of Mrs. Marsha Fisher. Nichole was last year's second grade winner of the Invention Convention. Nichole learned that she was the Georgia 2nd grade winner in September. In October, she found out that she was the 10-state regional winner for Invent America! Her invention, the "Night Helper", is now being considered for the National Invent America competition.

Since her invention has been in the news, Nichole has been on 2 local television news shows: Midday in Cordele and Town & Country in Albany. Mrs. Fisher is in the process of planning this year's Invention Convention. The competition is scheduled for February 24, 1994. Mrs. Fisher would like to have participants from all classes, including TAG and Enrichment classes. She hopes teachers will allow their students to enter this year's competition. In the meantime, we wish Nichole all the best with her winning invention.

Accelerated Reader at Sarah Cobb

On Monday, November 15th, posters appeared all over Sarah Cobb: "AR is coming!" Students were asking "What is AR?" Guesses abounded. Friday, November 19th was the kick-off day for Accelerated Reader at Sarah Cobb. Students gathered around the flagpole. Mrs. Daniel's fourth grade class paraded around with posters. These posters gave clues to what AR was going to be. Ms. Brooks' third grade class presented predictions made by students about what AR might be. One hundred balloons were released and the fun has begun.

Accelerated Reader is a computer program where students can take tests over books that they have read. Students will earn points for each book test passed and receive prizes for attaining certain levels. The Sarah Cobb PTO is supporting this reading improvement program by purchasing the incentives. Thank you PTO. So Sarah Cobb Students, JUST READ, READ, READ!

Sarah Cobb Study Groups

Sarah Cobb's quest for school improvement is continuing. Meetings were held to discuss our plan for improving student achievement with teacher study groups. On October 26th and November 9th parents were invited to hear plans for a weekly early release day for Sarah Cobb students. Under this plan all students would be dismissed at 1:30 each Wednesday. Parents have responded to surveys about childcare needs for such a day. We appreciate your support and cooperation. If you have any questions or concerns, please call the school.

National Children's Book Week

During the week of November 15th - 19th, Sarah Cobb celebrated National Children's Book Week. Several classes decorated their doors with a scene from their favorite book. Some classes decorated bulletin boards or walls. During the week we had people from the community read to various classes. Several classes celebrated by making bookmarks, book jackets, mobiles, and dioramas. Wednesday, November 17th was "Book Character Dress Up Day". Students and teachers dressed up as a character from their favorite book. On that day we had characters like Daniel Boone, Paul Bunyan, Harriet Tubman, and Miss Viola Swamp in our school. It was a lot of fun!

SOURCE: Reprinted by permission from Sarah Cobb Elementary School, Americus, Georgia.

Georgia Department of Education
Werner Rogers, State Superintendent of Schools

Public Information and Publications Division
2052 Twin Towers East • Atlanta, Georgia 30334
(404) 656-2476 • Fax (404) 651-9330

November 12, 1993

<u>For immediate release</u>

State Board Grants Waivers for System Innovations

Increased opportunities for teachers to study and plan together...

A plan that will allow teachers to govern all aspects of their school's operation...

Two innovative approaches to increasing the number of students who complete school...

An expanded teacher evaluation program...

These are the latest approved programs in the State Board of Education's continuing effort to encourage flexibility and innovation in local schools and districts by granting waivers of specific rules at the request of local boards of education.

The board granted the five waivers at its November meeting: two for Americus City Schools, one for Calhoun City, one for Glascock County and one for Stephens County. All were approved for three years contingent on annual progress and evaluation reports by each school district to the state board.

⟶ **At Sarah Cobb Elementary School In Americus,** one school day per week will be shortened to allow school faculty two hours per week to study, work and plan together to create integrated instruction across curriculum lines and to have weekly grade group meetings. Four days per week, the instructional day for students will be from 8:30 a.m. to 3:10 p.m. The fifth day will be from 8:30 a.m. to 1:30 p.m., allowing teachers two hours that day for group work. Students will receive a total of 1,750 minutes of instruction per week, 250 minutes more than the 1,500 minutes required by the state board.

ATLAS Summer 1997 Institute
" From Theory to Practice: Tools for Implementation"

Memphis, TN

Memphis City Schools has identified performance assessment as a tool to be used in all schools.   The schools that have all faculty in study groups have a unique opportunity.   How can study groups affect the implementation of performance objectives?

SCHOOL: *Locke Elementary*

STUDY GROUP MEMBERS: *Johnsie Pippin , Mary Seifert, Arlena Mabery, Glenda Ellis , Marilyn Yeager*

YOUR ANSWER TO THE ABOVE QUESTION:

Study groups can enhance the implementation of performance assessment by providing a non-threatening and safe arena for practicing and evaluating our own progress. By working together, we can discuss the development of tasks and the necessary teaching and practicing opportunities needed prior to assessment. We can also better differentiate between those skills best evaluated in this manner and those best served by another. The "theory" of more heads being better than one is definitely a plus in using study groups for this purpose.

SOURCE: Reprinted by permission from Locke Elementary School, Memphis, Tennessee.

WIRED STUDY GROUP

Action Plan

Volume 1 Issue 1

Students Need
To

1) Use technology as a tool for work

2) Use software designed to be instructional in nature - to teach or remediate.

3) Use the internet to locate resources with out plagiarism.

In Our Study Group Teachers will:

1) Locate software that supports the ATLAS project design.
2) Review available software for appropriateness.
3) Demonstrate competency in using various technological resources.
4) Plan for the use of technology with the team approach.
5) Demonstrate how to use the Internet for instructional purposes.
6) Practice using the computer.
7) Locate new Internet cites which will benefit the students' productivity.

INTENDED RESULT OF THE STUDY GROUP: To increase the level of proficiency in the student needs listed above, as evidenced on/by/in:

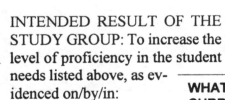

Rashad Sharif
Melody Sias-Linsey
Jackie Brotchner
Patricia Porchiran
Judith Nahlen
Jess Feldman

Team Projects.

Exhibition Production.

Accessing information from the Internet.

Creating new materials.

WHAT WILL BE THE CONTENT OR CURRICULUM OF THE STUDY?
     This would be the materials and other resources the group will use. Review software that is appropriate for use with ATLAS projects. Professional periodicals, magazines, catalogs, research for other schools, TLC programs for training, other NASDQ initiative schools, faculty training on site, Investigate web sites that offer resources for students.

Booker T. Washington High School, Memphis, TN
Elsie L. Bailey, Principal

Booker T. Washington H.S.
Wired Study Group

URL Review

Site Address: *http://www.classroom.net*

Major Content Area: *Classroom Connect Web Site for*

Minor Content Area: *educators*

Grade Level: *K-12*

Publisher: *Classroom Holdings*

Content Standards:
Standard Area   Number
Language Arts Standard 3
_____
_____
_____

Reviewer's Comments: *Classroom Connect offers this free website for educators; it has a multitude of free online resources. Through the G.R.A.D.E.S. database there are 183 links to reference materials such as the Macmillan Information SuperLibrary; College Net; On-line Books Page; Research-It!; New York Times; Virtual Library GEOGRAPHY Links; Web-Louvre-Live from France; Ask Eric; numerous encyclopedias and dictionaries. The Searching Page offers clear and easy to understand instruction on how to conduct a search on the internet as well as a link to numerous search engines.*

Reviewed By: *Brotchner*

SOURCE: Reprinted by permission from Booker T. Washington High School, Memphis, Tennessee.

Study Group Log
Monday, September 22, 1998

Group Members:

Lorene Schaffner	Margret Diede	Peggy Nordwell	Marilyn Enloe
Steve Deutsch	Lynn Holmes	Jan Dionne	

Today's Discussion:

We agreed on the following Group Norms.
- Group members need to be on time (3:45) and prepared with notebook.
- Ideas will be respected and not judged; our group will be a safe place.
- We will listen to one another.
- "Talk here, stays here" within our group.
- We will take time to slow down the "race pace" of the day with reflection, sharing and quiet music.
- Our discussions and work will be directly tied to instruction and to student performance.
- Everyone will have an opportunity to talk and to share their work.
- The group's agenda for the next meeting will be set at the end of a meeting and it will match what our Action Plan states that we will do.
- We will have regular debriefing times to check how we are doing and what is or what is not working for our group.
- Each member will share an equal part in the working of the group, such as:
  - group leader
  - hosting a meeting in their classroom
  - planning the agenda for the next meeting
  - bringing treats

Next Meeting:

Friday, Sept. 26 in Margret's room. We will work on our Action Plan and decide on the organization of the notebook we will keep on our work. We hope to begin our work on the First Steps Writing books so we will need to bring those books with us to the meeting.

Concerns and Recommendation:

Not any so far.

Classroom Application:

Not there yet.

Highland Terrace Elementary School
Shoreline School District
Seattle, WA

SOURCE: Reprinted by permission from Highland Terrace Elementary School, Seattle, Washington.

STUDY GROUP ACTION PLAN
October 6, 1997

GENERAL CATEGORY OF STUDENT NEEDS: *Math writing*
(Content area writing)

SPECIFIC STUDENT NEEDS	TEACHER NEEDS
1. Students need to write about math	1. Read First Steps books on explanations, recounts, and procedures
2. Students need to increase the math content in math writing	2. Get sample of math writing from students
3. Students need a complete understanding of math concepts	3. Compare grade levels/classes of math writing
4. Students need a complete understanding of math processes	4. Look at samples of the Benchmark I and II tests. What are the expectations?
5. Students and teachers need to know strategies to solve problems	5. Get copy of Benchmark II example test (Mark Jewell)
6. Students need to know how to sequence math events	6. How are the standards applied to math writing in the tests?
7. Students need to know specific math vocabulary to be able to write	7. Always do #11 in Try It in the math book.
	8. Math series rubrics
	9. Have students do a pre and post test–we need to find a test the 5/6 haven't done
	10. Create vocabulary quizzes and context sentences for math vocabulary
	11. Have the fourth grade teachers tell us what they know about the Benchmark I tests and scoring

INTENDED RESULT OF THE STUDY GROUP: To increase the level of proficiency in the student needs listed above, as evidenced on:

• improved results on the benchmark one and two tests
• better use of math vocabulary

WHAT WILL BE THE CONTENT OR CURRICULUM OF THE STUDY? This would be the materials and resources (people, speakers) we are aware of that may help us.

• Assessment rubrics in the math series
• Try it #11
• Mark Jewell
• Standards book with ideas and samples
• Benchmark one test practice book
• Fourth grade teachers

R. Randles Study Group Highland Terrace
Shoreline School District
Seattle, WA

SOURCE: Reprinted by permission from Highland Terrace Elementary School, Seattle, Washington.

Study
Teams
Affect
Rising
Scores

Reach For The
STARS
At
Northside Elementary School
Versailles, KY

Note: To fit with Northside's school theme, STARS, the faculty decided to call the study groups "study teams". STARS with its acronym, Study Teams Affect Rising Scores, was displayed throughout the school.

SOURCE: Reprinted by permission from Northside Elementary School, Versailles, Kentucky.

What's going on when school dismisses early on Wednesday?

Whole-faculty problem solving unfolds on seventeen Wednesdays this year to improve the curriculum and instructional practices. Faculty members are meeting in groups of four to six individuals to address needs identified in the school transformation plans.

Boyle County Middle School teachers are (1) revising the mathematics curriculum with an eye to elementary and high school expectations. Teachers are consulting with other mathematics departments and are considering the formation of a county-wide mathematics forum; (2) compiling an inventory of computer software and determining needs to better support the curriculum; (3) developing high level questioning skills; (4) examining classroom management skills in an effort to improve classroom efficiency, effectively resolve discipline problems, and provide resources to be shared with other teachers; (5) developing strategies to improve writing across the curriculum; (6) developing inter-disciplinary units that combine studies from different subject areas; (7) devising strategies to motivate students.

Perryville Elementary groups are studying (1) struggling readers, (2) the technology curriculum, (3) arts and the humanities, (4) the school climate, and (5) preschool parent awareness.

Junction City Elementary groups will (1) create a stronger parent volun-

Reading strategies are the focus of two groups at Perryville Elementary. Reading Recovery diagnostic strategies for the regular classroom and the creation of a video to assist parents who help their children with reading are two ideas being studied. In a future meeting, a textbook representative will share materials designed to help struggling readers. Members of the group include (from Left) Robyn McAfee, Delmer Warren, Cathy Camic, Margaret Moore, Ruthie Young, and (not pictured) Shelia Brummett.

teer program, (2) develop materials and conference forms to help parents better understand the Kentucky Early Learning Profile, (3) study the science curriculum, new state core content, and 95-96 KIRIS released questions.

Woodlawn Elementary groups are (1) developing writing improvement strategies, (2) enhancing arts and humanities instruction, and (3) strengthening the science curriculum.

Boyle County High School teachers have organized to (1) develop end-of-course examinations within the disciplines, (2) address ways to improve writing portfolios and assessment, (3) examine exit criteria for the class of 1999, and study Southern Region Education Board report recommendations pertaining to (4) computer/technical education, (5) science/agriculture/physical education, (6) English/fine arts education.

Perryville primary teachers (from Left) Gayle Best, Marilyn Holderman, and Sue Rodman are addressing the problem of primary students who are too old for preschool but lack necessary primary skills. The law does not allow five year olds to remain in preschool.

Manipulative ways to introduce algebraic equations are among the concerns of this group at Boyle County Middle School. Also, a curriculum alignment with elementary schools is needed to prepare students for seventh grade pre-algebra. Gail Wilson (not pictured), Betsy Hogan, Danny Daugherty, Jody Metcalfe, Ralph McKee II, and Jeff Reese comprise this group.

SOURCE: Reprinted by permission from Boyle County Board of Education, Danville, Kentucky.

What's going on? *continued from page 6*

Arts and Humanities concern this group at Woodlawn Elementary. Brainstorming produced a pilot practice to reinforce in the regular classroom music concepts that are presented in music class.

Drop Everything And Listen (D.E.A.L.) provides ten minutes per week for review of music concepts such as tempo, dynamics, patterns, and repetitions. The group plans to try a similar practice for art concepts.

Members of this group include (from left) Tammy Spratt, Kathy Clark, Joan Czarniecki, Ann Preston, and (not pictured) Max Pope.

Aligning the curriculum with the state's new core content and writing course syllabi have been the focus at Boyle County High School. Science teachers, for instance, examined science, math, reading, and writing course content and concluded that the science curriculum does a good job of addressing the core content recommended by the state. Science teachers are (from left) Nita Morgan, Bart Bredar, Kim Monaghan, Dianne Oliverio, and (not pictured) Karry Williams.

Parent volunteerism is the focus of this group at Junction City Elementary. Members visited four schools in Barren County to bring back information that will help develop a more active volunteer program for Junction City. A volunteer handbook, orientation program and an awareness campaign are being prepared. Veteran Boyle volunteer Harriet Stuart will share organizational ideas used at other schools. Members are (from left) Connie Johnson, Marla Poyner (back to camera), Jerry Leber, Linda Elmore, Cathy Lanham (parent), Jane Pennock, and Barbara Crain.

Boyle County Schools *Insights* is published by the Boyle County Board of Education as a service to the commmunity.

Address inquiries to
Paul Elwyn
Director of Communications
Boyle County High School
1637 Perryville Road
Danville, KY 40422
phone 606-236-5047 ext. 29
fax 606-236-7820

 Boyle County Schools

People making a difference!

Boyle County Schools *Insights*
Boyle County High School
1637 Perryville Road
Danville, KY 40422

Non-profit Org.
U.S. Postage
PAID
Danville, KY
Permit No. 18

**RESIDENT
R001
PERRYVILLE, KY 40468**

References

Birmbaum, R. (1988). *How colleges work: The cybernetics of academic organization and leadership.* San Francisco: Jossey-Bass.

Bradley, A. (1993, March 31). By asking teachers about "context" of work, center moves to the cutting edge of research. *Education Week, 12*(27), 6.

Branson, R. (1987). Why the schools can't improve: The upper limit hypothesis. *Journal of Instructional Development, 10*(1), 7-12.

Conner, D. (1993). *Managing at the speed of change.* New York: Villard.

Covey, S. (1990). *The 7 habits of highly effective people.* New York: Fireside.

Fullan, M., Bennett, B., & Rolheister-Bennett, C. (1990). Linking classroom and school improvement. *Educational Leadership, 47*(8), 13-19.

Fullan, M., & Steigelbauer, S. (1991). *The new meaning of educational change.* New York: Teachers College Press.

Guskey, T. (1990). Integrating innovations. *Educational Leadership, 47*(5), 11-15.

Hall, G., & Hord, S. (1987). *Change in schools: Facilitating the process.* New York: State University of New York Press.

Joyce, B., & Calhoun, E. (1996). *Learning experiences in school renewal: An exploration of five successful programs.* Eugene: University of Oregon Press. (ERIC Document Reproduction Service No. EA 026 696)

Joyce, B., & Showers, B. (1995). *Student achievement through staff development.* New York: Longman.

Joyce, B., & Weil, M. (1994). *Models of teaching.* New York: Prentice Hall.

Kaufman, R., Herman, J., & Watters, K. (1996). *Educational planning: Strategic, tactical, and operational.* Lancaster, PA: Technomic.

Levine, D., & Eubanks, E. (1989). *Site-based management: Engine for reform or pipedream?* Manuscript submitted for publication.

Lewis, A. (1997, May/June). A new consensus emerges on the characteristics of good professional development. *The Harvard Letter, 13*(3), 3.

Little, J. (1990). The persistence of privacy: Autonomy and initiative in teachers' professional relations. *Teachers College Record, 91*(4), 509-536.

Little, J. (1993, Summer). Teachers' professional development in a climate of educational reform. *Educational Evaluation and Policy Analysis,* 129-151.

Louis, K.S., Kruse, S.D., & Marks, H.M. (1996). Schoolwide professional community. In F. M. Newmann (Ed.), *Authentic achievement: Restructuring schools for intellectual quality.* San Francisco: Jossey-Bass.

Murphy, C. (1991). Lessons from a journey into change. *Educational Leadership, 48*(8), 63-67.

Murphy, C. (1995). Whole-faculty study groups: Doing the seemingly undoable. *Journal of Staff Development, 16*(3), 37-44.

Murphy, C. (1997). *Training handbook for whole-faculty study groups.* Unpublished manuscript.

National Staff Development Council. (1994). *National Staff Development Council's standards for staff development.* Oxford, OH: Author.

Richardson, J. (1996, October). School culture: A key to improved student learning. *The School Team Innovator,* 1 & 4.

Riley, P. (1994). *The winner within.* Encino, CA: Berkeley Books.

Rosenholtz, S. (1989). *Teacher's workplace: The social organization of schools.* New York: Longman.

Saphier, J., & King, M. (1985, March). Good seeds grow in strong cultures. *Educational Leadership, 42*(6), 67-74.

Senge, P. (1990). *The fifth discipline: The art and practice of the learning organization.* New York: Currency.

Webster's NewWorld Dictionary (2nd ed.). (1986). New York: Prentice Hall.

Wieman, H. (1990). *Man's ultimate commitment.* Denton, TX: Foundation for the Philosophy of Creativity.

Recommended Reading

Blanchard, K., Carew, D., & Parisi-Carew, E. (1990). *The one minute manager builds high performance teams.* Escondido, CA: Blanchard Training and Development.

Calhoun, E. (1993). Action research: Three approaches. *Educational Leadership, 51*(2), 62-65.

Charles, L., Clark, P., Roudebush, J., Budnick, S., Brown, M., & Turner, P. (1995). Study groups in practice. *Journal of Staff Development, 16*(3), 49-53.

Hord, S., Rutherford, W., Huling-Austin, L., & Hall, G. (1987). *Taking charge of change.* Alexandria, VA: Association for Supervision and Curriculum Development.

Joyce, B. (1991). The doors to school improvement. *Educational Leadership, 48*(8), 59-62.

Joyce, B. (1992). Cooperative learning and staff development: Teaching the method with the method. *Cooperative Learning, 12*(2), 10-13.

Joyce, B., & Murphy, C. (1990). Epilogue. In B. R. Joyce (Ed.), *ASCD yearbook: Changing school culture through staff development.* Alexandria, VA: Association for Supervision and Curriculum Development.

Joyce, B., Murphy, C., Showers, B., & Murphy, J. (1989). School renewal as cultural change. *Educational Leadership, 47*(3), 70-77.

Joyce, B., Wolf, J., & Calhoun, E. (1993). *The self-renewing school.* Alexandria, VA: Association for Supervision and Curriculum Development.

LaBonte, K., Leighty, C., Mills, S., & True, M. (1993). Whole faculty study groups: Building the capacity of change through interagency collaboration. *Journal of Staff Development, 16*(3), 45-47.

Little, J. (1981). *School success and staff development in urban desegregated schools: A summary of recently published research.* Boulder, CO: Center for Action Research.

Louis, K., & Miles, M. (1990). *Improving the urban high school: What works and why.* New York: Teachers College Press.

Miles, M., & Huberman, M. (1981). *Innovation up close: A field study.* Andover, MA: The Network.

Murphy, C. (1990, October 16). *The role of the central office staff in restructuring.* Keynote address at the International Society for Educational Planning, Atlanta, GA.

Murphy, C. (1991). The development of a training cadre. *Journal of Staff Development, 12*(3), 21-24.

Murphy, C. (1991, October). Changing organizational culture through administrative study groups. *Newsletter of the National Staff Development Council,* 1, 4.

Murphy, C. (1992). Study groups foster school-wide learning. *Educational Leadership, 50*(3), 71-74.

Murphy, C. (1993). Long-range planning for individual and organizational development. *Journal of Staff Development, 14*(2), 2-4.

Murphy, C. (1997). Finding time for faculties to study together. *Journal of Staff Development, 18*(3), 29-32.

Murphy, C., Murphy, J., Joyce, B., & Showers, B. (1988). The Richmond County School improvement program: Preparation and initial phase. *Journal of Staff Development, 9*(2), 36-41.

Raywid, M. (1993). Finding time for collaboration. *Education Leadership, 51*(1), 30-34.

Sarason, S. (1990). *The predictable failure of educational reform: Can we change course before it's too late.* San Francisco: Jossey-Bass.

Showers, B., Murphy, C., & Joyce, B. (1996). The River City program: Staff development becomes school improvement. In B. R. Joyce & E. Calhoun (Eds.), *Learning experiences in school renewal: An exploration of five successful programs.* Eugene: University of Oregon. (ERIC Document Reproduction Service No. EA 026 696)

Southern Regional Education Board. (1994). *High schools that work: Site development guide #4, staff development.* Atlanta, GA: Author.

Index

CORWIN
PRESS

The Corwin Press logo—a raven striding across an open book—represents the happy union of courage and learning. We are a professional-level publisher of books and journals for K–12 educators, and we are committed to creating and providing resources that embody these qualities. Corwin's motto is "Success for All Learners."